SOCIAL MARKETING

SOCIAL MARKETING

New Imperative for Public Health

by Richard K. Manoff

PRAEGER

New York
Westport, Connecticut
London

Library of Congress Cataloging in Publication Data

Manoff, Richard K.
  Social marketing.

  Includes bibliographies and index.
  1. Health education — Marketing — Social aspects.
2. Mass media in health education. 3. Marketing —
Social aspects. I. Title.
RA440.5.M34   1985   362.1'042   84-18279
ISBN 0-275-90143-2 (alk. paper)
      0-275-91673-1 (pbk.)

Library of Congress Catalog Card Number: 84-18279
ISBN: 0-275-91673-1

First published in 1985

Praeger Publishers, 521 Fifth Avenue, New York, NY 10175
A division of Greenwood Press, Inc.

Printed in the United States of America

∞

The paper used in this book complies with the Permanent
Paper Standard issued by the National Information Standards
Organization (Z39.48-1984).

10 9 8 7 6 5 4 3 2

This one is for Lucy
because she made me write it.

Acknowledgments

The author of a book incurs many debts that are difficult to clear because there is no proper coinage for settling obligations of inspiration, instruction, and experience on the one hand, and loyalty, interest, and support on the other. I am indebted to many friends, associates, and family members on all counts. These are privileged covenants and I am proud to acknowledge them publicly.

Dr. Martin Forman of AID and Alan Berg of the World Bank, though my juniors in years, were the mentors who stimulated my interest in world nutrition and food problems almost two decades ago. They provided my first social marketing opportunities. I am one of the grateful beneficiaries of the vision and courage with which they are fortunately abundantly supplied.

I have also been favored with enriching collegial relationships. Though I take full responsibility for the words of the book, I cannot take credit for all the ideas or material. I have been a member of an unusual team of gifted people. Marcia Griffiths, senior vice president of Manoff International Inc. and director of our Washington office, has been, since 1977, my closest ally. Her dedication to the social ideals of our work, her unremitting devotion to quality, and her stubborn defiance of compromise with either have been a joy for me.

Dan Lissance, who joined Manoff International after years as a senior management executive with Richard K. Manoff Inc., our U.S. advertising agency subsidiary, has proved, as I knew he would, an able recruit for social marketing. His advice and observations have been most helpful to me while writing this book.

Perhaps no one has been closer to the book than Ginny Wilmot, my longtime assistant and standard-bearer, whose devotion has been above and beyond the call. I would have sunk in the morass of my own manuscript a hundred times had not Ginny swooped down in the nick of time to rescue me from contradiction, inconsistency, and obscurity. My publishers, impressed with the quality of the manuscript, now know on whom to bestow their blessings.

To Marie Call, my other invaluable assistant, goes a special expression of gratitude. Her highly intelligent handling of the many business details that I am normally burdened with freed much of my time for writing. To Elizabeth Nobbe, of our Washington office, my thanks for her love of writing that made me love it all the more, her passion for ideas and the doggedness in carrying it out.

To my son, Robert Karl Manoff, the well-known editor and writer, I owe a deep debt of gratitude for his perceptive advice in organizing the book so as to enhance the reader's grasp of its content. And to the many, many friends I have made in "the work"—in the field, in governments, universities, hospitals, and health centers, the media, AID, the World Bank, UNICEF, WHO, the Ford Foundation, and elsewhere—my gratitude for all they have given me and for what we have been able to accomplish together.

Richard K. Manoff
New York

Contents

Part I

Background and Theory
of Social Marketing

1

Introduction

As recently as 15 years ago, the suggestion that marketing could play a role in public health education was certain to be rejected by health professionals with arguments such as: marketing is the enemy; even if it weren't it is a commercial strategy irrelevant to health education; at best, it is a promotional, not an educational, tool; and there are no hard data to prove otherwise.

Several critical events have since produced a marked change of attitude. The 1969 White House Conference on Food, Nutrition, and Health included a panel on "Popular Education: How to Reach Disadvantaged Groups Through the Media of Mass Communications."[1] This was perhaps the first time a major professional gathering acknowledged marketing's possibilities, if only peripherally. Bold recommendations issued from panel four, including a radical proposal for recapturing for public use 10 percent of all TV and radio time from station licensees.

The signs were growing for some time. Enterprising health and nutrition educators reported encouraging results from use of the mass media. Several efforts in developing countries had won the support of USAID, the Ford Foundation, and CARE. True, these were simply mass media campaigns employing advertising techniques, unsupported by target audience analysis, market research, message design and testing, media analysis, effectiveness tracking, etc.—all the disciplines that make up the marketing mix. Nevertheless, their promising results exerted a positive influence on professional attitudes.

If one event could be considered decisive, perhaps it was the historic 1978 United Nations conference at Alma-Ata, where the principles of primary health care were officially enunciated. Until then, health programs were a disconnected aggregation of vertical interventions with independent infrastructures often competing rather than collaborating with each other. Alma-Ata articulated the principle of integration, a single primary health care intervention of interdependent strategies with a common objective. The Alma-Ata declaration designated "education concerning prevailing health problems and the methods of preventing and controlling them" as the *first* of eight essential activities in primary health care.[2] Five years later, when the thirty-sixth World Health Assembly (WHO) devoted its technical discussions to the subject of "New Policies for Health Education in Primary Health Care," one of the 14 recommendations gave particular emphasis to the mass media. Some 300 delegates from 140 countries took part. As reported by one observer

> In general, the participants were in full agreement of their evident influence . . . [this despite] the unrealistic attitudes in not comprehending the values of mass media in the history of health education. . . . It is necessary to take diverse measures to encourage collaboration among health professionals and the media to assure a free and continuing flow of information between the two and to organize appropriate programs for the use of the media.[3]

Alma-Ata also underscored the role of the community in programs for its benefit and repudiated the doctrine of health paternalism implicit in plans designed unilaterally by authorities and handed down to communities as faits accomplis. These principles of program integration and community-based planning would revise for all time the strategies of public health promotion. Though few realized it at the time, these changes were soon to win for marketing an acceptance undreamed of a few short years before. For Alma-Ata had declared as fundamental to public health the selfsame elements that had been evolving in the marketing process for more than half a century. This could not have been apparent to the Alma-Ata participants, but those patient advocates of a role for marketing were quick to perceive it. Aware of the special advantages of marketing, they were convinced its adaptation to public health was merely a matter of time. And now, with Alma-Ata, its time had come.

Marketing's gestation had been prolonged even in the commercial world. As recently as 50 years ago, the consumer marketplace was controlled by the salesperson, whether the manufacturer's representative to the wholesaler or the retail employee urging merchandise onto the consumer. Product differentiation was limited because little was known about diversity in consumer preferences. Product uniformity was the mode—a mass market could be satisfied by a mass product. The strategy of product extension to expand the market was yet to be invented. The consumer was inhibited by the limited offerings of the salesperson. The salesperson depended totally on the manufacturer. The entire process was dominated by the factory.

What the factory produced, the sales force sold. Gradually, alert salespeople came to sense that the marketplace had a dynamic of its own, that not all consumers shared the same tastes and life-styles, and that these differences had a bearing on consumer demand. Moreover, this demand was always in flux. A twin opportunity existed: diversifying existing products and introducing new ones. Not even bread was sacred. The market could absorb as many varieties as there were consumers willing to buy them. The enterprising baker needed an alert sales organization attuned to consumer differences and marketplace changes.

This fine tuning distinguished the marketing staff from salespeople. The latter continued to peddle the output of the factory. But the former were not content merely to sell but to conceive of what new products the marketplace could absorb and to convince the factory to make them. Power inevitably shifted from the factory to the market, from the production to the marketing executive. The old order was now reversed; the factory produced what the marketplace demanded. Since consumer perception was the key to success, techniques for surveillance of consumer behavior became priority requirements.

The ultimate outcome is modern marketing with its components of market and consumer research (i.e., the focus group interview, the market segmentation study, target group analysis, etc.), advertising (i.e., product positioning, creative strategy, message design and testing, media strategy and planning, effectiveness tracking, etc.), and distribution and its array of dealer-loading and sales-promotion devices. The preeminent premise is the principle that the consumer is key and consumer perception is the fundamental wisdom. It is, in essence, the unfolding of a commercial Alma-Ata.

Some of its practitioners also saw the inherent possibilities of marketing for such social marketplaces as public health. In effect, some years before Alma-Ata, they began a crusade for the notion among health professionals but any reference to marketing almost always provoked instant antagonisms. There were exceptions, to be sure, the more notable by their small number included: Dr. Martin Forman of USAID; Alan Berg, of the World Bank; Dr. Nevin Scrimshaw of M.I.T.; Drs. Derrick and Patrice Jelliffe of the University of California in Los Angeles; Dr. Michael Latham of Cornell; Professor Doris Callaway of Berkeley; David Davis of the Ford Foundation; Indir Gujral, then minister of state for information and broadcasting in India; the late Bill McIntyre of USAID; Dr. Joan Gussow, of Columbia University; Robert Choate, the businessman turned nutrition advocate; Dr. Jean Mayer, Professor of Nutrition at Harvard, now president of Tufts University; Drs. Nathan Maccoby and Wilbur Schramm of Stanford; Dr. I.B. Mantra, director, Nutrition Education Component, Indonesian Nutrition Development Program; Dr. Lukas Hendrata, director of the Indonesia Sejahtera Foundation; Dr. Florentino Solon, executive director, Nutrition Center of the Philippines.

The resistance was not without some justification. The overmarketing of products like cigarettes, nonnutritious frivolous foods, breast-milk substitutes, and unnecessary drugs had come to symbolize the marketing process at its worst (or, best?). The radio and television hawking of such products debased the image of the mass media as antagonistic to social goals and inappropriate for loftier use.

Ironically, marketing was no newcomer to the health profession. The pharmaceutical industry with the collaboration of the medical profession had been making positive use of it for decades. The proliferation of proprietary drugs, in both the ethical and over-the-counter markets, could not have been possible without it, and even the most vehement critics would not deny the considerable social benefits received. Yet there is a qualitative difference between the promotion of commercial treatment items and the social marketing of health education and products devoted to disease prevention. Neither the pharmaceutical industry nor the medical profession has been notable for such effort. Economic dynamics favor treating illness rather than preventing it. We have yet to devise a system to secure economic rewards for prevention comparable to those earned for cure.

Professionals interested in exploiting marketing's potential sought to define its independence from commerce, to distinguish the method from the message, to urge its use for better messages. But health educators persisted in the use of traditional academic methods and materials. The reach and the frequency with which they could deliver their messages to the target population were limited by their number. Moreover, the biomedical orientation with problems rather than with consumer perceptions limited the capacity to motivate and overcome resistances. It was ironic because most marketing theory was borrowed from anthropology, sociology, social psychology, communications theory, and their research techniques. Marketing was a new synthesis of these elements, wedded to the use of the modern mass media. The theoretical underpinnings had little to do with soap and cigarettes. They provided a capability for insight into group behavior and motivations, target audiences, and attributes, and for designing responsive message and media strategies.

The times are demanding new approaches to health education. Populations are massive. School systems are proving inadequate everywhere, plagued by budgetary problems and assaulted by dissonant educational messages from other sources. Curricula have become engorged with ever-growing subject matter. The electronic hypnotism of cinema, radio, and television has preempted a major share of public attention and intellectual energy.

Surely, the time has come for the educators to reclaim the tools of their own invention and to break new ground. This is a call to social marketing: to carry on the struggle for a better-informed, healthier public with every new means. No other public concern demands this intervention more acutely. Public health is increasingly vulnerable to antagonisms in the environment, the food system, and life-styles. Health statistics on obesity, heart disease, stroke, and awareness of the relationship between environmental neglect and disease (as well as good diet and health) confirm the case. The central issue of the technical discussions at the thirty-third session of the WHO Regional Committee for Europe was the creeping powerlessness to resist the ill effects of social and environmental influences on life-style.

> Life-styles are . . . not simply individual decisions to avoid or accept certain health risks. There are limits to the choices open to individuals— limits imposed by their physical, social and cultural environment and by their financial means. Much depends, therefore, on how easy it is for people to choose one way of life rather than another.[4]

One participant pointed out, "We must stop blaming people for poor health behavior when, in fact, it is the social environment which is at the root of the problem."

Not surprisingly, the earliest uses of social marketing may have occurred where it was least expected, in developing countries. They may have far less-sophisticated marketing and mass media apparatuses, but they are also less rigid in managing them. Their mass media are far more available to public service than those in the United States. Americans are familiar with the pattern of scheduling PSAs (public service announcements) in the wee hours of the night or the morning. So cynical is the practice as to have inspired one wag to rename it *people sound asleep*. Furthermore, social marketing in the United States has been haphazard. We have few examples of a total social marketing approach. Ordinarily, advertising is an important component of the marketing process designed to maximize its success and minimize the risk of failure; virtually all public service advertising campaigns have been designed without probing research, pretesting messages, or tracking studies.

What follows is a response to the rising interest in social marketing, how it evolved from marketing, and how it can be employed for the public health in developed as well as developing countries. Problems may differ from country to country and within countries. But the social marketing of public health is a systems approach with universal application regardless of problem or local situation.

There is a logic to the flow of the book starting from background and moving on through history to theory, practice, case histories, and, finally, a delineation of barriers that could spell futility to social marketing unless they are first eliminated. The logic of this sequence need not dictate the way one chooses to read the book, however. For that reason it has been organized in three parts.

Part I: Background and Theory of Social Marketing embraces an introduction to social marketing's background (Chapter 1) and a discussion of the communications gaps in public health education that make it necessary (Chapter 2). The nature of marketing (Chapter 3) prepares us for examining the role of social marketing in public health education (Chapter 4) and its primary tool, the mass media (Chapter 5). Part I might be dubbed the what-it-is-and-why-it's-necessary section.

Part II: Putting Social Marketing to Work describes the steps in the development of the social marketing plan with emphasis on the research functions (Chapter 6); its execution, including the lessons learned from experience (Chapter 7); the steps in carrying out its two major components, the media plan (Chapter 8) and message design (Chapter 9), including the theory behind the resistance resolution model, the disciplines of message design, and, in accordance with both, an analysis of a typical message from a social marketing project in the Philippines. Part II is the how-to section of the book.

Part III: Social Marketing: Cases and Caveats presents four actual case histories on different problems from two developed and two developing countries (Chapter 10), and then examines the social, economic, political, and environmental impediments to social marketing efforts and the initiatives required to remove them (Chapter 11). Part III is a combination of here's-how-it's-worked and when-you-shouldn't-ever-try-and-why section.

The reader may want to read selectively, going first to Chapter 9, for example, because of an overriding interest in message design. The book may be meaningfully read this way without recourse to preceding chapters but that will depend on each reader's knowledge and experience.

Notes

1. White House Conference on Food, Nutrition and Health, section IV, panel four, Washington, D.C., November 1969.

2. *Declaration of Alma-Ata. Alma-Ata 1978. Primary Health Care,* report of the International Conference on Primary Health Care, Alma-Ata, U.S.S.R., September 6–12, 1978, WHO, Geneva, 1978.

3. Senault, R., honorary president, International Union for Health Education (IUHE), thirty-sixth World Health Assembly, Geneva, October 1983.

4. *Life-Styles and Their Impact on Health,* report of the thirty-third Session of WHO Regional Committee for Europe, EUR/RC33/Tech, Disc./1.

2

The Communications Gap in Public Health

While the analogy is far from exact, the role of education in public health programs is somewhat akin to that of marketing in the commercial world. Until recent decades, public health was concerned with the structural elements of disease—lurking dangers in the environment and bacteriological causes of disease—just as emphasis in the food business was on production. Modern, high-tech professionals have a shorthand term to describe these polarities: basic equipment is the hardware and the creative programs to which it is put are the software. In business the factory is hardware and marketing is software, in the same sense that the latter plays the critical role in programming a factory's output. In public health, the medical establishment could be said to be the hardware for the conquest of disease with software programs of therapy and prevention.

These software efforts have not always been appropriate or timely. Just as the production manager with a proprietary attachment to his machines was made uneasy by the growing power of the marketplace over product decisions, so the medical establishment for years has resisted those public health strategies it could not control.

The notion that public health need not depend on medicine or the ministrations of health professionals is not new. It predates the new awareness more than 100 years ago of the bacteriological causes of disease that first gave prominence to medical research and intervention. Until then the medical profession had little science to go on and public health officials focused their activities on environmental concerns. Modern epidemiology owes a debt to John Snow who, in 1854 to 1855, was the first to identify water supply as the means of cholera's transmission by clinical observation in London a whole generation before the cholera vibrio was identified by Koch. While inspecting the homes of those who had died

9

from cholera, he was led to examine their water sources. When correlated with the deaths this is what his inquiry revealed:

Cholera Mortality in London
(Four Weeks Ending August 5, 1854)[1]

Water Company	Homes Supplied	Deaths	Rate 1000 Homes
Southwark & Vauxhall	40,046	286	71
Lambeth	26,107	14	5
All others	287,345	277	9

Snow was able to establish that Southwark & Vauxhall were tapping the polluted waters of the Thames downstream; Lambeth, the unpolluted river upstream.

With the expansion of scientific knowledge into the bacteriological etiology of disease came a redirection of emphasis to the individual; medicine and personal hygiene thus set the stage for a conflict of interest between public programs and private medical service. According to Starr, "Doctors fought against public treatment of the sick, requirements for reporting cases of tuberculosis and venereal disease and attempts by public health authorities to establish health centers to coordinate preventive and curative medical services."[2] In giving emphasis to medicine, this shifting focus lessened attention to the environment with unfortunate consequences even to this day.

This history suggests that the conception of public health as a vertical program may have been ill advised. Halfdan Mahler, the director-general of WHO, has declared that

> the great technical and scientific advances of the past 30 years have not brought about truly significant improvement in health. . . . [We] see that the great improvement in health in Europe during the 19th century came about not through better medical care but through provision of better working conditions, better sanitation, better nutrition and housing, fostered by vigorous political action.[3]

Public health's orientation then was with engineering, not medicine, but the emergence of bacteriology preempted public health attention. Such preemptions have characterized public health history. Infatuated with new discoveries, it has always shown a readiness to be seduced by the latest strategy that then dominated its era.

The Eras of Health Education

One historian has discerned three such eras. The first, from 1840 to 1890, was an era of empirical environmental sanitation. It was dedicated to the improvement of water supply, sewerage, and sanitation on the premise that dirt and filth were the source of contagion long before the etiology was clear. The second was a brief 20-year period that ended in 1910 of concentration on bacteriology and a war against the germ sources of disease. But the discoveries of pathology did not simultaneously produce disease-specific remedies. The result was an atavistic adaptation of previous environmental sanitation procedures—fumigation and quarantining of disease. The third era, emerging about 1910, was typified by primitive efforts at disease prevention. The two major strategies were education in personal hygiene and regular medical examinations. The focus was still on combating bacterial sources of infection but with more precisely designed weapons. The targets were tuberculosis, venereal diseases, and illnesses affecting infants and children.[4]

We have since entered a fourth era characterized by heightened awareness of the relationship of diet and life-style to health. This new public health has its roots in such discoveries as preventing scurvy with limes in the British Navy, rickets with vitamin D, and pellagra in other food deficiencies through the work of Joseph Goldberger. It gained momentum with nutrition research and vitamin identity and function. Public awareness of life-style factors dates from World War II and its aftermath: the influence of exercise and diet on health; the connection of cigarette smoking to cancer, heart disease, hypertension and stroke; and the relationship of stress to morbidity.

Emphasis shifted to the preventive role of education as a behavior-change strategy to modify diet and life-style. Science, the hardware of public health, was still to be relied on, but the software of education became the major strategy for health improvement. The demand was not only for more education but also for better methodologies to enlarge its reach and impact. To those sensitive to the implications it became plain that the old pedagogy was inadequate for education's new responsibilities. Past assumptions about the content of messages and the means for their delivery needed reappraisal. Was the traditional classroom model sufficient to satisfy the need for broader reach to target populations? Were the old materials designed for small literate groups appropriate to massive effort? What other channels of education were accessible to public health efforts? Such questions put all previous educational strategies under stern review. Though the implications were not immediately apparent, it was clear that public health education would never be the same. Use of other educational strategies was inevitable. Among these the mass media loomed large.

Orthodoxy succumbs reluctantly. Public health and nutrition institutions are no exception. Public health officials' intolerance of the mass media was deep-seated; they disdained the media's commercial pedigree. The notion that they could be useful for education was considered unseemly. But the issue could not easily be turned aside. The shortcomings of traditional practices were becoming increasingly apparent.

The Shortcomings of Traditional Methodologies

By 1970, the Applied Nutrition Program (ANP) had been operating in India for ten years, funded by the government, UNICEF, and FAO (U.N. Food and Agriculture Organization). Under the ANP the farm-extension worker (*gram sevak*) was assigned the additional task of nutrition education to rural people. The program had covered 900 (roughly 18 percent) of the 5,000 development blocks into which Indian villages were grouped. This coverage was exemplary given the task of training, equipping, and motivating under the constraints of poor transportation and limited funds. Yet the number of people covered by even this attempt at nutrition education was equivalent to half the population increase over the same period of time (approximately 24.8 percent, a rate of 2.5 percent per annum).[5]

In Turkey, the medical profession had opposed authorizing nurses and midwives to insert intrauterine devices (IUDs) under the national family planning program. But in April 1983, a bill was passed to allow this important service to areas outside the large cities and towns. According to one doctor sympathetic to this authority, "The medical schools teach Western medicine so the students learn about the diseases of the rich but they do not notice the problems of most in their country."[6] Controlled studies in IUD insertion showed no better performance (absence of complications and side effects) from doctors than from trained midwives.[7]

But sanction of midwives' services to rural areas did not resolve the problem of how to get them to go. Here the stumbling block was "the lack of incentives for health care personnel to work in the rural areas of the Third World," according to one observer of the situation in Nigeria.[8] Dr. B. Williamson, chief medical officer of Sierra Leone, agreed that "there is very little inducement; salaries on the whole are very low." Dr. W. S. Boayue, WHO program coordinator in Liberia, declared that "it all boils down to a matter of money." But more than a personnel shortage was involved. Were sufficient personnel available, there would still be the problem of how to persuade rural people to come forward and accept their service.

These are typical problems in all countries, many of which exceed even India's and Turkey's population growth rates. They dramatize the need for techniques to improve health service and education delivery at a rate at least commensurate with population growth. Even in developed countries where growth rates may be below population replacement, the problem is qualitatively the same. The high cost of formal systems and the shortage of qualified personnel pose the same issue of inadequate reach to target populations. Moreover, the preeminent concerns of modifying diet and life-style put even greater emphasis on education than on structural factors in the food and health system.

It is a situation in which the realization has grown that health and nutrition educators preoccupied with the technical demands of their profession and incapable or unwilling to adapt to the new health education could not be left to their old devices. The 1969 White House Conference on Food, Nutrition and Health declared that "nutrition education is too important to be left to the nutritionist alone. It is also the job of the professional communicator."[9] This bold but hardly startling observation was not intended to give professional offense when it was elaborated at the Western Hemisphere Nutrition Conference III in 1971

> Nutrition educators have labored on their own for too long, over-burdened by the professional demands of the communicator. They cannot be their own best communicator, anymore than communicators can be their own best nutritionists. They need the mass media. And they need help to use them properly.[10]

These words received a mixed reception. The mass media and the reach-and-frequency (advertising) technique were attacked as commercial devices unsuitable for education because of their limited capability for audience feedback.

We have come a long way since. The theme of the sixteenth annual meeting of the Society for Nutrition Education in July 1983 was "Promoting Health Through Nutrition: Cooperative Ventures" and prominent among the topics was "Health Promotion and Working With the Media." The profession has since come to appreciate that for many aspects of health education the mass media have an incomparable utility.

The Feedback Question

As to feedback, not even traditional educational systems have remained immune to criticism. Witness this recent comment: ". . . the amount of feedback . . . in the average classroom or lecture hall is also very limited. I believe research shows that in the average classroom the lecturer or teacher communicates with about 5 or 10% of her class or group at any one time."[11]

The subject of feedback suffers from feedback confusion. Despite all that has been written and said, it is not clear what function we expect of feedback. Its etymology seems to make clear that feedback is important for the insights it produces for refining messages and improving materials. The question, then, is how to produce the richest insights. Is the face-to-face learning situation best or is it in a test with target audiences in their own environment, removed from the restraints of the educational process?

Social marketing places emphasis on testing in advance all concepts, messages, and materials for total, deliberate feedback. Once learning begins, it stresses monitoring the process for two continuing interdependent and indispensable feedbacks: to measure progress toward objectives and to add to the reservoir of target-audience insights. Periodic tracking studies ascertain whether the effort is having its effect and how it might be improved. This programmed feedback is fundamental to social marketing as its systemic mechanism for improvement and contrasts with the individualistic modifications that may emerge from the haphazard feedback of the face-to-face model. And with the latter there is no guarantee that the educational insight will be shared with the system. More likely, this personal feedback to each teacher for his or her own use is bound to create individualistic, idiosyncratic approaches to health education. The danger of message dissonances from teacher to teacher and group to group is very real.

It is also important to note, however, that simultaneous feedback is possible with certain radio and TV formats. It was ingeniously afforded in the 1960s by India's "Radio Farm Forum." In these programs, so invaluable to the Green Revolution, on-air discussions between farmers and technicians were broadcast to rural listening groups early in the morning before work started in the fields. Questions and comments were fed back to the program and used in subsequent broadcasts as well as for program improvement.

Marketing Style Versus Substance

While regard for marketing techniques in the new health education has grown, the tendency has been to mimic the style of commerce in ways

that betray ignorance of marketing's true functions. The fifty-seventh annual meeting of the American Dietetic Association featured a teaching
demonstration by a professor of nutrition from Syracuse University. It
was fashioned with rock music, disco staging and strobe lights, costumes,
and entry and exit by the professor on a motorbike. The aim was to give
education a now context, presumably to make it relevant to student life-
styles.[12] And the April 17, 1974, *Wall Street Journal* reported on its front
page efforts of colleges to stimulate student interest by utilizing television
gag writers to revise teaching materials.[13] These bizarre schemes may
amuse students but do they also aid learning? Has the intellectual content
been reduced to accommodate the entertainment?

Social marketing's impetus is entirely in the other direction. It opposes this invasion of the classroom by cultural styles exploited on the
mass media. Instead of the school as an extension of television entertainment, social marketing seeks to make television an annex of the school
with emphasis on enlightenment.

Advocates of social marketing contrast the sophistication of food
manufacturers in using marketing techniques with the traditional
methods of nutrition educators. "Food manufacturers and their advertisers have changed eating patterns," said Joan Gussow of Columbia University, a former president of the Society of Nutrition Education. "Until
we in nutrition education understand how they have achieved this . . . we
can teach the four food groups until we are blue in the face . . . while
American eating habits go down the drain.[14] According to nutritionist Dr.
Jean Mayer, president of Tufts University and chairman of the 1969 White
House Conference on Food, Nutrition and Health, "the basic four have
been a catastrophe. . . . People think protein is meat so they disregard the
protein to be found in the milk group. Fruits and vegetables have nothing
in common, yet they are linked together. It's counterproductive."[15]

Comprehension Gap: The Case of the Food Groups

Even its staunch advocates have had trouble with the food groups
concept. When Caroline L. Hunt, associate specialist in food and nutrition, U.S. Bureau of Home Economics, first introduced the concept in
1917, it was a five-group model.[16] During World War I the U.S. Department of Agriculture made it seven groups. With peace, four years later,
the basic seven was no longer found suitable and was reduced to the basic
four. Some countries use as many as four different groups for differing
education levels or socioeconomic classes. Japan and Poland, with three-

group systems, added a fourth a decade ago in maternity and child-wel-
fare cases. South Africa prefers the basic four but added a fifth, compris-
ing fats, for its low-income classes. Italy's different ministries use different groups at the same time. The group number around the world varies
from three to thirteen.[17]

As an educational technique, food-grouping systems illustrate the
comprehension gap created by outmoded message-design concepts.
They are cumbersome, complicated, and confusing in their focus on a device rather than on substance, on groups of foods rather than on the foods
themselves. In the United States, we have added to the confusion by
changing their number at least three times. Knowledge of the foods and
why they are important is lost in the clutter. Despite widespread teaching
of the basic four, most U.S. school children classify food as sweet or
nonsweet though sweets are not a category. Beans are placed with vegetables (a not illogical decision) rather than with meats and fish (a proper
nutrient decision); potato chips are grouped with pretzels and crackers
rather than with vegetables (not entirely indefensible). Some 42 percent
of the children identified dairy products as a discrete group.[18] Foods overlap groups. Corn is grouped with carbohydrates, yet for many of the poor
in Latin America and among the Hispanics in the United States, it is a
major source of protein.

Clinging to outmoded message concepts reveals serious misconceptions about message design despite the availability of well-tried principles
(see Chapter 9). It is also true of message materials. Because health
educators have relied primarily on interpersonal communication, their
materials are designed for face-to-face delivery to small audiences (i.e. flip
charts, posters, pamphlets, slides, overheads, etc.). They are heavily
weighted in favor of the printed word, a disadvantage in developing
countries where literacy is the exception. Such materials also pose logistical problems even in the developed countries. Every message needs a
medium and the only guarantee that a leaflet will be delivered is the
presence of a human being to get it there. With awareness that health
education is a combination of message, material, and medium comes the
realization of how lacking in sophistication are its methods.

The Awareness Gap

Deficiencies in message, materials, and media produce an awareness
gap as the history of the U.S. food stamp program attests. In the year after
the 1969 White House conference, a Nixon administration study revealed
that stamps were used by only 16 percent of those eligible. The McGovern

Select Senate Committee on Nutrition reported a 22-percent figure, still far below expectations and legislative intent.[19] The poor participation was ascribed to local prejudice, inefficiency, and indifference of officials and to public ignorance.[20] But these ancient traits of human behavior are proper targets for education that in this instance were either insufficient or inappropriate. A proper effort would have identified the barriers and set out to level them by taking the issue to the public—to rescue it from the doldrums, to keep public officials faithful, and to arouse popular awareness.

In September 1974, citizen groups instituted lawsuits against the responsible government agencies. These actions drew attention to the marketing problem; the product was not properly marketed either to its target audience (the eligible public) or to its distributors (the responsible officials).[21] An exquisite opportunity for social marketing was missed despite the existence of a successful precedent. Such a food stamp social marketing campaign was tried in New Mexico late in 1970 by the Office of Economic Opportunity and the Department of Nutrition of the University of New Mexico. The objective was "to create awareness of the availability of various food aid programs and to motivate those people who are eligible . . . to take advantage of the programs." Using radio, TV, and the press under the theme of "The Right to Eat Right," the campaign was addressed to food stamps and school breakfast and lunch programs. Within six months food stamp participation had more than tripled and school feeding programs were virtually universal.[22]

The experience illustrated that social marketing can create broad public awareness of critical public health issues on a farther/faster basis using well-crafted, consistently delivered messages, to ensure maximum comprehension by target audiences.

The Materials Gap

While acknowledgement of this untapped potential has grown, understanding of how to use the technology has languished. Much confusion still persists about the uses of the media and the nature of its materials. More than a decade ago, Congress mandated AID "to expand and strengthen non-formal education methods." AID comments on its responsibilities under this mandate

> Most non-formal education (NFE) takes place outside the classroom. AID spends more than $40 million. . . . Materials are usually low cost and simple much as photonovellas, comic books, pamphlets, audio cas-

settes, games, manuals, posters and flipcharts, but *television, radio, video tape, film, slide shows and multi-media packages are also often used* (author's italics).[23]

This forward-looking statement is not without its contradictions. It is hardware oriented, defining nonformal education in terms of technique rather than process. It adds confusion by lumping television and radio together with materials, disregarding TV and radio as media. Moreover, they are presumed to be more expensive, which is not necessarily true (see Chapter 8).

Characterizing the mass media merely as NFE techniques considerably depreciates their value. Their effectiveness depends on strategic decisions of the social marketing process. Employed grossly on the basis of an arbitrary judgment, misuse of the mass media is an abysmal waste and helps perpetuate misconceptions about their usefulness.

Thus, we have a range of communications gaps that enfeeble public health education. Foremost is the reach-and-frequency gap between audience and authority. The old ways of health education are proving inadequate to modern demand whether in developed or developing countries. Large numbers of people are not being reached with appropriate messages or frequency. There also are gaps between:

1. The two cultures of the target audience and the health professional
2. Educational assumption and popular perception
3. Educational content and such realities of the environment as deleterious practices in the marketplace
4. The dissonant messages from responsible authorities
5. The health care system and large numbers of the needy who are unmotivated to avail themselves of its facilities
6. The emphasis on and competition between curative services and the rising need for prevention

Social marketing provides the health educator with a unique capability for bridging these gaps.

Notes

1. Snow, J., *On the Mode of Transmission of Cholera*, second edition, Churchill, London, 1855 (reprinted Commonwealth Fund, New York, 1936). Cited by J.M. Last, *Public Health and Preventive Medicine*, eleventh edition.

2. Starr, P., "The Laissez-Faire Elixir," *The New Republic,* April 18, 1983, p. 19.

3. Mahler, H., director-general, WHO, *Rescue Mission for Tomorrow's Health,* an interview, *People,* vol. 6, no. 2, 1979, IPPF, London.

4. Starr, P., *The Social Transformation of American Medicine,* Harper & Row, New York, 1982.

5. Manoff, R.K., *Social Policy and the Uses of Public Media for Nutrition and Health Education,* prepared for the Commission on Critical Choices for Americans, the Rockefeller Foundation, November 1974.

6. Tansey, G., "The Midwives of Cubuk," *People,* vol. 10, no. 3, p. 12, IPPF, London.

7. Financioglu, N., *Turkey's Liberal Law,* ibid., p. 29.

8. Kabba-Diallo, F., in *West Africa,* Nigerian expatriate-owned weekly, London, June 20, 1983.

9. White House Conference on Food, Nutrition and Health, October 1969, report on Recommendations of Panel IV-4.

10. Manoff, R.K., *The Role of the Communications Specialist: The Reach-And-Frequency Use of Mass Media,* Western Hemisphere Nutrition Congress III, August-September 1971.

11. Cain, J., *Health Education by Television and Radio,* (ed. M. Meyer), K.G. Saur, Munich, 1981.

12. Short, Dr. S.H., *Nutrition is Alive and Well at College,* presented at fifty-seventh Annual Meeting of the American Dietetic Association, Philadelphia, Pennsylvania, October 10, 1974.

13. Lancaster, H., "Ever Hear the One About the Professor and the Gag Writer?" the *Wall Street Journal,* April 17, 1974.

14. Gussow, Dr. J., *Nutrition Education—Is There Any Other Source?* sixty-fourth Annual Meeting of the American Association of Home Economics, June 1973.

15. Quoted by William Rice in The Los Angeles *Times* from The Washington *Post* News Service, October 19, 1973.

16. Hunt, C.L., *Food for Young Children,* U.S. Department of Agriculture Farmers' Bulletin 717, 1917, Washington, D.C.

17. Manoff, R.K., *You May Be Teaching Nutrition, But Are They Learning?* American Dietetic Association fifty-seventh Annual Meeting, Philadelphia, October 10, 1974.

18. "Children Devise Own Food Groups," *Nutrition Week,* May 12, 1983, p. 6.

19. This study by two West Point instructors, Captain Terrence P. Goggin and Captain Clifford Hendrix, was commissioned by the White House in the summer of 1969 for President Nixon. They submitted their final report in early February 1970. George McGovern, then chairman of the Senate Select Committee on Nutrition, commented: "It is accurate to say that the report was suppressed for some considerable time." It covered an eight-week study of fifteen countries in New York, Mississippi, Missouri, and California.

20. Rosenthal, J., "Food Programs Called Deceptive," the New York *Times,* June 3, 1970.

21. Kihss, P., "Suits in Seventeen States Charge Failure to Enlarge Food Stamp Programs," the New York *Times,* September 24, 1974.

22. This effort was the brainchild of Robert Choate, the nutrition advocate, and was executed by Richard K. Manoff Inc., an advertising and marketing agency of which the author was the founder and chairman. The Citizens for the Right to Eat Right in Santa Fe, New Mexico, was the local sponsoring organization established expressly for the effort.

23. AID Resources Report, May-June, 1983, No. 28.

3

The Nature of
the Marketing Process

Early on a Monday morning some 40 years ago, an enterprising young executive at the Welch Grape Juice Company (now Welch Foods Inc.) dropped a memo onto the desk of his superior. He had agonized over it for weeks, finally ignoring his wife who warned him not to make waves. The memo was a proposal to market a frozen concentrated version of grape juice. Welch's credo was quality; its symbol for more than fifty years was the famous bottle of Welch's Grape Juice. His superior wasted no time in telling him that the idea was a sacrilege.

"Adding three cans of water won't reconstitute this product to Welch's Grape Juice, now, would it?"

"No, sir, but the label would make that clear."

"But the reconstituted drink would be only 50-percent grape juice with sugar added."

"Added sugar is necessary to restore the brix imbalance." Brix was the acid-sugar relationship. He had at least done his homework.

The older man impugned his sanity. "You would risk the Welch name for quality in a reckless gamble for dubious gain?" He gave a sermonetic recital of company history. Conveniently overlooked was the recent decline in its fortunes. The young man noted but ignored the omission.

Instead, he said respectfully, "Research shows that grape juice is consumed by less than 5 percent of the population as infrequently as once a year. Women dilute it with water."

"Nothing new. Many people like it that way."

"Exactly. So why not offer a *superior* diluted drink to begin with and at half the price?"

"It wouldn't be Welch quality. Besides, it would cannibalize bottled juice sales." That was a moot question. And the young man knew it.

"Indications are that it will appeal to a different consumer. It could expand our market and increase, not cannibalize, our business." Waving the memo, he saved the best item for last. "Calculations show a better return per ton of grapes."

For the first time the older man noticed the names of others who had been copied on the memo. It was obviously a pressure play and turning it down could prove awkward to explain later.

"What about a small market test?" the young man asked quietly, the sweet taste of victory on his tongue.

Welch's Frozen Grape Juice was one of the food marketing successes of the post-World War II era. Modern marketing was still in its infancy and its devotees approached their tasks with much trepidation. With little theory and less fact to go on, what they needed most was raw courage and chutzpah. Pioneering successes emboldened others and, gradually, the accumulating experience became systematized. The idea of line extension, the innovation of our young Welch executive, is now marketing custom. No professional overlooks it today in formulating the annual marketing plan. This is true for all the elements in what is now known as the marketing mix.

Perhaps the most successful new food product of the decade is Tostitos, a snack from Frito-Lay with sales of $140 million during its first year in 1980 and $165 million in 1981. It is a variation on the older Doritos and was feared at first by some Frito-Lay executives as a potential cannibal. John Cranor, vice president of Marketing, shrugged cannibalism aside, declaring: "For some reason the marketing community is enamored with the notion of cannibalization and seems to be absolutely terrified of it. . . . As long as a legitimate consumer niche exists, someone else will fill it, if I don't."[1]

The original bottle of Welch's Grape Juice has since been extended to:

1. A canned ready-to-drink product (less grape juice, more quantity, lower price)
2. A carbonated soda (for the soft-drink market)
3. A powder (the Kool aid belly-wash set)
4. A bottled white grape juice (a different grape, flavor, and color)
5. A bottled red grape juice (a variation on the original purple)
6. A canned fruit punch (for the exotic palate)
7. A canned apple-grape drink (for a share of the apple-drink market)
8. The frozen concentrate ("a more healthful soft drink" for the choosier, more upscale, young family market)
9. A number of failed entries whose promise was not fulfilled in the marketplace

Market Expansion or Share-of-Market?

Each line extension represented a new appeal to a distinctive consumer segment that had been unresponsive to existing versions (or uses) of the product. The reasons for the appeal might include the form of the product; price; cost-per-ounce; the package; convenience in storage, handling, preparation, or serving; image; or other factors uncovered by research. The Welch's premise was that grape flavor in a drink was more popular than its form. Different people like grape in different ways, at different cost levels, with differing personas. Either Welch got there first or the competition would. Realization of full market potential demands a strategy of product-form diversity. The market leader is in the most advantageous position to seize the initiative and has the most to gain. Thus, market expansion and/or share-of-market are the chief preoccupations of the marketing executive, the two strategies the marketing mix is designed to implement.

Ask an automobile manufacturer for the rationale behind the model in his line and he will talk about them in terms he uses to describe people. He views his product in the profile of a consumer type on the assumption that it represents a worthwhile market. Don't expect an impassioned disquisition on its engineering, which belongs to an era when performance made a critical competitive difference. Any modern auto gets you where you want to go easily and efficiently. The critical advantage is not in the car per se but in its public perception, in its image to the special consumer segment for which it was designed, priced, powered, styled, and advertised. An auto model rarely fails to sell because of poor performance. As with the Edsel, the reason is either a misconception about its target consumers or the failure of the model and its advertising to match image expectations.

The modern consumer goods manufacturer would no more conduct his business without marketing than without a sales force or a product. Each of these elements relies crucially on the others. Business achievement is increasingly a function of marketing skill, even with dramatic product innovations. Computer technology was well established when two young engineers perceived the opportunity for a desk-top unit for the small business and the home. Even the name they chose—Apple—was a homespun image breakaway from the arcane appellations of its engineering-dominated predecessors.

"The genius of the modern corporation is not invention," authors Barnett and Muller declared in a masterful examination of multinational enterprise around the world, "but the development and marketing of individual inspiration."[2] Business history tends to bear them out: Moulton's bicycle, Carlson's Xerox, Godowski's Kodachrome, Kellogg's corn flakes, Welch's grape juice, Clarence Birdseye's frozen foods, the Wright Brothers' airplane, etc. But behind each success is a marketing enterprise the inventor could never have done without. Warren Hirsh, the genius of the jeans business, put it plainly: "Everyone knows how to make good jeans. Jeans that fit. There are no secrets. All jeans are the same. The difference is how you market them."

Defining Marketing

Definitions of marketing, like all definitions, are notable for their omissions mainly because marketing is more process than proposition, a *how* rather than a *what* affair. This is so probably because marketing depends more on creative thinking than some marketing professionals are prepared to admit. Definitions rarely capture this elusive quality and dwell, instead, on matter-of-fact aspects. One view of marketing is of cut-and-dried market and consumer research and analysis by browbeating statisticians dubbed number tumblers by antagonistic creative types. Research is a vital part of marketing but by no means its major preoccupation. Nor is research by the numbers either the only method or the most productive. At the other extreme is the view of marketing as an advertising operation, the probable effect of advertising's visibility. This simplistic perception of the thirty-second TV commercial as marketing ignores the complicated decisions needed before advertising can be initiated. Two English communications professionals have put it well: "The important point . . . is that the whole process is *integrated* and makes use of the mass media as only one aspect, albeit a very important aspect of it."[3]

Marketing was defined in 1960 by the American Marketing Association (AMA) as "the performance of business activities that direct the flow of goods and services from producer to consumer."[4] There is nothing wrong with this definition except that what it includes is less important than what it leaves out. It took nineteen years to fix with this addition: "in order to best satisfy customers and accomplish the firm's objectives."[5]

The British, surprisingly, had forged ahead of American marketers in theory, at least, if not in practice. In 1966, fourteen years before the AMA, the British Institute of Marketing revised its previous definition by replacing "assessing consumer needs" with "assessing and converting customer purchase power into effective demand for a specific product."[6] By 1980, at least, on both sides of the Atlantic, marketing had assumed the responsibility of creating demand, not merely satisfying it.

But definitions are not helpful for understanding the how of the process. A state-of-the-art description is necessary. Peter Drucker tried with:

"Marketing is so basic that it cannot be considered as a separate function. . . . It is the whole business seen from the point of view of its final results, that is, from the consumer point of view."[7] Lee Adler acquiesced:
"The essence of marketing can be distilled into two concepts: *customer
orientation* and the *integrated use of all of a company's resources* to aid
and abet in supplying wanted goods and services at a profit to itself."[8] He
elaborated: "Marketing may also be perceived as a vast communications
system, giving information regarding product availability to consumers
while feeding back data regarding consumers' wants to producers."

Now we are getting somewhere, for it is that vast (*and special*) communications system to and from the consumer that is the quintessence of
modern marketing. In the years before our industrial maturity, movement of goods to consumers was narrowly confined. Economic systems
were primarily agricultural and food was the dominant commodity. Almost all markets were local and what they offered was indigenous produce. The marketing infrastructure of roads, transport, and storage and
distribution facilities was primitive. Nonperishable goods had a wider
geographic potential but supply was limited to what handcraftsmen
could produce.

The Consumer as a Study Target

Industrialization vastly expanded marketing opportunities for enterprising minds. Invention became the grist for the mill of industry; the factory became an instrument of limitless possibility for the manufacture of
clothing, household goods, and tools. The invention of canning gave
food a year-round availability to distant corners of the world.

Supply was limited only by demand so that the creation of demand
became an entrepreneurial preoccupation. The more ambitious discovered that their factories had a potential beyond the know-how of the production managers. They began to turn an ear to the market, to listen to the
tales of returning salespeople, of encounters with strange consumer practices, of complaints and criticisms. This ear-to-the-market was a critical
modification of business behavior. It was inevitable that the manufacturer
should *redirect strategy from distributing his products to markets with a
known need* (selling) *to identifying new consumer needs and wants, in-
venting the products to satisfy them, and designing the distribution system to markets for their delivery* (marketing).

Thus, with supply limited only by demand, the creation of demand
was then hobbled by ignorance of the dynamics of consumer motivation
and behavior. The new marketing manager was determined to explore

these "misty mid-regions of Weir."* This was a venture for which every human intellectual resource was to be conscripted: research, statistics, mathematics, economics, psychology, anthropology, sociology, communications, and more. It was a search for the El Dorado of the human mind, the mother lode of human desire and motive. The recourse was to direct investigation of individual behavior patterns. This intelligence, multiplied by hundreds and thousands of such observations, offered an exciting promise to the new marketing manager.

What made the enterprise difficult were the invisible barriers that block access to the human mind, the most intricate of all God's designs. Rare are they who are not victims of their own deceptions, who are capable of comprehending their own behavior. Self-perception is blurred by aspiration and camouflaged by guilt, and investigators can be led badly astray.

Their need turned the social scientist into the marketing manager's principal ally. Methods and techniques that had previously been the exclusive tools of academia now found commercial applications. Motivation research, a buzzword three decades ago, became a standard feature of consumer studies together with much of the panoply of social science interventions. The results are evident in the proliferation of new products in an endless array of ingenious packaging, at carefully determined price levels, in tailored distribution systems, and supported by advertising with a deliberate buying incentive and image appeal.

Almost 25 years ago, Ernest Dichter (if not the father of motivation research, certainly its most illustrious son) predicted that "cultural anthropology will be an important tool of competitive marketing."[9] Yet, Barnett and Muller expressed surprise that McCann-Erickson, the international advertising agency, should have surveyed professors of Latin American studies on "the eating habits of *campesinos* and the consumption patterns of the new urban middle-class family."[10] This is standard operating procedure. But the new marketing manager would prefer finding out first hand.

The "Coca-Colanization" of the world, as the French once put it, has been replicated with thousands of items from New York, Paris, and Tokyo to Nairobi, New Delhi, Abidjan, Lagos, Lima, Bogotá, and Lomé, with foods, appliances, clothing, pharmaceuticals, films, and television programs.

Success, according to Dichter's assessment two decades ago, depends on such awareness as only one Frenchman out of three brushes his teeth. Yet, a U.S. toothpaste company, unaware of French custom, failed with an advertising threat to men that if they didn't brush their teeth reg-

---

*With gratitude to Samuel Taylor Coleridge, the great English poet of nineteenth-century Romanticism.

ularly, they would develop cavities or would not find a lover. Presumably, if all Frenchmen suffered from bad teeth, the condition could hardly
constitute a handicap to amorous adventure. Frenchwomen had no alternative. Moreover, attitudinal research with anthropological methods revealed feelings of guilt about overindulging in bathing or the use of toiletries. The appeal was switched to fashion and chic with positive results.[11]

   There are a variety of research techniques for probing the consumer
mind (see Chapters 6 and 7). The anthropological method has a number
of variations. The focus group interview consists of informally structured
sessions with small groups of people (usually fewer than 12) in which the
moderator stimulates interchange with a set of guideline statements.
There is no rigidly structured questionnaire to confine the interviewer. It
is a qualitative technique to search for attitudinal insights as well as new
questions by stimulating response from consumers on their own initiative
rather than by the prod of questions. The individual in-depth interview is
conducted along similar lines in a lengthy session. Its advantage is its
exhaustive dissection of the subject; the disadvantages are its high cost in
time and money and the loss of the benefits of group interaction.

   The traditional quantitative technique with its prestructured questionnaire and scientific sample selection is valuable for ascertaining the
relative importance of responses. Each has its passionate partisans. One
Chicago researcher declared

> Your typical market research interview is a highly artificial situation. You
> have an interviewer asking very specific questions of a stranger who . . .
> has given almost no previous thought to what he's being questioned
> about. The subject winds up giving the answers he thinks he's supposed
> to give. The results can be expressed in terms of neat percentages, but as
> a practical matter, they're mostly useless.[12]

   This advocate of the anthropological approach insisted it was the one
way of uncovering true behavior patterns that are frequently at odds with
what people say. He cited cases. Research about peoples' thermostat-setting habits turned out to be badly mistaken. An anthropologic approach
with TV cameras in 150 homes showed that fixed thermostat setting was a
myth, with everyone in the family adjusting and readjusting it at will.
Conventional research for a new health food revealed that people "were
interested in detailed data on vitamin content. . . . Our panels showed
just the opposite: that what [they] really wanted was a general sense of
feeling good. . . . Ask people . . . if they want more information and they'll
say 'sure.' But that's not what sells them."

   The consumer study is the companion piece to product research that
seeks to arrange the perfect match between product and target consumer.
The concept test solicits consumer reaction to written descriptions of a
proposed product. Once samples are available, the product test subjects

them to consumer blind-product trials (no identification) against the competition or alternative formulations of the product, itself, by in-home-use placements.

Obviously, the ideal product with a significant desirable difference from existing brands is rare today, and most contenders for the market share offer little more than product parity. This puts a heavy burden on the other strategies of the marketing mix: price policy, packaging, trade sales policy, sales promotion, and, especially, product positioning, advertising, and media selection. When shredded wheat shifts to a theme of "the all natural, 100% whole grain cereal, rich in natural fiber" from a previous strategy of "taste and goodness," it is repositioning the product to take advantage of aroused nutrition consciousness. When Sunkist urged America to "Drink an orange for breakfast" years ago, they were repositioning the orange as a beverage for breakfast from its conventional place in the fruit bowl. Intrigued that some consumers were squeezing the orange for its juice, Sunkist saw potential in promoting that usage as a breakfast fixture.

When Lysol disinfectant was discovered to have uses its manufacturer had not divined, the product was repositioned to test their sales potential: use as a floor cleaner, a bathroom disinfectant, and, strangest of all, a feminine douche. Some proved popular enough to become line extensions: Lysol disinfectant spray—a room deodorizer; Lysol basin tub and tile cleaner; and Lysol toilet bowl cleaner. Not all products are so fortunate. Most of them offer no significant distinction, and positioning must rely on imagery to create consumer demand.

There were in 1984 some 53 million cigarette smokers in the United States with 214 variations in flavor, tar content, package, and length with and without filters to choose from. More than $1.5 billion is spent on advertising the images conjured up by marketing strategists.[13] The latest is value, a cheeky positioning for a product declared "dangerous to your health" by the U.S. Surgeon General. R.J. Reynolds' Century brand offers 25 cigarettes per package instead of 20 for the same money to attract "the smart shopper," a neat subterfuge for seducing people who would kick the habit if they were really smart. Philip Morris' venture into value is an investment in imagery, a silver box with gold trim for Benson & Hedges 100's Deluxe Ultra Lights and a black box with gold lettering for its new Players. The advertising reinforces the imagery appeal to a luxury market. This compulsive market segmentation is the outcome of marketing's insatiable quest for growth from diminishing population fractions. Liggett & Myers, unable to compete nationally, aims Superior and Dorado at the country's growing Hispanic population.

Martin J. Freedman of the Dancer, Fitzgerald, Sample advertising agency saw two strong opposing trends in recent new product activity— the expansion of nutrition-oriented foods on the one hand and gourmet items on the other. *Light* has become the key concept, he observed, whether in beer, where it means fewer calories, or in cigarettes, meaning less tar. But he found the most active category to be low-sodium foods; followed by low-fat, reduced-cholesterol products; high-fiber items and caffeine-reduced beverages.[14] The exploitation of nutrition awareness is simply another manifestation of marketing's primum mobile: give the consumers what they want. It is not industry altruism but the outcome of the new militancy of health and nutrition educators.

Market segmentation strategy has limits but they are not always foreseeable, so manufacturers, the hot breath of competition at their backs, feverishly stake out new claims. Prospecting is done through segmentation studies to analyze amorphous consumer groupings for smaller constituencies differentiated by life-style or psychographic attributes. These consumer segments may be described by such baffling descriptions as upward-striving, passive, inner- (or outer-) directed from psychology's lexicon. Whether such subtleties of segmentation have market potential depends entirely on what can be made of them through fantasy. The familiar values of fact, function, and rationality are inapplicable. Marlboro, originally a lady's cigarette, was transformed into America's number-one brand for both sexes with cowboy imagery.

But it is marketing more than the marketer that deserves the tribute for such successes. Marketers can be trained in a relatively short time to wield their tools. Most potent of all are the mass media, particularly radio and television. A prominent presence in these media accomplishes wonders. Procter & Gamble, the giant consumer marketer (Tide, Bounty, Pampers, Charmin), is famed for its insistence on product distinction and, lacking that, trying for it through creative advertising copy. But one distinction it is never without is media dominance. The saying goes that "what P&G may lack in creative brilliance, they more than make up for with media weight." All other things being equal, share-of-advertising determines share-of-market.

But good copy and media weight are wasted without effective distribution of product. Tostitos relied mainly on network TV for advertising delivery but its 10,000-person delivery system was

> the final ingredient in this recipe for success. They contacted every major supermarket and every little store up and down the street. . . . The whole effort was coordinated from the time it left production until it reached the store and that meant they got extraordinary results from their advertising. That's what marketing is all about.[15]

The advertising phenomenon is well known in the developing world. In Mexico, U.S. agencies own eight of the top ten advertising firms; in Venezuela, nine of the top ten. J. Walter Thompson is number one in Argentina, Chile, and Venezuela; number two in Brazil; and number four in Mexico. McCann-Erickson represents Coca-Cola in more than 50 countries. Brazil's largest cigarette manufacturer, 70-percent owned by U.S. and British interests, seeks six to seven million new smokers in the next generation "using TV advertising techniques recently banished from the U.S. airwaves."[16]

The former chairman of the National Biscuit Company (now National Brands, Inc.) in 1968 detected a "tendency for people all over the world to adopt the same tastes and same consumption habits" and just to make sure, he said, "We plan someday to advertise all over the world . . . [using] a communications satellite system."[17] Today, talk of global brands and global ads is commonplace. England's Saatchi and Saatchi ad agency runs full-page ads espousing the notion.

Those engaged in food marketing know TV, and not the grocery store, is the food marketplace and that selling is done on the airwaves and the store is merely a display case. *The medium has become the market.* This explains the astronomical TV expenditures of U.S. food companies. Of a total of $11.4 billion spent in 1982 for TV advertising, more than $1.8 billion was for food products—one dollar out of six. As a result, the average supermarket stocks more than 8,220 different food items, half of which did not exist 30 years ago.

According to A.C. Nielsen Company, the sales auditing firm, almost 6,500 new food products were introduced in the United States in 1982, about the level of activity for the past decade with a 1975 peak of 6,700 new items. But more interesting than the growth of new-product activity is the waning quality of its technology. "Most companies haven't been able to afford the capital investment required for research and development of high-tech foods," said Goody Solomon, a syndicated food columnist.[18] She quoted James Albrecht, a McCormick Company vice president that "people don't need anything in the way of new products," but companies do.

In veering from high-tech to less costly innovations, they rely on the strength of their brand names for launching line extensions (Grape Nuts with raisins, sliced Velveeta cheese, Oscar mayer weiners with cheese, soft Philadelphia Brand cream cheese, etc.) and companion products (Minute Maid apple juice, Jello Pudding Pops, Lipton's herbal teas, etc.). Consumer trends like the rising health and nutrition consciousness allow them to introduce products they would have dismissed less than two decades ago (salt-free baby foods, yogurts, low-fat milks and cottage cheeses, caffeine- and sugar-free soft drinks, vitamin-enriched and whole-grain cereals). "Let's make the most of the consumer good-will and confidence in our brands and products . . . rather than elect the more risky and expensive pioneering course," advised K.O. Carlson, a vice president of A.C. Nielsen.[19]

When the Association of National Advertisers queried its member companies in 1983 on managing new product development, 57 percent said they would put more effort into the strategic work of studying markets rather than designing products. This reaffirms management's inclination to give marketing preeminence over production. Brand names, not products, are the creatures of success, and brand names are marketing constructs of advertising images projected by the mass media.

But every action spawns a reaction. When management subordinates production, inevitably production must suffer. Indirectly, preoccupation with marketing may have had this deleterious effect. Complaints about product quality abound. One authoritative critic declared

> Gripped by a dogma called 'management science,' the schools have played an important institutional role in the erosion of competence for production. A generation of managers has been trained by our business schools to make money, not goods.[20]

By contrast, the Japanese have absorbed the management lesson that, while it directs production, marketing cannot make up for its deficiencies. Less than 25 years ago "made in Japan" meant product inferiority. Today, that image has been totally reversed. Japanese production quality is the envy of the industrialized world.

The Neutrality of Marketing

In its broadest—and, perhaps, its most meaningful sense—marketing is a rationale, a problem-solving systems approach for institutionalizing an idea, a product, a point of view, a public policy, a political party, or a candidate. Its component elements—research, mass media, etc.—have been borrowed from academia and the entertainment world, and combined into a system for powering business growth.

Like all systems, marketing is neutral but, like Zelig in Woody Allen's motion picture, it takes on the identity of its association so that the two become indistinguishable. This is essentially what happened in the commercial marketplace. The system took on the market's name and function so completely that it lost its identity for other purposes. Even when it is employed for other ventures, the tendency has been to call it by another name to avoid a crass commercial association. Use has been made of such euphemisms as social communications, nonformal education, social promotion, and political technology—virtually any label that avoids any hint of linkage to marketing.

Appreciation of marketing's neutrality as a thought system has grown with the understanding that its disciplines have much broader applications. Witness the American political scene where marketing has forever changed the country's electoral process. Gone is the one-on-one electioneering, the power of the local political club, the doorbell ringers, and the canvassers. The process has been automated and canvassing by the political machine has now been replaced by the reach of the mass media. At the seventy-ninth annual meeting of the American Political Science Association held in September 1983 in Chicago, Benjamin Ginsberg, professor of political science at Cornell University, said that the growth of political polling, spot television commercials, telephone banks, direct mail, and the campaign consultant is, in essence, a shift from labor to capital-intensive competitive electoral practices.[21] The genealogy is unmistakable.

The swelling advocacy for a new industrial policy exudes a marketing aroma in the language its advocates use and the ways they work to promote it. Lester Thurow, the M.I.T. economist, borrowed from marketing thinking in answering a query as to which industries should be selected for government investment. "You can't pick winners," he said. "You create winners."[22] One bill in Congress backed by those favoring industrial policy would provide an "initial task . . . to compile data on the competitive situation of individual American industries . . . then 'formulate a strategy' to restructure basic industries and enhance the emergence of new industries."[23] And how will this new idea be sold to the American public? Patrick Caddell, formerly President Carter's pollster, "believes that the blue-collar voters can be aroused with the right *selling proposition*." Another public opinion expert, William Schneider of the American Enterprise Institute, "agrees with Caddell on *the marketing of industrial policy*."[24]

Thus, the neutral power of the marketing method and its mass-media techniques are being widely used for other than the promotion of commercial products even though the view persists that it is useful only for that purpose. This is unfortunate and it is akin to the belief that wealth is the inherent right of the rich and can have no useful purpose for the less fortunate of the world. The thesis of this book is an argument to the contrary, both for marketing and the world's unfortunate.

Notes

1. *Advertising Age,* magazine/section 2, March 15, 1982.

2. Barnett, R.J., Muller, R.E., *Global Reach,* Simon and Schuster, 1974, p. 350.

3. McCron, R., Budd, J., *The Role of Mass Media in Health Education. An Analysis in Health Education by Television and Radio* (Ed. M. Meyer), K.G. Saur, Munich, 1981.

4. *Marketing Definitions,* American Marketing Association, Chicago, Illinois, 1960.

5. McCarthy, E.J., *Basic Marketing, A Managerial Approach,* sixth edition, Irwin, Homewood, Illinois, 1979.

6. Rogers, L.W., *Marketing in a Competitive Economy,* International Publishers, New York, 1965, 1969.

7. Drucker, P.F., *Management: Tasks, Responsibilities, Practices,* Harper & Row, New York, 1973.

8. Adler, L., *Marketing. The Encyclopedia of Management,* third edition (Ed. C. Heyel), Van Nostrand Reinhold Company, New York, 1982, p. 653.

9. Dichter, E., "The World Customer," *Harvard Business Review,* Vol. 40, No. 4, July-August, 1962, p. 113.

10. Barnett, R.J., Muller, R.E. op. cit., p. 30.

11. Ibid.

12. Barnett, S., vice president, Planmetrics Inc., as quoted in an interview with Frederick C. Klein, the *Wall Street Journal,* July 7, 1983.

13. Loeb, M., "Marketing: Giving Smokers Added Value is Tobacco Firms' Latest Idea," the *Wall Street Journal,* July 7, 1983, p. 31.

14. Association of National Advertisers, new product workshop, November 2, 1983, Roosevelt Hotel, New York City. Proceedings available from ANA headquarters, 155 East 44 Street, New York City.

15. *Advertising Age,* op. cit.

16. Barnett, R.J., Muller, R.E., op. cit., p. 144.

17. *Forbes* magazine, November 15, 1968, in an interview with Lee S. Bickmore (as quoted in Barnett, R.I.; Muller, R.E., op. cit., p. 31).

18. Solomon, G.L., "New Foods Proliferate Without High Technology," *Nutrition Week,* June 30, 1983, p. 4.

19. Ibid.

20. Melman, S., "Managers' Debacle," the New York *Times,* op-ed page, November 4, 1983.

21. Clymer, A., "Shift of Power to GOP Seen in Technology Use," the New York *Times,* September 3, 1983.

22. Blumenthal, S., "Drafting a Democratic Industrial Policy," the New York *Times Magazine,* August 28, 1983, p. 31.

23. Ibid.

24. Ibid.

4

Why Social Marketing is Important to Public Health

The appellation social marketing was not so much chosen as fallen into. At least that is the mutual recollection Professor Philip Kotler and I have of a series of conversations in the late 1960s. A marketing professor at Northwestern University, he had come to talk about my use of marketing techniques in nutrition and health education. He had a compelling interest in the same subject and was to write several papers on the subject.[1] The wording slipped easily into our talk. It was easy, obvious stenography for distinguishing our subject from its commercial counterpart. I have never been partial to the name choice, a reflection of the embarrassment instilled in me by academic disdain for any reference to marketing however gussied up by adjectival cosmetics. Phil Kotler, an academician of another stripe, was made of sterner stuff and stuck to his word-knitting. While I went on to give speeches about the seemingly less offensive "mass media . . . social change"[2] and Phil wrote about "social marketing . . . social change," we were nevertheless parsing the same principle. I went on to practice what we both preached but I never came up with an alternative moniker, though I searched far and wide. All the time the holy grail was in Phil's front yard. *Social marketing.* It's a relief not to have to hide anymore.

The early 1970s witnessed a deepening academic interest in the subject. But for the most part, it was a concern with whether marketing was truly marketing when uprooted from its commercial soil. One commentator on the subject was of the opinion that unless it was associated with marketplace transfers of goods for money, it couldn't be marketing.[3] No goods, no money, no marketing—as extreme a position to deny the name as I had taken to avoid it. But withholding the birthright cannot forestall the birth. The *Journal of Marketing,* by devoting its July 1971 issue to the subject, pronounced its legitimacy. The literature has since proliferated and so have social marketing's proponents. The timing was felicitous. Circumstances demanded a far greater public communications responsibility than ever from health professionals. Even for those who preferred to identify the function more precisely as education, the process required a communications system beyond the conventional classroom. The opportunity for social marketing was timely because it offered a disciplined systems approach for public health promotion and communications efforts.

And that is the essence of the matter. The uses to which the methodology is put do not determine or alter its nature any more than the nature of an automobile engine is altered when it is used for transporting schoolchildren instead of commercial freight. Efforts to constrain social marketing's application to some narrow spectrum of purpose are futile because they usually hinge on the interjection of some extraneous element. Look, a family planner might declare about a social marketing breast-feeding campaign, that's not a social marketing project because it does not embrace a product marketing component. Yet when the project is examined, it may very well include just about every other essential element. If all the disciplines of the process are employed on behalf of a health idea or a practice, should the absence of a product invalidate it? Or, should an unnecessary product be conceived merely to prove its legitimacy? Such useless iconography belongs to voodoo cults, not to social marketing, which is a process, a strategy for persuading adoption of an idea, a practice, a product, or all three. It behooves the social marketer to think product even when there is none because intangible ideas, practices, and services can be more evocatively dealt with in that fashion—as emotional products, as it were. Moreover, even most of these are literally products though they may not be packaged and sold as such. Breast milk is a product though we somehow never think of it that way. Teaching a mother how to enrich homemade weaning foods is an effort to urge her to make her own.

Marketing is a neutral methodology and social marketing is its adaptation to public health imperatives. The distinction between the two is in substance and objective but not in methodology. Social marketing of public health is not to be confused with the marketing activity of the new commercial health care and hospital corporations. These are business organizations whose raison d'etre is to market health products and services for the profit of stockholders. Theirs is a menu mostly of curative services and since marketing is meant to increase sales, their operations are indistinguishable from normal commercial enterprise. Their catering to health appeals should not obscure their real business objective. In fact, there is question as to whether their impact on public health is always beneficial. Until recently, private hospitals were always viewed with suspicion. "Now health care is frankly accepted as a business, and non-profit institutions are even being urged to become for-profit. Some of the people who talked about health care planning ten years ago now attend seminars on 'health care marketing.'"[4]

This form of health care marketing is under criticism since costs have soared astronomically. Between 1960 and 1970, health care costs in the United States increased from $142 to $334 per capita—a national gross increase from $26 billion to $69 billion. By 1981 costs had reached $1,225 per capita for a national total of $287 billion, a jump in 11 years from 5.2 to 9.8 percent of the G.N.P. The United States spends more of its national income on health than almost all other advanced industrial countries.[5] Paid curative health care is a major item of consumption and is increasingly subject to market forces.

Creation of demand seems a dubious strategy when only illness should be the deciding factor. Social marketing's objective is the advancement of public health. Its only goal is improved public health. It is primarily a disease-prevention strategy with some notable exceptions like the treatment of diarrhea. It is indirectly competitive with commercial health care marketing in that social marketing aims to reduce the market for curative services. It is a classic share-of-market contest in which those with therapies to offer are pitted against those who would diminish the need for them.

Social marketing is a strategy for translating scientific findings about health and nutrition into education and action programs adopted from methodologies of commercial marketing. The opportunity is worldwide; only the urgency of its need may vary. One in five children in Upper Volta in Africa dies before age five from measles, whooping cough, diarrhea, malaria, and tetanus. Yet, "all are preventable by vaccination or environmental hygiene and, above all, by a better diet."[6] Upper Volta is representative of many developing countries as well as of deprived areas of the most advanced countries. For example, infant mortality in Washington, D.C., at 29.6 per 1,000 births, is as high as Malaysia where the rate is 30.3. Debility and sickness levels in Arizona, Texas, and New Mexico, as well as the ghettos of New York City, approach those in Bangladesh.[7] The root cause is poverty but the poor diet and sanitation it breeds can be ameliorated with health education.

Even among more fortunate but still needy Americans, damaging dietary practices prevail. In 1977 to 1978 when the U.S. Department of Agriculture (USDA) workers monitored food consumption patterns of food stamp households to promulgate food-buying recommendations for its Thrifty Food Plan, they found fat consumption for all ages exceeded the 35 percent of caloric intake that the USDA set as its standard but many authorities consider too high. Cholesterol levels, particularly for men over 15, were very high, from 460 to 520 mg per day, as were sugar and sodium levels.[8] One in three children in the United States is reported by *Family*

Practice News to have higher than optimum serum cholesterol levels, which at age 14 is already considered a high-risk factor for coronary heart disease in later life.[9] In Canada, according to the June 10, 1983 issue of the *Journal of the American Medical Association,* infants with high-sodium diets continue that level of intake in later years, a pattern they received from their parents.

The recitation could go on interminably from country to country. Some are the undeniable product of poverty and remediable only by changes in the socioeconomic structure. But many are also the result of ignorance and its spawn of behavior patterns that run contrary to good health. A few, like cigarette smoking, may be considered beyond the reach of education since they are addictions. "Many smokers are nicotine addicts. . . . They may have started in control—using nicotine—but have been taken over by the drug."[10]

But this point argues for education, not against it. The task may be made harder but not impossible by the psychological barriers. Because of the high social cost of inaction, prudence suggests such efforts be tried. Past efforts to discourage cigarette smoking have relied mostly on widespread publicity in the mass media. It has had a perceptible impact that confirms the belief that antismoking messages can work and that the mass media can effectively deliver them. Until now, however, the basis for mass media exposure has been haphazard news stories selected by editors for their newsworthiness, not for their urgent social value. This effort cannot be sustained indefinitely. The day arrives when the story dies and the subject disappears from the press and the airwaves. There is no meaningful substitute for committed, disciplined public education about this health hazard, which, as Stepney reminds us, "is the biggest preventable cause of death and disease in the Western world."[11]

Doctors Are Not Enough

Even if the medical establishment was oriented toward disease prevention, the maldistribution of doctors is an insuperable handicap. One of the most affluent of U.S. communities, the Hamptons of Long Island, was designated by the U.S. Government "as having a shortage of primary health care physicians—one of about 4,000 underserved communities in the country. And it is the poor who have felt the impact of that shortage the most."[12] New York State, Easthampton, and Southampton raised a fund of $110,000 to help subsidize the solution—a physician for poor residents. The effort to recruit and establish him took three years and, in the interim, local doctors and nurses volunteered their services one night a week. This illustrates again the narrow interpretation authorities make of the health needs of the poor. The conventional response is for curative medical care but if health conditions in the Hamptons resemble those of most communities, then the pressing need is for prevention. If debatable, then the issue can be resolved with a study of the nature and extent of the services required, including investigation of the community's perception of its needs.

Because doctors fail to recognize work-related diseases or seldom report it to health authorities when they do, Harvard Medical School compiled a reference list of 50 sentinel health events to alert doctors to preventable work hazards.[13] Thus, kidney failure in a plumber should alert suspicions of lead poisoning. A cataract in a radar technician might mean excessive microwaves; in a baker, too much exposure to heat. But normal channels to the medical profession may not always be the most efficient way to make information operational. From a public health point of view, the medical school might have considered some means of bringing the information directly to those who make their living where health hazards are known to exist.

Dr. David Rutstein, principal author of the paper in which this list was reported, wrote that there are no plans to inform the general public, except through publicity in such newspapers as the *Wall Street Journal* and the New York *Times*.[14] The major objective is to raise awareness among physicians. Communicating directly with the public, he added, "is not Harvard Medical School's bag."

The question here is one of philosophy. Should the emphasis be given to marketing awareness to the physician or directly to those at risk? A sentinel health event (SHE) is defined as

> a *preventable* disease, disability, or untimely death whose occurrence serves as a warning signal that the quality of *preventive* and/or therapeutic *medical care* may need to be improved. A SHE is . . . occupationally related and whose occurrence may: (1) provide the impetus for epidemiologic or industrial hygiene studies; or (2) serve as a warning signal that materials substitution, engineering control, personal protection, or *medical care* may be required (author's italics).

The limitation of a physician-directed approach is that it must wait for the disease to strike before preventive measures can be taken. There is no guarantee that this will be a first-strike incident. It may be the first to be detected of dozens—perhaps hundreds or thousands. This preventive strategy is a reworked version of curative medicine and, as Dr. Rutstein and his coauthors made clear, "occupational disease, despite its profound impact directly and indirectly on all of us, continues to remain outside the mainstream of American medicine and health surveillance."

While a better-informed medical establishment is certainly to be desired, there is reason for emphasis on awareness in the work place so that the SHE may be prevented. This calls for alerting workers-at-risk and their employers and public officials if work place regulations are indicated. The medical scientist may not be the most effective agent for deciding policy to control risk. A social marketing analysis would identify the primary preventive agents and propose the media and message strategies necessary to reach them. The causative factors of all 50 SHEs are mostly well known. Why must action wait upon the sentinel health event especially in the light of an admittedly "inadequate educational background [of physicians] and the consequent diminished level of suspicion regarding the occurrence of occupational disease?"

Not all scientists agree with shielding the public from knowledge of health emergencies. Some instances are not without their humorous side. Three hamsters used for research into the dangerous Creutzfeldt-Jakob virus were found to be missing from laboratory cages. The community was notified. Dr. Jan A. Stolwijk believed it was important to do so even though the risk was minimal. Dr. Stolwijk is chairman of the Department of Epidemiology and Public Health at Yale University and has studied public perception of public health risks. He said: "In this profession it is not realities you deal with. Perception is reality."[15]

The Emergence of the Paramedical Worker

Countervailing marketing forces are called for to unsell unnecessary consumption of medical services—a demedicalization of America, as it were—and to restore confidence in individual stewardship of health. Since the major share of illness is generally believed to be self-limiting, the highly specialized services of licensed physicians may not be as sorely needed as those of physician's-assistants and nurse-practitioners. "Data now show convincingly," said Donna Diers, dean of Yale University's School of Nursing, "that well-prepared nurse-practitioners can deal quite safely with 70 percent to 90 percent of the patient problems that occur in the office or ambulatory visit."[16]

In 1983, Dr. Albert B. Sabin, developer of the polio vaccine suffered paralysis and excruciating pain from ligamentous ossification near the spinal cord. After an operation to relieve it, paralysis set in and ten days later his breathing suddenly stopped. "He was saved by an alert private duty assistant hired by his wife. She was the least trained, the least educated, not even a nurse," Dr. Sabin reported, "but if she hadn't been there . . .?"[17]

Segments of the medical establishment oppose such complementary service. The president of the National Association of Pediatric Nurse-Practitioners charged that the American Academy of Pediatrics "felt we would be in direct competition for the same dollar. . . . But we're not. We want to deal primarily with the common problems of childhood. The big stuff, intensive care, we're more than happy to leave to them."[18] But Dr. Gerald R. Gehringer, president of the American Academy of Family Physicians, in forecasting a surplus of 130,000 physicians by the year 2000, declared that "the doctors are going to be out there competing. We certainly don't need another level of health care." Perhaps he is overlooking the likelihood of a different view from "we," the public. On the other hand, the Institute of Medicine of the National Academy of Sciences, after a two-year study, recommended expanded training of nurse-practitioners because "they are willing to provide primary care . . . where physicians at present do not practice."[19]

A bill to permit nurse-practitioners to handle "simple medical problems" was introduced into the New York State Legislature in 1983. Ashley Montagu, who styles himself an old medical school teacher, declared his support in a letter to the New York *Times* on June 7, 1983 because

> Most problems that come to medical attention are quite simple, easily diagnosed and effectively treatable by any appropriately trained individual. . . . The truth is that most conditions with which the physician is confronted require no knowledge that is beyond the grasp of any intelligent human.

The tragedy of this debate is that the real issue is obscured—the public health gaps in prevention activity and outreach to underserved communities demand new strategies for health education and service delivery. It is a worldwide problem. West Africa has been characterized by "snail-like progress in switching to a primary health care system [using lower-level medical personnel] and in the low priority given to [preventive] health."[20] A Brazilian public health official elaborated on the need for more paramedical workers. He presented an interesting case showing the correlation between declining child mortality and the rising supply of medical auxiliaries (paramedical workers) in several countries around the world, concluding that the value of paramedical workers may be decisive.[21]

Mary H. Griffith, a health educator in rural and urban areas of Bangladesh, stated

> Even an illiterate CHW (community health worker) can learn the early treatment for simple ailments and spare the doctor the majority of patients. . . . And because she lives close to her patients, she is in a position to help them prevent disease in the first place. She does not aspire to

move out to the cities . . . as doctors generally do. Part of the village and
its life, she feels a sense of responsibility born of her own identity.[22]

Even in the cities "people have no ready source of health information
about either preventive health or low-cost remedies. . . . The need is . . .
not so much for more curative personnel as a trusted source of practical
health information and guidance."

It used to be that oral health was the one positive claim of developing
countries. Twenty years ago, the WHO index (average number) of de-
cayed, missing, and filled (DMF) teeth of a 12-year-old boy or girl was 1.0
for most less-developed nations and as high as 10.0 for the developed.
Today, the index is 4.1 (5.0 for urban areas) for the Third World and 3.3 for
developed countries. Industrialized countries have one dentist for every
1,000 people; the Third World countries, one for every 20,000 to 100,000.
According to USAID, the training of more dentists is prohibitively expensive and is not considered a practical answer. Primary health care workers
trained in preventive measures and oral health assistants are considered a
more practical strategy.[23]

In Turkey, "the medical system follows the Western pattern but fails
to meet the needs of many people. Most doctors are in private practice
and as recently as 1980, 59% of doctors were concentrated in the three
largest cities where only 20% of the population lives."[24] A system of midwives that began in the early 1960s sought to make up for the deficiencies.
The midwives inserted IUDs and conducted the routine medical procedures of measuring blood pressure and hemoglobin levels, checking for
signs of albumen and slow toxemia, and offering health education, and
instruction in nutrition and environmental health, including the building
of latrines, and the need for safe water and clean houses.

Much of the health education for mothers—information on essential
foods, food preparations, sanitation practices, etc.—can be provided by
simple educational inputs. This justifies very short units of communication designed to reach larger audiences via radio and television. For this
reason, there is a close philosophical kinship between the auxiliary health
worker and social marketing. Each, in its own way, is an ingenious strategy to extend the reach of health services; medical care on the one hand,
health education on the other.

What we have at hand is an opportunity to restore balance to the marketplace with a prevention strategy of education and a primary health
care delivery system manned by those who can be trained in less time and
lower cost. The social marketer and the primary health care professional
are professional blood relations.

Though marketing has demonstrated its usefulness for social goals, it
is rarely carried out with the skill and thoroughness characteristic of the
commercial world. Most applications look like, sound like, even appear

like the real thing but the resemblance is superficial, often little more than a borrowing of marketing's reach-and-frequency use of the mass media (see Chapter 6). These are public service advertising campaigns executed without marketing's disciplines. Results are usually inconclusive. Social marketing is a holistic system of interdependent parts. When they are not all working, function is impaired and the whole adds up to less than the sum of its parts.

The Disciplines of Social Marketing

The developing world is scarred with inappropriate transfers of technology. Blame for Africa's food crisis has been ascribed by more than one authority to development models that fail "to provide a convincing understanding of the motivations of rural people and the role of technological change. . . . Development is an historical, social, political, technical and organizational process which cannot be understood by means of a single discipline."[25] These words could serve as a fitting preamble to the declaration of principles for the interdisciplinary approach of social marketing:

1. Identify the health problems and the marketing and message actions required for their solution.
2. Establish priorities, select affordable efforts, and set up a deferred schedule for all others.
3. Analyze the distinct marketing/message activities needed for each problem/solution.
4. Pinpoint the target audience for each marketing/message action.
5. Conduct the necessary research on each marketing/message concept to determine current target audience attitudes and uncover potential *resistance points.*
6. Establish objectives for each target group and each marketing/message action.
7. Design the marketing/message actions.
8. Test the marketing/message actions for acceptability, implementation, comprehension, believability, motivation, and conviction.
9. Revise and retest the marketing/message actions as necessary.
10. Construct the marketing/distribution and message/media patterns to achieve maximum target audience reach and message frequency.
11. Coordinate and harmonize with all ongoing related programs.
12. Track the impact of each marketing/message action and modify according to findings.

Identifying health priorities is essential to conserve limited time, energy, and money. Health authorities, plagued with many problems, are tempted to deal with all the priorities at once, dissipating energies over more ventures than can prudently be handled. The priority principle is needed everywhere. John Maddox, editor of the 114-year-old science weekly, *Nature*, declared

> Establishing priorities is a continuing problem. In medical research, for example, individual hospital doctors decide what developments will be pursued. . . . If there were a more objective look at our priorities in medicine, far less would be spent on prosthetic technology—new kinds of hearts—and much more on prevention.[26]

Dr. Cecile de Sweemer, associate director of the Christian Medical Mission and recently an associate professor at Johns Hopkins University, asserted "that primary health care must tackle priority diseases, and high risk groups (mostly women and children) so as to give the optimal benefit for the limited resources available."[27]

Identifying priorities requires discipline. Too often general familiarity with local health conditions inspires false confidence and arbitrary judgments that are frequently wrong. Personal observations need to be verified by surveys or the records of health centers and hospitals. The kind of information helpful to maternal and infant health decisions has been set forth by the Food Research and Action Center in Washington[28]

1. Number of low-birth-weight babies
2. Infant mortality rate
3. Maternal death rate
4. Number of premature infants
5. Anthropometric measures
6. Clinical signs of nutrient deficiencies
7. Leading causes of death
8. Disease-specific death rates
9. Most common childhood diseases

Solutions are difficult to find. An approach effective in a limited area may not be relevant for wider application. It may require more personnel and funds than are available, a weakness of pilot programs that fail to take expansion budgeting into account. Food aid is sometimes viewed as a hindrance that perpetuates hunger and poverty to be reserved only for emergency relief situations. The adage is cited about the wisdom of teaching a man to fish so he can feed a nation instead of giving him one only to feed himself.

Solutions can be counterproductive of other activities. Halfdan Mahler, head of WHO, recalled suggesting to the minister of Health of India that

> We can treat tuberculosis for one-five-hundredth of what it costs in Europe on one condition: that you will close down all the hospitals treating tuberculosis on an institutional basis today because we need those funds to go into the ambulatory treatment of tuberculosis. "You must be crazy," she replied, implying that such a move was politically impossible, that popular opinion would never permit the removal of such a facility.[29]

Mahler's observation was that "Development expenditure cannot be permitted to perpetuate the existing malpractices. . . . It's not so much the quantity of money but the way it is spent that is important. . . . In Nigeria some 90% of the health spending is in the big city hospitals."

Rigid custom and entrenched opinion can be obstacles. The social marketer must be sensitive to the local political struggles and should waste no time in head-on contention. The situation calls for arbitration. The best mechanism is research, and agreement by all parties to enter into research is tantamount to a commitment to abide by the findings. An informed basis for making strategic decisions is all the social marketer needs.

Health educators debate whether the purpose of health education is to educate or to persuade. One member of the Health Education Council of England was adamantly against "trying to persuade people to change their behavior—what we should be doing . . . is telling people the facts and letting them make their own minds up." Others on the council disagreed, believing such a position to be "sheer hypocrisy, [that] . . . we should be . . . trying to persuade people to behave one way rather than another way."[30]

The social marketer avoids debate, knowing that a fixed approach is a useless abstraction in the real world. Social marketing aims grow out of analysis of problems, not solutions arbitrarily decided beforehand. Shall we be shackled by a telling-the-people-the-facts-and-letting-them-make-their-own-minds-up strategy against cigarette smoking? Or, glory be, having been given five spots a week in prime time television on all three major networks in the United States, should we not throw ourselves into designing the most informative and the most powerfully persuasive messages possible? Who would keep dubious faith with a pledge to inform given the chance also to persuade?

True, there are unresolved health issues, like the relationship of a high-fat diet to cancer. The message may have to be a presentation of the facts because people have a right to know the risk so they may decide for themselves. This debate typifies the danger of reducing experience to rigid models. In social marketing, strategic decisions emerge from problem and target audience analysis, and since no two problems or audiences are exact, it follows that approaches may differ in significant yet unpredictable ways.

When asked the question, "Which is the appropriate responsibility of the health educator, to inform or to persuade?"—the social marketer replies, "When, with what and to whom?" For social marketing, the valid model is a simple construction of a chain of interconnected actions whose links are not unbreakably forged to each other. They can be rearranged when circumstances dictate. The project becomes the model but it may not be valid for any other. For the same problem at another time and other target population, the project could be modeled differently though its elements may be recognized from its predecessors.

The past has been described as the future's prologue. But in communications, modeling, rigidly patterned on the past, comes perilously close to legislating the future of a process unconstrained by the natural laws governing more predictable phenomena. Imposing a preconceived communications matrix on a new and radically different situation can be futile or, even worse, paralyzing to the young communicator and stultifying to the old.

I have witnessed the painful efforts of communications apprentices in the Philippines to design messages for changes in knowledge, attitude and practice in exactly that sequence—a separate message for knowledge, another for attitude, still another for practice—because they insisted this is what they had been taught. They could vividly remember the model—oh, how many we have seen like that!—and struggled slavishly to follow all its lines and arrows, to occupy every box, circle, and configuration of its construction. While the model was intended merely to explain the nature and flow of the process, the students took it as a religious ritual for executing it. And why not? If this is how people learn, they reasoned, why not teach that way?[31] But not all theorists even agree that this is necessarily the way people learn or, at least, that the learning occurs in separate and discrete stages. Cartwright suggested from his research a long time ago that messages serve different purposes depending on the target audience. The process by which we learn does not necessarily progress in linear fashion from knowledge to attitude and, if effective, to practice. Some messages may accomplish all three simultaneously with certain individuals of the target audience.[32]

Modeling zealots may suggest that either (or both) the instructor or the model was poor and that the modeling theory should hardly be held responsible. But granting this does not eliminate the danger to which our young Filipinos fell prey. Modelers, too, are victimized. Fearful of being faulted at some future collegial gathering for modeling omissions, they become enraptured with detail and a compulsion to leave nothing out.

What may have been useful as a graphic depiction of a simple concept (see Chapter 9 for the Resistance Resolution Model) becomes a Procrustean bed. To students who are always asking the how-to question, the model provides a welcome answer. They seize it as a template for slavishly tracing their way.

By contrast, social marketing assumes the communications process is an organic experience whose disciplines define directions, not to fix predetermined paths. In social marketing, paths become clear once the directions are taken. We cannot foretell the precise way each step relates to the next or the effect they have on each other. We know only that each step must be taken or else the process will falter. It is clear from experience that knowledge need not precede attitude change, nor must either or both occur before behavior is altered. Perhaps in some emotionally charged situations, they may occur simultaneously and without reason or knowledge. Behavior may be modified by extraneous circumstance unrelated either to knowledge or attitude (sudden peer pressure among teenagers) or faith-induced diktat (the anti-breast-feeding doctor). Other researchers reported the possibility that "the whole concept of attitude change [may be] useless in practice."[33] They argue that there is no clear evidence that the sequence from knowledge to attitude to behavior change necessarily operates, that the linkage is far from certain and if it exists at all it may be fortuitous.[34]

In this belief born of experience, the social marketer may be at odds with theory derived from experiment. It is doubtful that more experiment or debate will ever resolve the issue or that the resolution would be worth the effort. The social marketer believes that experience, not theory, offers the most useful instruction, that each effort deepens our understanding of how to make the next one better. This may increase the cost of learning but it also enhances the value received. In the end, market experience may be more cost effective than theoretical experimentation. In the latter with its intricately designed studies, realities are often distorted by special arrangements.

The mothercraft centers of Haiti, established some years ago to rehabilitate severely malnourished children, called for extra services of medical and health care personnel, special accommodations, and food supplies. The purpose was not only to improve the health of the children but also to educate mothers in nutrition as a preventive measure. The strategy proved impractical for achieving these objectives—there was simply not enough money or personnel to operate the number of centers required to come even close to dealing effectively with these problems.[35] A social marketing approach would have ascertained in advance the dimensions of the problems, the funds, and personnel required to handle the load. It would have revealed the full inputs required for effective curative intervention as well as the inconsistency in using rehabilitation as a prevention strategy.

What each such case reminds us is that the experience is special and may not be projectable. Isn't this why so many successful pilot projects fail to fulfill their promise when expanded to new territories? There is some mysterious seed we sow in pilot project plans that inevitably bear the bitter fruit of futility. The pilot plan seems to assume a life of its own and to seduce us into arrangements to underwrite its success. The original aim slowly begins to shift. The health care system gets souped up in ways not affordable on a larger scale. More trained personnel and funds are made available to the program than could proportionately be mustered for its extension. The real world now becomes idealized in ways that will make the experience inapplicable to other communities no matter how representative it was to begin with. The original aim is trampled in the drive toward success. The pilot has been illicitly transformed into a winner.

Social marketers take a more realistic view of such enterprise. Even the terminology reflects our intent. The difference between test market and pilot program is more than a matter of verbiage. A test market is ab initio an open commitment not to rearrange local conditions. Social marketing's discipline is to authenticate existing circumstances and to keep them that way, to prevent the slightest change in prevailing values before the program begins. *The program is the one exclusive alteration.* The full-scale future extension budget for people and funds is determined in advance and a pro rata share is established for the test. Thus, the social marketer establishes in advance what a full national extension will entail. With success, the administrators know they can afford the price of multiplying it.

But even with success, the social marketer is not constrained to replicate the experience exactly. Only the approach—the disciplined process of research, planning, execution, and evaluation—remains intact. All else—the product (if there is one), the strategies of messages and media, the materials—are subject to change in the new territory. Only research can determine how much of the test market experience may be applicable.

Thus, social marketing's dedication is to action and experience. What we may generalize from that experience, what may be called social marketing theory (though I wince at the words) is supported by observations from direct involvement and in most respects, though by no means all, by results. Social marketing results, however, are usually audits of program effectiveness. They can rarely be extrapolated for evaluating such elusive social elements as message design. On such matters, the social marketer again falls back on experience. He or she tests messages in natural and, to the maximum degree possible, unaltered surroundings and reviews their impact in the course of the campaign. We learn from this how to revise current messages and to make better ones in the future but we do not make the lessons articles of fervid religious faith. We refer to them as lessons learned, principles, disciplines, or insights (we even recoil from blind reverence for labels) but we are reluctant to sculpt them into overladen models that, like the graven images of a faith proved false, have to be smashed so we may free ourselves to learn from fresh experience.

Target Audience Identification

Target audience identification is a more subtle exercise than even many sophisticated commercial marketers appreciate. Despite many years in marketing, I am still amazed at the broad demographic brush used to paint target audiences, for example, women between the ages of 19 and 45. Even for a product of wide appeal, such a broad target range would include many who are not prospects and obscure the marketer's aim on many who are. Such factors as health, economics, life-style, convenience, and image are necessary to differentiate targets if sharply focused message and media strategies are to be devised.

Health education usually needs to address more than one public because the issues have implications for public policy, the media, and professional relationships. In the Brazilian breast-feeding promotion program launched in 1982, eight separate target audiences were identified, each for reasons vital to the objectives.[36]

1. The doctor—to be informed of the benefits of breast-feeding and to be encouraged to engage in technical research
2. The health services—to be informed and educated on breast-feeding practices and the health of the mother so as to become information vehicles for the mother
3. The hospital—to introduce new practices and to revise old ones
4. The infant food industry—to implement the objectives of the WHO/UNICEF International Code for the Marketing of Breast-Milk Substitutes
5. Industry (in general)—to comply with existing laws affecting breast-feeding: provision of crèches in commercial establishments with more than 30 employees and a three-month maternity leave
6. The community—to offer psychological support for families and to provide support facilities for breast-feeding mothers
7. Government officials—to initiate new policies
8. The mother—to promote longer duration of breast-feeding and to encourage its initiation among those who might be disinclined or discouraged to do so by engaging the mass media and the educational system

Even within the mother group, the Brazilians were to discover psychosocioeconomic segmentation. Women who worked outside the home had different concerns from those at home. For the latter, economic status proved to be a differentiating factor. Those who could afford infant formula had to be appealed to for reasons that were irrelevant to the economically disadvantaged.

Another illustration is offered by the debate among WHO and UNICEF officials over the promotion of oral rehydration therapy (ORT) for treatment of diarrhea. The difference of opinion hinged on whether home preparation should be promoted in addition to the prepackaged salts. Though WHO's ORT packets represented a significant cost improvement over intravenous therapy, they were too costly to provide to every family; the 50 million packets produced each year would serve under 5 percent of all diarrhea cases.[37] The annual need for oral rehydration salt (ORS) packets by 1990 was estimated at 750,000,000. The manufacture and logistics of distribution represented a staggering task. It was obvious that both product strategies were essential, for we were dealing with at least three distinct target audience segments: those who would decide to buy; those who would decide to make at home (either because they could not afford to buy, had no access to a free supply, or actually preferred to make it); and those with access to a health center where they could obtain it free. To ignore this target segmentation reality would have limited the objectives in advance.

Health workers felt strongly about the homemade formulation. N.H. Anita of the Foundation for Research in Community Health in Bombay, said, "It is not desirable to depend on ORS packets and . . . preference should be given to rehydration using materials like salt, sugar and bicarbonate or rice or coconut water . . . available even in the poorest home."[38] He cited the limited shelf life of ORS packets, storage problems (rodents and termites), limited supply, and inability to obtain more on short notice. When "ORS packets are given to the first few and the rest advised the home remedy . . . [they] feel that they have been left to fend for themselves, with what they now consider a counsel of despair." In Project Piaxtla, a villager-run health program in the mountains of Western Mexico, preference was for the home preparation. Packets, the villagers decided, "cost more and create more dependency than when a special drink is made in the home with local sugar and salt . . . the . . . health team prefers that families make their own rehydration drink without having to depend on either packets or spoons from the outside."[39]

Message Design

This question has obvious implications for message design (see Chapter 9). The social marketing message cannot be designed without up-front research of target audiences' perceptions of problems and solutions. Academicians know such research as formative evaluation, the procedure to help form the activity and provide the baseline. This is distinct from summative evaluation or data gathering for evaluation. The techniques may be qualitative or quantitative or a combination of the two. But the need to understand the workings of the human mind makes qualitative research invaluable to the social marketer. One doctor engaged in rural health care for more than 23 years declared that "people's perceived needs in health care are moulded by the culture and its understanding of health and wholeness. . . . The professionals need to become acquainted with the concepts and with the healing methods that can be derived from them."[40]

The commercial marketer has made a unique adaptation of the technique, the focus-group interview (see Chapter 6). This informal, loosely structured (but deftly guided) group device for penetrating to deep-seated attitudes relies on group interaction, which can be more revealing than individual responses. "Communication is a social act," according to William S. Howell. "In the most basic sense this implies that what occurs in participants is not as significant as what they produce together. . . . Interaction theory is needed to cope with the Third World, which is a result not of what participants do, but of the chemistry of combination. The effort to interact generates something quite unique that exists independently of those making the effort."[41]

The testing of messages and the determination of optimal media and distribution plans when products are involved need such inquiry. A priori notions are invalid without testimony from target populations. But focus groups are not always possible in the villages of the world. The alternative is the in-depth interview. Sometimes, a modified focus group of two or three people is possible. There should be no rigid rules about this, no more than about the focus-group technique itself. Its value lies in improvisation and, therefore, relies on the sensitivity and creativity of the moderator.

The Scope of Social Marketing

We see that social marketing is more than research, product design and distribution, diffusion of information, or the formulation and implementation of a communications strategy. It may include introduction of a new product (e.g., oral rehydration salts), the modification of existing ones (e.g., iodized salt), restricted consumption of others (e.g., cigarettes, infant formula), and promotion of structural change in existing institution (e.g., food stamps, hospital practices). Social marketing may be exclusively educational (e.g., sodium reduction) yet still be obliged to do missionary work with food companies for sodium-reduced products. While social marketers may not have to arrange it, they have an obligation to suggest that responsible parties do their share, just as the commercial marketer makes sure the salesperson gets the merchandise to the stores before advertising commences.

When a product is involved (e.g., contraceptives), authorities have a comparable obligation to see that an appropriate communications component is provided for. Tuluhungwa of UNICEF made the point: "It is not the diffusion of the famous cement slab but the change of attitude toward excreta disposal that may 'force' a person or family to construct, use or maintain a pit latrine. It is only when we change peoples' attitudes that they realize their old methods of disposal are not conducive to good health."[42]

In social marketing no component is more important than others. Relative importance is not fixed but varies by task. I have known failed campaigns with good communications components but inadequate field preparation and vice versa. By 1974, an antidiarrheal campaign in Nicaragua had been limping along for years. One of the serious problems turned out to be the oral rehydration formula to be made at home. It included bicarbonate of soda, though virtually no village *tienda* had it in stock when social marketers checked. The formula was promptly modified without reducing its effectiveness. This was eminently preferable to forcing distribution for bicarbonate of soda in the face of little other demand.[43]

Conversely, a successful product in Sierra Leone was not given all the communications support it deserved. This was the case of the palm oil press, a remarkably effective, appropriate technology introduced to six villages as an aid to women.[44] Unfortunately, reports of its success scarcely carried beyond official channels. Had an appropriate marketing program been devised, the benefits could have been extended to thousands more women. A social marketing approach would have embraced these steps:

1. Ascertain how women in other villages could obtain presses
2. Evaluate existing maintenance and repair manuals for their use and revise accordingly
3. Research and analyze the experience of the women in the pilot villages and get their reactions and recommendations for changes
4. Convert this tracking into media materials featuring a case history (e.g., what women in six villages of Sierra Leone did with the palm oil press) for delivery by appropriate means (radio, mobile film units, MCH centers, etc.) to women's groups throughout the region

Though social marketing is essentially a free-market methodology, communist countries resort to it. Despite draconian measures of Communist China to limit family size, the government found it necessary to conduct a Chinese version of a social marketing program. Even with "the mind-boggling array of controls that communist society can muster, the job of curbing China's population growth hasn't been easy," one official declared.[45] Thus, even total control of the state apparatus did not ensure compliance with policy when it infringed on normal human behavior. Social marketing helped to neutralize opposition and to reshape deeply ingrained attitudes.

Family planning officials in countries without China's autocratic controls face an even more difficult challenge. In most, "family planning services do not yet reach a majority of couples at risk of pregnancy. . . . Between a quarter and a third of births probably would not occur if every child born were a wanted child. . . . Most Third World couples still want families of four or more children."[46] In essence, social marketing is a strategic system for dealing with such social problems. Research and testing are its planning tools; communications, its primary executional mechanism.

A Prevention Strategy

Typical prevention messages are simple and direct—demanding little technical preparation. They depend as much on emotive, persuasive power as on information. They are directed to behavioral and life-style traits of the affluent as well as to the special concerns of the less fortunate. Social marketing is tailor-made for this task. The objectives have proved worthwhile. The *Journal of the American Medical Association* reported on the effects of a program of stress management and a low-fat diet of fresh fruit and vegetables—and without the usual inclusion of aerobic exercises—on a group of 23 individuals with ischemic heart disease. In 24 days, the patients had lowered cholesterol levels 20 percent, angina attacks by 90 percent, and 18 of them were able to reduce or quit the use of antihypertensive medication.[47]

Jean Mayer pleaded for the study of biology because "it provides an understanding of evolution and the working of the human body essential at a time when so many diseases can be prevented better than they can be treated. . . ."[48] The charge "that physicians do not want to worry about prevention because it is tedious and boring,"[49] may be exaggerated but the fact remains that much of prevention is beyond their power. People seek medical advice after illness occurs, not before. One does not call on a doctor for wellness. Even if doctors were eager to do more about prevention they are not a public voice. The power of social marketing is its use of a public voice—the mass media, the most potent of all. It would not be necessary if person-to-person outreach were possible through a corps of professionals large enough, adequately trained, and equipped for the task. But there are never enough people or funds. Even the best examples are inadequate: China's barefoot doctors, Indonesia's *kaders*, Burma's *lethes*. Armed with a few weeks of education on selected problems, they fan out through millions of villages administering to the routine health needs of rural populations. They are sorely needed. WHO reported one doctor for 84,350 people in Ethiopia, for 27,950 in Zaire, for 11,420 in Kenya. One look at doctor distribution and the picture darkens. Few doctors locate in needy areas, neither in developing countries nor in the poor rural sections and urban ghettos of industrial nations.

These workers need the support of social marketing. In addition to adding outreach, it bolsters morale ("they mentioned us on the radio") and reinforces the messages workers deliver. It is a form of refresher training for the health service corps. It supports them, too, by influencing targets like public officials, by influencing attitudes on legislation and social policy initiatives. And the public voice is available everywhere, especially radio. The case for the mass media has been put succinctly: "Given the fact that we are never going to have enough conventional teachers in whatever subject, that the only possible way we are going to educate our people whatever country we come from whatever political system we work under, is to give the mass media a part to play."[50]

There is little reliable information about radio in the Third World but, thanks to the transistor, there are few countries in which it has not penetrated deeply (see Chapter 5). The rural radio now has a mass audience estimated at 60 to 70 percent of the rural population of even the poorest countries. Not all are regular radio listeners nor do they necessarily own their sets. Radio listening is a community experience. Reception comes from neighbors' sets or community systems. This fragmented listening pattern makes the scatter pattern of the reach-and-frequency technique of commercial advertising ideal. Longer programs have their value but only when there is confirmed audience interest based on research into popular preference rather than on authorities' opinions of what the target should listen to. The unmotivated comprise a sizable segment of targeted populations. This is the same problem faced by the message designer. Facts no more speak for themselves than the right radio and TV programs automatically attract desired audiences (see Chapters 6, 8, and 9).

Even in developed countries like the United States, social marketing use of the mass media is still in its infancy. Witness our handling of health emergencies. Dioxin-related illnesses were first noticed in 1962 by Dr. Joseph Brodkin, a local physician, in a chemical plant in Newark, New

Jersey, and brought to the attention of the U.S. Public Health Service and New Jersey health officials. He also wrote up his findings "in the Archives of Dermatology in June 1964."[51] Confining the account to a professional journal was tantamount to silence on a problem that extended beyond the one in Newark to all factories where the danger needed to be guarded against. Thousands of workers and their families have since paid dearly for the failure of health authorities to make the issue public. Another benefit would have been an earlier invoking of appropriate regulations. What this experience pleads for is the cultivation of a social marketing attitude. Scientists are not equipped to decide what people ought to know or how to inform them. Scientists communicate through professional journals to enlighten each other, not the public. Their language is arcane; the exchange, hermetic. Yet much information important to the public appears in these journals and should be disseminated to the public in terms they will understand.

Three officials of the U.S. Food and Drug Administration reported that the American public in 1982 was no more aware of the potential dangers of caffeine to the fetus than it had been two years before. After comparing surveys from both years, they concluded that "reasonable steps to inform the public of the possible risk seem in order."[52] The incidence of adolescent childbearing in the United States is one of the highest of all industrialized countries. Only Hungary and Rumania have a higher rate among 30 countries studied by the Alan Guttmacher Institute. Justice Thurgood Marshall, rendering his opinion in a U.S. Supreme Court decision, noted that "adolescent children apparently have a pressing need for information about contraception." The New York *Times*, in editorializing on that decision declared that

> Teenagers need education in birth control through schools, community groups and advertising. They need easy access to contraceptives. They—and their progeny—do not need to be made victims of a revolution that occurred before they were born. . . . Many parents are understandably saddened by the sexual precocity of their youngsters. But the social issue is not whether their behavior is wrong but whether responsible adults are treating them right.[53]

A 1978 report described information to teenagers as scarce and largely inappropriate. Pregnant teenagers or those who suspect pregnancy have great difficulties obtaining information through public information channels.[54] Such channels are mostly inadequate, inappropriate, or incorrect. Teenagers confronted with the first symptoms of pregnancy find it difficult to obtain information they need to comprehend their situation or what to do about it. The mass media consistently abstain from offering information so as to avoid the charge of abetting immorality. The result is that public silence blankets a subject on which millions of teenagers urgently need to be informed. The relaxed sexual environment in the United States makes matters worse. The mass media freely portray the new sexual liberation in dramas, talk shows, feature films, and even the news. Late night public access channels on cable TV drool with explicit sex. Teenagers, certain to be well represented in the viewing audiences, receive a patent invitation to engage in the exhibited joys.

What they are not given—what the media shy away from—is what they need to know to avoid the tragic consequences. Teenagers have, in effect, been given the right to drive without a license. Political scientist Bernard Cohen put the matter succinctly: "The press may not be successful in telling people what to think but it is stunningly successful in telling its readers what to think about." This is true about all media, of course, but it is not a question of success or failure as Dr. Cohen suggests. It is a deliberate policy to avoid instruction on ticklish issues. The media will give all sorts of advice to its audiences—cooking shows, consumer fraud, traffic and weather advice—but not on matters that may involve them in controversy.

Surely, an ingenious group of social marketers—or those who aspire to be—should be able to put their minds to work on devising an acceptable formula forward-thinking media officials could accept as a basis for their active involvement. In the early 1970s when my advertising agency, Richard K. Manoff Inc., was asked by the Advertising Council to create a national family planning campaign for Planned Parenthood/World Population, we were unable to obtain network approval of such language as "contraceptive", "pregnant teenager", "unwanted child." A few years later, though, Rhoda, heroine of one of the top ten TV shows, had to ponder the advisability of an abortion, sharing the agony of her decision on the air with millions of viewers.

This change in media respectability standards was speeded by the Population Institute. Having designated TV writers and producers as their targets, the institute proceeded to market family planning to them through special workshop luncheons in Hollywood and New York. These bridgings of the gap between health professionals and the media have made the latter more accessible to public health education.

Even industry is not always aware of the other uses to which marketing can be put. The rising cost of medical care in the United States has become an enormous financial problem for business. A typical experience was that of Thomas J. Lipton, Inc., whose employee health plan by 1983 had grown to almost $10 million annually from $5.8 million in 1980, more than 70 percent in less than four years. In addition to new rules to reduce hospitalization and surgery costs, the company urged its employees to become "more aware of ways to save on health care . . . by learning to be smarter shoppers and . . . understanding that treatment is no longer the only health care focus. More and more we stress wellness, prevention of accidents and illnesses and self care."[55] This is a national business problem. It warrants a broad-scale education effort by business organizations and insurance companies combined. A social marketing effort, supported by a consortium of industry associations, could generalize the problem, making each company's effort more effective. It would minimize potential friction between labor and management over the issue.

The highly sophisticated Social Marketing Program for retail contraceptive sales has been in operation since 1975 in Bangladesh, organized jointly by the government and Population Services International with funding from USAID. More condoms are currently being distributed and sold through this successful program than the government is giving away free through its family planning and health centers. The program also markets birth control pills and vaginal foam tablets (see Chapter 10). Similar programs operate in India, Thailand, and Sri Lanka and are under consideration in Pakistan and Haiti, among others.

Numerous nutrition education projects use marketing techniques but rarely full social marketing application. But this is largely a function of time and experience and of word of more successful programs spread through the workshops, seminars, and publications of the World Bank, USAID, and the United Nations. The International Nutrition Communication Service, a consortium of three nongovernmental organizations, was created by USAID to provide technical assistance to developing countries. Requests for social marketing aid continues to grow.[56]

A decade ago, few would have foreseen widespread acceptance for social marketing among health professionals. Actual programs, however, are still relatively sparse. Because more work must be done in social marketing than in the isolated mass communications of the past, financial requirements are greater. So, obviously, are the demands for personnel with the necessary level of skill. Thus far, there has been no great migration of marketing professionals from the commercial world. The income disparity is hardly encouraging. Until such time as the public health schools see fit to make social marketing a curricular imperative, trained social marketers will remain in short supply. Even among those willing to make the move, many will not be suited to the change. There are marked differences in purpose, content, style, and philosophy between the two worlds. Social marketing's target populations generally exist outside the cash marketplace in an environment that is socially, psychologically, and culturally different. Progress is slow and results much more difficult to come by. Expectations are short and waiting times long. Not everyone finds the difference in substance and style easy to accommodate. Whereas social marketing chooses substance over style, commercial marketing's emphasis is quite the reverse. The latter is mostly preoccupied with the promotion of parity products, and its messages are short on substance and long on mood and images. The change takes an adjustment and not many have chosen to chance it.

Whose Responsibility?

These realities explain social marketing's slow emergence. The pace will quicken with efforts made through the collaboration of health professionals, governments, schools, the media, and industry. This raises the question of whose responsibility it is. The assumption that it belongs to health professionals has involved them in matters for which neither their training nor their experience have prepared them. The impact of the mass media has put much of their educational influence beyond the professionals' reach. These critical changes have produced a mandate for a new, responsible collaboration to replace past superficial cooperative arrangements with the food industry. Food companies have been actively involved in nutrition education.

The headline of a Best Foods (CPC International) health advertising series for its Mazola margarine asked: "Is there something your heart isn't telling you?" It referred to the information that "around 60 million Americans are afflicted with elevated blood pressure . . . yet, detection is simple: a quick, painless check by your physician." The ad went quickly to its major point, namely that a dietary program to lower elevated blood pressure "featured foods high in polyunsaturates, particularly Mazola Corn Oil." The rest was an unvarnished pitch for the product's "natural sources of cholesterol-free polyunsaturates."[57]

Pfizer Pharmaceutical conducted a Healthcare advertising campaign. The series consisted of 12 ads on diabetes, hypertension, angina, geriatrics, life-style, cancer, and "best years" and are for the reader who was dubbed "the most important partner" in health care. The ads on diabetes were typical. "Your doctor [who] orders your tests and makes the diagnosis [and] all those who discover, develop and distribute medicines complete the partnership." The advertising strategy of this partnership campaign was obviously threefold: to alert the consumer to the diabetes danger and to encourage medical checkups; to build respect for and confidence in doctors and Pfizer; to enhance Pfizer's standing among doctors. The ultimate objective for Pfizer was increased sales for its ethical diabetes pharmaceutical business.[58]

The food industry has for years offered schools a wide variety of teaching aids. The federal government and state and city health agencies sponsor a broad range of health and nutrition activities. Health and nutrition news and advice appear regularly in newspapers and magazines. Radio and TV programmers have discovered there is an audience for such material and have been offering it increasingly, if not generously, in the better hours. The Cable Health Network offered a 24-hour service of health news and advice, seven days a week, to more than 1,300 cable systems with over 13 million households (more than 15 percent of all U.S.

homes with TV). CHN then merged with ABC Video and Hearst and was renamed Lifetime Network. This gave it a charter for coverage beyond medical health and fitness to other critical behavioral factors.

These are positive developments but they are, nonetheless, arbitrary and unreliable activities, independently entered into and unrelated to each other. Those in charge are motivated by special, at times narrow, interests sometimes at odds with one another. (This includes government agencies: USDA food and nutrition projects are hamstrung by departmental loyalties to agricultural and meat- and dairy-producing constituencies, viz. the Dietary Guidelines.)[59] Information is pouring out but it has become difficult for the public to sort out the sane and sensible voices in the rising noise level.

We have become victims of a grotesque irony: *in order to get informed we have to be informed.* How else can we distinguish right from wrong information, balanced from distorted counsel? Those already informed become more so; the uninformed end up more bewildered. The gap between the haves and have-nots widens and the healthy get healthier. Only government programs and cooperating voluntary groups give major attention to disadvantaged populations. The mass media and the food companies tend to focus on problems of the affluent, reflecting their marketplace orientation. A decade ago the Food Council of America and Family Circle Magazine issued a "catalogue of nutrition education material developed by the home economics departments of major food companies, associations and retailing organizations."[60] These aids have become the mainstay of thousands of schools, a de facto acceptance of food companies' decisions on the form and content of teaching materials. Much of this material is an unabashed promotion for company brands but teachers have little choice. Either they accept it or do without. Industry material is colorfully and attractively designed. Even an objecting teacher swallows hard and accepts it.

The material focuses on food groups and balanced diet concepts. Hardly any reference is made to the dietary aberrations of fat, sugar, and salt overconsumption or to the snack-and-soft-drinks excesses that have produced a generation of food groupies and made a balanced diet more elusive than ever. In 1982, per capita consumption of soft drinks in the United States advanced to 419.5 twelve-ounce units, more than tripling the rate of consumption two decades before.[61]

Occasionally, exceptions like the Dietary Guidelines occur and cannot be avoided in this material. But even that singular victory evaporated under heat from industry groups whose products were unfavorably affected. Obviously, priority health and nutrition issues have a difficult time. Much of what must be urged on the public is an unselling of some product. This explains the general retreat to the neutrality of the balanced diet and the food groups. Controversy is avoided but at the sacrifice of impact on major problems. Cooperating sources are many and their assistance is sizable but the issuing stream of material is bland and of dubious worth. Nutrient education is a favorite noncontroversial subject. But nutrient deficiencies are of a low level among narrow segments of society. It seems ill advised to have them displace attention to more pressing concerns.

Even the forms of the material predetermines their limited usefulness. Most of it is posters, booklets, film strips, and teaching kits specifically designed for person-to-person use. Little of it is designed to be disseminated directly to the public as part of a deliberate program of information and advice making use of the major media. The food industry spends more than $3 billion in mass media to advertise its products, more than a billion on television, alone. But its efforts in behalf of health and nutrition education are not nearly so aggressive. Yet, awards are made annually by panels of teachers for the best materials found of most value in the classroom. Equally earnest endeavors to encourage more aggressive actions with more meaningful messages in the major media are virtually nonexistent. Considering that sound nutrition's most powerful opposition comes from the commercial food system, the struggle is an unequal competition. It is not without a typical free enterprise irony. One of the nutrition educator's key supporters is also, in another guise, an overwhelmingly powerful opponent who reserves his best weapons for himself.

The issues companies deal with are dictated by product sales, not public urgency; the message is short on education and motivation and long on public relations. This should come as no surprise. The objective of business is more business and marketing costs are replenishable only from the profits of business success. Marketing cannot, therefore, be wasted. This is legitimate business behavior and it is naive to criticize a business for conducting itself like a business. The appropriate focus is on more realistic sources of social action. Federal, state, and local governments are foremost among these. Others, like business, have roles to play. But these must be defined in terms of what can be reasonably expected in a free society. On such a basis, productive collaborations have a real chance of being built.

The need is there as de Sweemer contended: "The poorest communities do not have the necessary resources. . . . For them to feel a sense of partnership with professionals and government, a real contribution must be made by the larger national community."[62]

Notes

1. Kotler, P., Levy, S., "Broadening the Concept of Marketing," *Journal of Marketing,* 33/1, January 1969, pp. 10–15 and Kotler, P., Zaltman, G., "Social Marketing: An Approach to Planned Social Change," *Journal of Marketing,* 35/3, July 1971, pp. 3–12.

2. Manoff, R.K., "The Media and Social Change." An address before the annual meeting of Planned Parenthood Federation of America, Inc., San Antonio, Texas, October 23, 1972.

3. Luck, D., "Broadening the Concept of Marketing—Too Far," *Journal of Marketing,* 33, January 1969, pp. 53–55.

4. Starr, P., "The Laissez-Faire Elixir," *The New Republic,* April 18, 1983, p. 19.

5. Ibid., p. 20.

6. Knight, D., "Lively Beginnings in Upper Volta," *People,* Vol. 10, No. 3, 1983, IPPF, London.

7. "Child Survival—A Fair Start For Children." A paper prepared by the Ford Foundation to describe its Fair Start Program for children in the United States, January 1983.

8. *Nutrition Week,* Vol. 13, No. 33, August 25, 1983, Washington, D.C., p. 1.

9. Ibid., p. 2.

10. Stepney, R., "Why Do People Smoke?" *New Society,* London, July 28, 1983.

11. Ibid.

12. Winer, M., "Shortage of Doctors in Hamptons Limits Medical Care for Poor," the New York *Times,* June 30, 1983, p. B1.

13. Rutstein, Dr. D.D., et al., "Sentinel Health Events (Occupational): A Basis for Physician Recognition and Public Health Surveillance," *American Journal of Public Health,* Vol. 73, No. 9, September 1983.

14. Dr. David D. Rutstein in a telephone interview with Daniel M. Lissance of Manoff International Inc. on October 25, 1983. Dr. Rutstein, now retired from the faculty of Harvard Medical School, made clear that he could speak only for himself and not for the institution.

15. "A Yale Lab, Three Hamsters and a Hunt," the New York *Times,* October 19, 1983, p. B2.

16. Freudenheim, M., "Doctors Battle Nurses Over Domain in Care," the New York *Times,* June 4, 1983, p. 1.

17. Boffey, P.M., "Sabin, Paralyzed, Tells of Death Wish," the New York *Times,* November 27, 1983, p. 26.

18. Freudenheim, M., op. cit.

19. Ibid.

20. Kabba-Diallo, F., in *West Africa,* Nigerian expatriate-owned weekly, London, June 20, 1983.

21. Dr. Joao Bosco Salomao in an interview with the author in Sobrandinho, Brasilia, while on a mission to Brazil for USAID, May 16 to 26, 1972.

22. Griffith, M.H., "Urban Health Workers in Search of a Role," *Future,* 1983, first quarter, p. 43, IPPF, London.

23. "Accent on Development," *Horizons,* USAID, Vol. 2, No. 8, September 1983, p. 1.

24. Tansey, G., "The Midwives of Cubuk," *People,* Vol. 10, No.3, 1983, p. 12, IPPF, London.

25. Eicher, C.K., "Facing Up To Africa's Food Crisis," *Foreign Affairs,* Vol. 61, No. 1, Fall 1982, p. 159.

26. Maddox, J., "Scientists and Responsibility," an interview with Alfred Balk, *World Press Review,* July 1983, p. 31.

27. de Sweemer, C., "Reaching the Village," *People,* Vol. 10, No.3, 1983, IPPF, London.

28. Doyle, J., "How to Use Health Status Information in Hunger Monitoring," supplement to *CNI Weekly Report,* December 23, 1983.

29. Mahler, H., director-general, WHO, "Rescue Mission for Tomorrow's Health," an interview, *People,* Vol. 6, No. 2, 1979, IPPF, London.

30. Cain, J., assistant controller, Educational Broadcasting, British Broadcasting Corporation, London, and a member of the U.K. Health Education Council in a statement on "Health Education by Television and Radio—Some Dimensions of the Conference Theme" before the International Conference on Health Education by Television and Radio, Munich, Germany, November 1980.

31. This experience took place in a message design workshop during a Manoff International consultancy in connection with "Radio Nutrition Education—Using The Advertising Technique To Reach Rural Families: Philippines and Nicaragua," final report, December 1977. The result was a redesign and retesting of messages conceived in a more flexible creative climate (see example of one of these in Chapter 8). This project was supported by the Office of Nutrition, Technical Assistance Bureau, Agency for International Development, Washington, D.C.

32. Cartwright, D., "Some Principles of Mass Persuasion," *Human Relations,* February 1949, pp. 253–267.

33. McCron, R., Budd, J., "The Role of the Mass Media in Health Education: An Analysis," in *Health Education by Television and Radio,* (Ed. M. Meyer), K.G. Saur, Munich, 1981.

34. Halloran, J.D., "Attitude Formation and Change," presented to a conference on Attitudes and Health Education, University of Dundee, September 1977.

35. The background for this reference is to be found in a "Report from Haiti on Mothercraft Centers" prepared for the Working Conference on Nutrition Rehabilitation Centers in Bogotá by Dr. William Fougere, Gladys Dominique, and Linda D. Gonzalez. Unfortunately the report is undated. However, references to it are found in my letter to the *American Journal of Clinical Nutrition* 28: December 1975, pp. 1345–1346, in answer to a letter from Dr. Kendall W. King (*American Journal of Clinical Nutrition* 28: 435, 1975) and in "The Essential Communigraphic Component" (discussant remarks on the design of nutrition intervention programs) by this author, International Conference on Nutrition, National Development and Planning, M.I.T., Cambridge, Massachusetts, October 20, 1971.

36. Manoff, R.K., "The Brazilian National Breast-Feeding Program," report of consultant's visit, March 21–31, 1982, International Nutrition Communication Service (INCS), 55 Chapel Street, Newton, Massachusetts.

37. AID bulletin, *Horizons,* USAID, Vol. 2, No. 8, September 1983, p. 5.

38. Anita, N.H. in a communication to *Future,* the UNICEF magazine in India, 1983 first quarter, p. 5.

39. "Child-to-Child-Activities in Ajoya," in *Education for Health,* the newsletter of WHO, inaugural issue, 1984, p. 29.

40. de Sweemer, Cecile, op. cit.

41. Howell, W.S., "Theoretical Directions for Intercultural Communication," in *Handbook of Intercultural Communication* (N.K. Asante, E. Newmark, and C.A. Blake Eds.) Sage, Beverly Hill, California, 1979.

42. Tuluhungwa, R.N., "A Communications Strategy for Develoment," in *Health Education by Television and Radio,* (Ed. M. Meyer), K.G. Saur, Munich, 1981, p. 32.

43. Manoff International Inc. was the marketing consultant to the government of Nicaragua in 1974 on this campaign to teach village mothers how to prepare the ORT formula at home.

44. Manoff, Richard K., consultant to ATRCW from October to December, 1976, in the development of a communications program for women's development in Africa. The palm oil press experience was proudly referred to by officials as an example of what could be accomplished by women for themselves. But at the time, there was little appreciation of how to roll out this success elsewhere through social marketing.

45. Bennett, A., "China Cajoles Families and Offers Incentives to Reduce Birth Rate," the *Wall Street Journal,* July 6, 1983, p. 1.

46. Jacobsen, J., "Promoting Population Stabilization: Incentives for Small Families," *Worldwatch Paper,* No. 54, Worldwatch Institute, Washington, D.C., June 1983.

47. As reported in an advertisement by Rodale Press in the New York *Times,* op-ed page, July 26, 1983.

48. Mayer, J., "A Basic Curriculum," the New York *Times,* op-ed page, June 21, 1983.

49. Ibid.

50. Cain, J., "Some Problems Faced by Broadcasters," in *Health Education by Television and Radio—Some Dimensions of the Conference Theme,* (Ed. M. Meyer), K.G. Saur, Munich, 1981.

51. Blumenthal, R., "Doctor in Jersey Cited Ailments at Dioxin Plant," the New York *Times,* June 7, 1983, p. B5.

52. "Consumer Update," *CNI Weekly,* August 4, 1983, p. 5.

53. "When Children Bear Children," editorial, the New York *Times,* August 1, 1983.

54. Ambrose, L., "Misinforming Pregnant Teenagers," *Family Planning Perspectives,* 10/1978/1, pp. 51–53, 57.

55. From a presentation to employees of Thomas J. Lipton, Inc., on health care cost containments, July 1983.

56. The INCS consortium comprises the Education Development Center (EDC), Save the Children Federation (SCF), and Manoff International Inc.

57. "Is There Something Your Heart Isn't Telling You?" an advertisement in a new health advertising series from Mazola margarine, Best Foods Division, CPC International Inc., the New York *Times,* October 19, 1983, p. C8.

58. Healthcare Series (advertising campaign) available from: Pfizer Pharmaceuticals, P.O. Box 3852, Grand Central Station, New York, New York 10163.

59. U.S. Senate, Select Committee on Nutrition and Human Needs, *Dietary Goals for the United States,* Washington, D.C., 1977.

60. "Catalogue of Nutrition Education Material", compiled by Family Circle Magazine in cooperation with the Food Council of America, June 1973.

61. *Sales Survey of the Soft Drink Industry,* (1982), National Soft Drink Industry Association, Washington, D.C.

62. de Sweemer, C., op. cit.

5

Mass Media:
Social Marketing's Primary Tool

Automated contact is so routine a part of our lives that we are no more conscious of it though we depend on it just as we do on the air we breathe. It is, of course, the product of mass communications in which human beings are terminals in a dizzying network. The individual now has a reach to far more people and places but the contact is entirely non-direct and nonconnected. Thus, though we live in vastly enlarged human communities, interpersonal communication may, in fact, be shrinking. Much of the increasing alienation of the individual in modern society may be traced to this effect of the mass media.

Since one is either a sender or a receiver, communication is almost entirely one way. We may be acquainted with each other, but since we are confined to the passive role of audience and spectator, the terms of human association and exchange are radically altered. It takes very little imagination to see the implications for social change—or no change. The possibilities range from stultification of the status quo to its overthrow. Recent history has given us ample evidence of both. It is no wonder that revolutionary forces occupy radio and television stations first when seizing the reins of government. Indeed, the two are often indistinguishable.

The late Edward R. Murrow of CBS once said

A communications system is totally neutral. It has no conscience, no principle, no morality. It has only a history. It will broadcast filth or inspiration with equal facility. It will speak the truth as lightly as it will speak falsehood. It is, in sum, no more no less than the men and women who use it.

Viewed in this light, the mass media are clearly a strategy for shaping social policy and belief. The uses to which they are put depend on the answers society frames to questions like: What are our social goals and how shall our communications media be employed for their realization? It is possible for the media to neutralize change, to be employed for endless presentation of the current mode rearranged in diverse combinations to give the appearance of social dynamism without, in fact, disturbing the underlying social structure. One formula for such a use of the mass media is a continuous serving up of entertainments to divert audiences from the legitimate and clamoring social concerns of the day. It is also possible for the mass media to pursue the opposing strategy: to identify these concerns and exhort people to rectify the causes, to educate society in the pursuit of positive personal and social goals, and to reject goals that are repugnant to the public welfare. The mass media, like all human inventions, will do as we direct, and herein lies the central consideration of social policy governing the uses to be made of them.

The Penetration of the Mass Media

DEIR AL QAMAR, Lebanon, Nov. 1—Naef Saad, 87 years old, stood in front of Bus No. 1, waiting to be evacuated from this Christian town under siege. In his right hand he clutched a plastic bag containing all he had left in the world: a Sony portable radio and a clump of earth from Ramhala, his home village some 15 miles from here. "I'm old," he explained. "I know I will never see my village again."—the New York *Times,* November 2, 1983.

The evidence of mass media penetration is everywhere to be seen— in rooftop TV antennas, portable radio sets that are our inseparable companions, newspapers and magazines, billboards and hoardings, cinemas and the multitudinous minor media that have forever upset the balance of the social ecology.

More than ten years ago a U.N. organization paid its acknowledgment to the transistor revolution, saying,

Small inexpensive transistor radios abound in the developing world. Today, it would not be unusual to see a Masai tribesman in Kenya or a gaucho on the Argentinian pampas listening to a transistor radio while tending his cattle. Nor, for that matter, would it be extraordinary to observe residents of equally remote regions of Africa, Asia and South America doing the same thing. Where illiteracy is high and newspapers are scarce, radio has become the primary link to the outside world. It communicated information and new ideas, thereby especially widening the horizons of those in the lower socioeconomic classes. Moreover, radio awakens these people to new opportunities and in so doing is a major force motivating them to acquire the education and know-how that will enable them to improve their conditions.[1]

This is true no matter in what part of the world one lives.

The impact of radio today is immense. As a result of transistors, there are radios in even the most remote corners of the planet: an estimated 1.5 billion of them, six times as many as in the mid-1950's. This represents the most direct means available of reaching vast numbers of people on a regular basis.[2]

Vladimir Lenin once predicted that international radio could be "a newspaper without paper and without frontiers."

One may not find TV outside the cities of Indonesia, India, Kenya, and Ecuador, and radio's audience may come in large measure from group listening over amplified public facilities or around neighbors' sets. But TV and radio's coverage far exceeds official reports. In India, data on radio-set ownership are from licensing records that even officials say grossly understate the situation. India, in the British tradition, requires an annual license for every set. The result is an active underground market in smuggled radio sets, swelling the reported number in operation perhaps 10 to 20 times. For example, a study conducted by the National Institute of Community Development in Hyderabad as far back as May 1968 found radio penetration in the villages to be far greater than official figures would have indicated.[3] The average number of working radios was found to be 20 per village. Projected nationally, this would suggest 11 million radio sets for the estimated 550,000 villages of the country. Yet, according to license registrations, there was a national total of only 10 million sets, including urban areas in which set ownership was known to be concentrated. The transistor also has made the radio set relatively inexpensive, as little as 60 or 70 rupees or about $6 or $7. Battery replacements are a problem for villagers, making the distinction of a working radio important.

This universality of the mass media and their growing domination of our lives are dramatically reflected in some life-style indexes in a country like the United States. There are 85.4 million homes in the United States[4] and 98 percent of them are equipped with a TV set[5] that is on for about seven hours a day.[6] More than 55 percent have two or more sets.[7] During the average weekday winter evening, about 63.5 percent of the people in this country are in total surrender to their TV sets and the material it has to offer.[8]

From the age of two or three, the average child watches three hours of TV after school each day and four hours a day on weekends—a total of 21 to 25 hours a week. This is more time than will have been spent in elementary and high school combined by age 18. By the time the child enters kindergarten, more time will already have been spent with TV than will be devoted to earning an undergraduate college degree. By the age of 65, the average American will have watched TV for 3,000 24-hour periods—or more than nine full years.

But TV is only the half of it. All in all, the average American spends approximately 2,600 hours a year with all forms of spectator entertainment. Almost half—1,200 hours—is spent watching TV. Radio absorbs 900 hours; newspapers, 218; and magazines, 170. Books, regrettably, receive only ten hours of attention; tapes and records, 68; the movies, 9; and sporting events, 3. All cultural events combined (plays, operas, concerts) are given 3 hours.[9] Assuming 8 hours a day for work, 8 for sleep, and 3 for eating and other body functions, by the end of the year, the typical American is left with a depressing total of 45 hours, or less than 2 days a year to devote to all the other living concerns.

This is the Media Life and considering what comprises most of it, is it any wonder that Media Man and Woman are left with a deepening disinclination to deal with the concerns of their lives? Moreover, given such a gargantuan preemption of our time and attention, would it not seem surprising if the mass media have had no perceptible qualitative influence on our beliefs and behavior? Yet, Gatherer et al, as a result of an assessment of 49 mass media projects in health education reported that "there is a common assumption that the mass media have a powerful influence on our lives. However, these evaluative studies have shown that their effect is not very great, especially upon the individual."[10]

Such a finding conflicts with the simple evidence of our eyes the day after a single prime-time TV newscast reported new findings confirming the relationship of high sodium intake to hypertension and heart disease. We witnessed an instantaneous consumer reaction in the food stores. Even if it is not long lasting or permanent, we are on uncertain ground when we conclude that the effect of mass media is limited. One TV announcement or even ten cannot guarantee indelibility. Only continuing mass media exposure, like continuing education in the schools, can promise lasting significant behavioral effect. Even Gatherer et al, conceded that "the long-term effects over the decades of a continuing media campaign . . . in helping to bring about a gradual change in the climate of opinion and thus in the definition of acceptable behaviour should not be underrated." There is evidence, they suggested, that "there may be a steady but slow incremental change over the years though other factors as well as the mass media may have helped to bring this about." The social marketer believes that "other factors" always help and never seeks to rely exclusively on the mass media, viewing the enterprise as needing a collaboration, not a competition, of media.

Other circumstances militate against mass media effectiveness and health education in general. If appropriate products are not available in the food stores—salt-free baby food, for example—the consumer gradually relapses into old ways despite the readiness to change. Health and nutrition educators must take a broader view of their obligations and become involved in public policy issues and the practices of the marketplace. This is the educational embrace envisaged by social marketing.

Evaluating the Influence of the Mass Media

Communications researchers have been engaged for years in assessing the real influence of the mass media on behavioral change. Much of this research has proved inconclusive as Flay[11] and others have observed. The preponderance of the research suggests that the mass media have limited potential for changing behavior, although there have been some notable exceptions—the Finnish North Karelia Project[12]; the Stanford Three Community Project[13]; the Indonesian Nutrition Improvement Program[14]; the Bangladesh Social Marketing Program[15]; the Philippines Iloilo Nutrition Education Campaign[16] (see Chapter 10). Flay acknowledges, however, that the deficiency may be with the inability of available research models to measure the impact of the mass media rather than with the mass media's incapacity to deliver it. This may be another demonstration of the reality denial effect that hampers our efforts to reconstruct a whole reality from a restricted view of its parts. Projecting this view then magnifies the distortion and we can never be certain of what produces it. Is it because significant elements may be absent from our field of view yet present in the area beyond it? Or, because the elements, though present, are not discernible to us? Or, if discernible, are they overlooked?

In social research we deal with restricted samples (perilously subject to error, especially in developing countries) and patterns of inquiry limited to the known questions. Even under the most rigorous approach our confidence must waver at the thought of all the unprobed areas—the unasked questions—that defy our best efforts. Which of them may hold the key to the whole reality of what we seek to know? In the novel, *Daniel Martin* by John Fowles, the hero deplores the limitations of the camera because it "denies the existence of what it cannot capture." And who can deny that a photograph, even the most starkly realistic, is at best only a fragment of the reality it seeks to represent and, thereby, excludes from our view much that could make a difference to our understanding?

Given the limitations of research and of researchers, it is plausible that, like Daniel Martin's camera, research denies the existence of what it cannot measure. And there is much that is missing from evaluations to date of mass media programs in health and nutrition education. Almost without exception the research model—what Flay refers to as "the information-processing model"—confines itself to measuring the impact on knowledge, attitude, and behavior of the medium, assuming that message's design quality has a fixed value and is not also a variable to be measured. Thus, when evaluation reveals little or no impact from a mass media project or the results are indecisive, the conclusion invariably is that the medium has failed to fulfill its purpose.

But the failure may lie elsewhere. The message may have been ineptly designed for any number of reasons: misidentification of the target audience, insensitivity to cultural considerations, failure either to deal effectively with audience *resistance points* or to have identified those points in advance, internal message dissonances, and problems of clarity or comprehension (see Chapter 9). The media plan may have been misdirected: inappropriate media selection for the target audience or the message, inadequate media exposure or media mix (see Chapter 8).

Mass media impact is determined by message quality and the exposure the message is given in terms of audience focus and reach and frequency of delivery. No evaluation can afford to overlook these factors. Admittedly, these are difficult measurements to make considering the elusive nature of message design in which the creative contribution is so important. But this is why the social marketer places emphasis on message design and media research and planning. The premise is that the force of the medium is determined by the message and the pattern of its delivery. Success or failure summarily ascribed to the media may, in fact, be more accurately assigned to the message, its delivery, or both. Thus, the aim of evaluation should be not only to measure results but also to evaluate the components of the process (see Chapter 6).

The evidence is that the mass media can be effective in health education under prescribed conditions and disciplines. We believe there will be more such evidence as the social marketing skills of health and nutrition professionals improve. Techniques for message design, media scheduling and mixing, and in estimating appropriate exposure levels will improve with practice. To bring this about, health educators will have to give increasing attention, as McCron and Budd pointed out, "to *formative* rather than to *evaluative* research."[17] By shifting the focus of their evaluative studies to this area, communications researchers would be offering the health educator invaluable assistance.

Not all communication theorists doubt the influence of television as an important source of social learning. Bandura is not neutral on the subject,[18] and Liebert, Neale, and Davidson have a similar conviction.[19] Surveys conducted both with the public and with primary care physicians in Northern Florida in 1978 indicate the health education impact of the mass media. When asked how health education should be provided, the physicians' first choice was the elementary schools followed closely by the mass media. Their predilection was substantiated by the consumer survey. More than one-third of the respondents said they had "been influenced in their child-rearing practices, personal and family health habits . . . by information which they had received in newspaper/magazine articles and ads and via TV commercials."[20] Still others, in readily accepting TV's influence on health and nutrition practices, devoted their attention to pinpointing the blame. For example, a 1980 report in the *Journal of Communication* of a study of both television advertising and programming suggested "that nutritionists and other groups concerned with food messages on television may have been overly hasty in singling out advertising as the major culprit in the promotion of poor nutritional habits and that greater attention ought to be paid to program content as a source of food messages."[21]

The big worry about TV keeps growing as was evident at the first Everychild Conference in New York in September, 1983. "I think many are alarmed over the fact that kids are getting information from television or computers and not books," the director of the Children's Book Council declared, but Dr. George Gerbner, dean of the Annenberg School of Communications, reserved his concern exclusively for TV. He said that "other proliferating technologies are simply new stores in the supermarket of television."[22] Gerbner estimated that "by the time a typical American child reaches adulthood, he or she will have received more than 30,000 electronic 'stories.' These have . . . replaced the socializing role of the preindustrial church in creating 'a cultural mythology' that establishes the norm of approved behavior and belief."[23] One nutrition educator from Harvard's School of Public Health pointed out that because characters on TV soap operas are always "wolfing down doughnuts and coffee or swigging alcoholic beverages,"[24] TV programs should incorporate better health practices in the life-styles they portray.

Radical positive changes in the American life-style have taken place over the last two decades and it would be utterly devious to deny major credit to the mass media. True, they have been the result of increased perception of the relationship of life-style to health but how could this have been accomplished if it had not been publicized by the mass media? Those who fault the capability of the mass media to persuade behavior change will have a hard time with this one: a U.S. government survey conducted jointly by four federal agencies in 1982 and 1983 revealed that jogging, now the activity of 26 percent of the people in the survey, "was so insignificant 20 years ago that it was not included in the first survey."[25]

Dr. Leonardo Mata of Costa Rica credited a mass media campaign with helping to reduce the incidence of diarrhea in his country "causing a sharp drop in infant mortality."[26] As a result, he believed that what was needed "is an educational revolution to change the attitude of women, not only through the schools, but also with the mass media. Some aspects of life are not dependent on changes in food habits. Life-style changes—a veritable revolution—have brought about drastic, positive changes in individual and societal behavior.

The likelihood is that skepticism will die hard and researchers will continue to probe the question long after it practically ceases to exist. It is an intriguing exercise that many, if not all, communications researchers are reluctant to abandon. Like a worked-out gold mine, it keeps beckoning the jejune with tantalizing visions of hidden treasure. As far back as 1969, a rural health study in Costa Rica explored the interrelationship between formal education, mass media exposure, and child feeding. One objective was to determine whether radio-listening and newspaper-reading in general have a positive effect on child-feeding practices. This is tantamount to implying that the mass media could exert such an influence even when they convey no child-feeding messages, a classic instance of erecting a straw man. The study directors knocked it down when they concluded that the mass media have "little direct impact on modern health practices but have an important indirect impact as vehicles for education which does have a significant direct effect on health practices."[27] Social marketers have known this from long experience. The mass media are the means, not the meaning of communication.

On occasion, research conclusions confuse cause with effect. This is the case with at least two studies in which adolescents who spend time with TV public affairs programming were found to be better informed on the subject.[28] The researchers concluded that the primary effect of TV viewing was to stimulate interest in learning and acquiring information.[29] This is tantamount to saying that those interested in public affairs are interested in public affairs and know more about the subject than those who are not. Moreover, since public affairs programs on TV are essentially informational, how, on that basis, can the medium be expected to deliver anything more? How does this warrant the implication that TV is incapable of more profound educational purpose? Unfair.

The Special Case of the Dietary Guidelines

The question as to whether the mass media are capable of causing behavior change should have been satisfactorily answered for all time by the experience with the evolution of the Dietary Guidelines in the United States. The matter came to public attention in the early 1960s and 1970s as a result of congressional hearings, federal agency reports, and public advocacy by individuals and lobbying groups. The identification of the most serious national health risk factors focused public attention on cigarette smoking; obesity; high fat, sugar, and salt consumption; and the importance of exercise. The press, radio, and TV seized on these as a "good story".

The promulgation of the dietary guidelines in 1980 was a direct result of this activity and of the subsequent intervention of the Select Senate Committee on Nutrition, chaired by Senator George McGovern. It was an historic episode and health and nutrition education were never to be the same. Attention shifted from the traditional instruction of a balanced diet to life-style and dietary imbalances that had been identified with the most serious health problems in the United States—heart disease, high blood pressure, cancer, and stroke.

Until that time, food manufacturers had always disdained nutrition as a sales incentive. "Nutrition just doesn't sell," was the pat answer of the industry to urgings that it make nutritional improvements in the food supply. In fact, the record of many failed efforts to do so justified their indifference. Suddenly, all had changed. A sizable consumer segment was forming in the marketplace seeking appropriate food products. Cigarette advertising was ended on radio and TV by legislation, undoubtedly stimulated by heavy popular pressure and the astonishing support of the tobacco industry seeking desperately to ward off the threat of counter-commercials under the Fairness Doctrine. Food advertisers, who only a few short years before had considered nutrition claims worthless, were now feverishly rushing on the air with new commercials proclaiming the values of the low-fat, low-cholesterol content of their brands. New no-salt, sugar-free, low-fat, and high-fiber products proliferated in unprecedented numbers as though the health risks they were intended to combat had been newly discovered and their life-style and dietary etiologies identified for the first time.

The cause of this about-face was the involvement of the mass media. No previous health story, except for critical outbreaks of disease or other health emergencies, had ever been given such focused, sustained attention by the media, particularly by the most powerful of all, TV. The media invasion was total—in news programs, panel shows, cooking shows and columns, cookbooks, and, most of all, in food advertising, itself.

Only the most skeptical can doubt the extent and nature of this revolution in America's food and health habits. The behavior of millions of individuals and of major segments of the social and economic structure was altered. The food system has been radically affected. The evidence is everywhere—in the spreading prohibition of cigarette smoking in public places, a ban that would never have been tolerated in the past; in the proliferation of nutrition-oriented foods on supermarket shelves and in the advertising to support them; in the changed restaurant menus; in the growing acceptance of exercise as an essential daily routine. Only the most obdurate social commentators continue to deny the indispensable role of the mass media in this transformation.

Why There Are Not More Special Cases

It is not likely that such a change could take place again soon for the convergence of circumstances that made it possible was largely a matter of good luck, not of planning. Militant advocates like Robert Choate, Joan Gussow, Michael Jacobson, Charles Arnold, Beverly Winikoff, the Community Nutrition Institute, the Ralph Nader activists, congressional leaders like Senators George McGovern and Ted Kennedy, and hundreds of others mounted a barrage of policy conferences and special events designed to capture media attention. The media seized upon this health news as a "good story".

But "a good story" is an unreliable strategy for public health education because it depends on media whim and is subject to competition from other news events. It is thus uncontrolled, sporadic, and subject to the judgment of those whose first interest is news, not public health. The two are rarely compatible. Public health education cannot be effectively carried out without use of the mass media in the fashion of the commercial marketer. That means planned use of the media to deliver well-designed messages consistent with predetermined strategies.

The soft drink industry has been able to achieve startling success through deliberate, consistent marketing with strategic planning carried out year-in, year-out without let up. By 1982, according to the National Soft Drink Association's annual report, per capita soft drink sales amounted to 419.5 12-ounce units, more than one a day for every man, woman, and child in the United States! This marked a steady rise in 20 years to a three-fold increase.

It is specious to argue that health and nutrition objectives are far more complex to achieve. This may be true in some, but not in most, cases. Certainly, in nutrition we are dealing with the promotion of foods that are no more complicated than those of the commercial world and, in fact, are offered to the consumer through the same channels. To argue that Coca-Cola is easier to sell than fruit juices, for example, is conveniently to forget how strange its flavor was when it was first offered to the public. The mass media have figured prominently in Coca-Cola's success because their use has been uninterrupted, continuous, and consistently monitored and analyzed for decades.

This is not to say that case histories of health and nutrition successes do not exist. In addition to those mentioned earlier (the Finnish North

Karelia Project, the Stanford Three Community Study, the Indonesian Nutrition Improvement Program, the Bangladesh Social Marketing Program, and the Philippines Iloilo Nutrition Education Campaign), there are other notable examples of mass media impact on behavior change: the Academy for Educational Development's Mass Media Health Practices Projects in Honduras and Gambia. Certainly, much past experience has been less than successful. But the reasons may have more to do with the failings of health and nutrition professionals than with the mass media. The latter are merely tools requiring special knowledge, skill, and experience in their employment.

Most often, the health educator's inadequacy is with message design—including the preparatory stages of concept testing and consumer knowledge and attitude probing—and with media strategy and planning. McCron and Budd declared that this may be because "health educators have not yet achieved the optimal formula for harnessing the potential of the mass media in health education. In this interpretation the problem is essentially one of technique (such as message construction and delivery)."[30] The attitude of media as a tool capable of doing its work with a minimum of management is no more relevant to the mass media than it is to the hammer. How often is the need to design a message for radio or TV met with an arbitrary decision to make a jingle as though this popular advertising format is appropriate for any effort in these media? The demands of health education messages are different from those of commercial products, and message mimicry, without point or purpose, produces almost certain failure. Once again McCron wisely suggested that this may be because all too often "health education campaigns stress the *advertising* aspect of the process, at the expense (or neglect) of the *marketing* aspect."[31]

How often are media campaigns scheduled for a short burst of four, six, or eight weeks as though the schedule of learning achievement can, like the baking of a cake, be set in advance? How often are messages aired on radio and TV without regard to target audience requirements? While this is usually because of the indifference of station operators, it behooves the health educators to have the necessary know-how to overcome it. The public media have a public-interest obligation to provide such service in a meaningful way, but only enlightened health educators can help to keep that performance in accordance with the highest standards of media professionalism.

Some Questionable Assumptions of
Mass Media Evaluation

Much of the research in health education mass media campaigns is based on questionable assumptions that are not always articulated but almost always implied.

Questionable Assumption #1. The mass media are monoliths and their impact is measurable without recourse to evaluation of message design, the length of the media schedule (continuity), or the frequency of exposure (media weight). Until they are given a message to deliver and a schedule to manage its delivery, the mass media are neutral entities. It is the message, combined with media weight and continuity, that determines media effectiveness, not vice versa.

Questionable Assumption #2. Messages have a uniform value entirely dependent on media effectiveness for their impact. This is the converse of QA #1 and is invalid for the same reasons.

Questionable Assumption #3. The duration of mass media campaigns is immaterial to their effectiveness. This is a typical flaw of most evaluations. The author has examined scores of campaigns without uncovering one that made a determined effort to analyze the media's audience reach, frequency, and continuity or to evaluate the implications of such intelligence on the outcome of the campaign. For the most part the typical evaluation disregards significant differences in media weight, reach, frequency, and continuity and confines itself to measuring impact on the target audience, which cannot be meaningfully interpreted without evaluation of these values. A true evaluation analyzes the process, assessing the relationship of all parts to the whole; it cannot merely be an audit of results with no insight into what was right or wrong. At best, we are sometimes offered conjectural possibilities totally lacking in the kind of rigorous substantiation that researchers ordinarily oblige others to provide.

Questionable Assumption #4. There is no qualitative difference among the mass media in terms of potential impact on the target audience. Mass media projects are frequently imprecise in the selection of media and undiscriminating in their categorization. Leaflets, posters, and films are often classified as mass media along with radio and TV, and this indifference to comparative media values is reciprocated in the typical evaluation. Many of the projects and their accompanying evaluations reported in the literature fall into this category. Not one has come to the author's attention that makes a serious attempt at assessing comparative media values in relation to the results attained.

Questionable Assumption #5. Radio, TV, newspaper, and magazine exposure is a gross quantity unaffected by channel selection and program adjacencies on radio and TV or by the choice of publications and the positions messages are assigned in them. The assurance that messages will be efficiently delivered to their target populations obliges the health educator to identify the stations, programs and the print-media sections with the highest concentration of desired viewers, listeners, or readers. Once again, evaluations rarely, if ever, make this differentiation a subject of their analysis.

Some Safe Assumptions About the Mass Media

The social marketer's familiarity with the mass media has led to some reasonable assumptions about their power. Here then, even at penalty of having them challenged, is the distillation of one social marketer's judgment regarding mass media possibilities as borne out by his experience and attested to by others.

The mass media carry a special authority. We all sense, and even research confirms, that what is heard over radio or seen on TV or in the cinema or read in the newspaper or a magazine or viewed from the prominence of a public poster carries a special impact no individual is capable of delivering on a face-to-face basis. While the latter may have greater personal persuasion, the mass media carry an institutional impact on the individual that can be an invaluable communications asset or what French and Raven called a "great resource of power."[32]

Mass media assure thorough control of the message. This is true in every medium. Since message conception and design are of primary importance, the most desirable means of communication is the one that guarantees that our message will be delivered intact every time in every medium. Wherever and whenever and from whomever the message, it is always heard the same way. It quickly becomes a common experience. Word-of-mouth is accelerated. The impression grows that something important is happening because it is evident wherever you go and to almost everyone you know.

Mass media lend a cumulative impact to the message. Intermedia consistency of the message produces a measurable psychological advantage. The result is that the impact of the *whole* campaign is far greater than the mere arithmetic sum of its messages. This is communications synergism and the seasoned social marketer knows the joy of its blessings. Kline and Pavlik referred to the "ubiquitous nature" of the mass media, which "constantly bombard us with messages, even when we seek to avoid them."[33]

Mass media reach the masses. They can take the message further than any other medium at any given time. And they have an undiminishing capability for doing it again and again for the same message.

Mass media telescope time. They have a maximum further-faster capability. No factor is more valuable for urgent health education objectives.

Mass media influence other major audiences in important ways while directing a message to its target audience. Though directed, for example, to mothers, a nutrition message will be seen and heard by farmers who learn of the special emphasis on selected foods; by government officials and legislators whose support for new food policies is always necessary; by private businesspeople, who are always eager for new food-processing opportunities where a demonstrated need exist; by children, often their own most effective spokespeople with their parents in behalf of their wants; by teachers and other public servants whose participation in the educational effort is essential. The chain conceivably could link all essential population segments.

The mass media campaign enhances the effectiveness of all other methods employed in health education. The nutritionists, the farm agents, the mobile vans, the traveling puppet theaters, the song and drama groups, and the schools are all involved with a sense of solidarity that is the inevitable impact of the mass media and is not obtainable as quickly in any other way.

A Glimpse of Mass Media's Future

During the 1980s, TV's total metastasis of the body politic will be completed by the video cassette and the video disc. Toward the end of the 1970s, Vice President Richard Sonnenfeldt of RCA predicted that, in a decade, a quarter to one-third of all homes would own a video disc machine, one-third would be receiving cable TV and twice as many would have signed up for paid TV. That estimate has already proved modest. Viewers not only have a wider choice of what to watch, they are also able to choose when to watch, free of the time-period dictatorship of media programmers. This time-shift viewing is creating a new mass media freedom.

With cable TV and the new space "birds," the communications satellites, hundreds of electronic highways have now been opened. Today, thousands of home space antenna scattered around the United States and Canada are tuned into one or another North American domestic satellite for their hundreds of TV programs. They are rapidly falling in price and, with a readily obtainable FCC permit, can be easily erected alongside the rooftop TV antenna. What this means is that no experience or information is beyond our ken. We are able to select any program, source of information, or service the way we select books from library stacks or merchandise from the shelves of stores. All this will be obtainable at home—a realization of "let-your-fingers-do-the-walking" never even dreamed of by the Yellow Pages people. We have the capability of electronic home delivery of newspapers as readout or printout with all their news, features, and, yes, advertising. It will be possible to tailor the paper to the neighborhood—even to the individual—and to deliver it on microfilm, eliminating the bulk of a newspaper.

Thus, though it may seem a contradiction of terms, what will take place in the future is the individualization of mass communications. The transistor, the great revolutionary breakthrough of just a few years ago, is already outmatched by the integrated circuit or microelectronics, which makes possible the reduction of the most sophisticated communications equipment to the size of your hand and portable anywhere—in your telephone, your auto, your pocket.

The Bell System awaits only a sizeable demand for picture phones or person-to-person television to offer it to the public. Facsimile transmission and telewriting already exist. Even computers have become as versatile in communications as humans. Their messages may be spoken or printed in diagrams or drawings. They can be spoken to and, unlike a lot of humans, they will always listen though they may not always be able to understand.

Teleshopping may dominate food distribution through cable TV, a microcomputer probably built into every new home like the plumbing, and a TV video display set. With this system, we can talk to the supermarket, the library, the bank. Qube, the two-way TV system tested in Columbus, Ohio, enables audiences to react to the TV station. The supermarket's inventory can be programmed to the home telecomputer on request so one can make a teleselection.

This foretaste of future communications technology makes one wonder how it will be used. The implications for education are bewildering. Integrated circuit modules for programming individual computers, coupled to home or school TV screens, are a reality. The use of holography—the projection of three-dimensional images by laser beams—will bring heightened reality to the TV teacher and the TV demonstration.

This industrialization of education will intensify because of inflation, resistance to higher taxes, and rising costs. In 15 years, it is estimated that the current four-year course of college tuition at a state university will go from $16,000 to $42,000. Efforts to curb such a rise will be reflected in costcutting technology in the classroom. Already, we have shrinking job opportunities for teachers, a surplus of qualified B.A. and Ph.D. graduates and a 9-percent drop-off over the last decade in teachers' education enrollment, according to the Department of Labor.

This industrialization of education may have its greatest impact on our youngest students. Early childhood education is destined to expand, though the percentage of childless women, ages 24 to 49, is now more than 50 percent, double what it was only a few years ago. The proportion of three and four year olds who attend preschool has tripled since 1964, from 10 to 32 percent. The increase in women's employment may cause this to rise to 50 percent in the next decade. Because so many mothers are working and the nuclear family has become more like an affinity group, day care for these children will have to shift its emphasis from mere custodial care to child development education, in which health and nutrition education will have a high priority in the face of declining federal, state, and municipal budgets.

Thus, social responsibility for health and nutrition education will be enlarged and the policies for executing that responsibility will become a primary concern of nutrition and health educators. Much of what needs to be taught to the American people from a very early age will come increasingly by courtesy of our airwaves, which will depend on public policies for their rule. Systems of mass communications can help develop minds; they can also degrade them. They can educate for health; they can impair it. They can enrich or they can impoverish our spirits. In keeping with this testament, the great technical and scientific advances in communications and education will not, of themselves, bring about significant improvements in health education and, therefore, in health status. The real hope for doing so is through fostering sound public policies to govern health education (see Chapter 11).

Perhaps the main public policy issue with respect to the use of the mass media for health education has to do with access, the availability of the media to messages from the health educator. The situation today is no better than it was more than a decade ago when a study revealed that health-related information on TV was offered only 7.2 percent of the time. Only 30 percent of this was useful while 70 percent was judged inaccurate, misleading, or both. Health professionals' services were virtually ignored. Two-thirds of the public service messages, virtually the only vehicle for useful health information, "were aimed at the relatively small population viewing television during the daytime hours."[34]

This situation is difficult and complicated. The public interest obligation of station licensees is not energetically carried out and health educators find themselves powerless to gain satisfactory access to this most influential medium for their messages. New social initiatives are clearly called for and they will not be easy to promote. The situation in the United States is, perhaps, the most complex. Involved are First Amendment implications, private ownership of station licenses, the Fairness Doctrine, the limitations of the Communications Act of 1934, the ambivalent history of the Federal Communications Commission, the dominance of the commercial advertisers, and the disinclination of legislators to engage in a battle with an industry whose political power is now supreme. Because the United States is a worst-case scenario of the problem, it brilliantly illuminates the access problem everywhere.

The Problem of Access: The U.S. Example

One hot August day in 1922 the builder of the new Hawthorne Court cooperative apartments in Jackson Heights, New York, had not seen a single sales prospect. The high-pitched monotone of a human voice from the crystal radio on the chest behind his desk was the only sound in the office. It gave him an idea.

The next day he was at the offices of WEAF Radio in New York. Would they sell him the time for an advertisement for his apartments? Torn between an offer of hard cash for a cold commercial announcement and the fear of breaking with precedent, WEAF came up with an ingenious euphemism. They would sell him a ten-minute segment for $50 to deliver a lecture in memory of Nathaniel Hawthorne and to talk about the joys of living at Hawthorne Court, named in memory of the famous author.

Fred Friendly refers to this incident as "the birth of the commercial" and "almost an accident."[35] The man, the time, and the place may have been an accident but the strategic event was inevitable—the logical conclusion to a laissez-faire, free-market-system policy in the operation of the public media. The rest, as they say, is history—the evolution of the network mechanism to supply the major portion of media content and the proliferation of TV advertising at an annual rate of $8 billion.

No one could have anticipated this commercial potential and the benefits it would produce for the marketplace. Nor could more than a few have foreseen the problems. But in recent years other voices have begun to demand that we claim the vast wasteland of TV with programs and messages designed to nourish self-esteem and self-reliance, especially when public health and sanity are involved. Though from different quarters and with divergent motivations, they raise a fundamental question of social policy: should exploitation of our airwaves be left to a free-market system that is failing to realize our hopes and intentions? Our policy thrust, in the public interest, has been clear from the beginning but definition and standards for implementation were left vague.

One consensus description of the legislative mandate of the Federal Communications Commission (FCC) is that it was deliberately left ambiguous. FCC commissioners

> were at once critics and accomplices of the new broadcast industry; they were regulators, but they could not be censors; the public tended to charge them with responsibility for the quality of a universal public service, and yet the Commission was denied the rate-making and standard-setting authority applied to public utilities by other regulatory agencies.[36]

In its famous blue book entitled *Public Service Responsibility of Broadcast Licensees* (March 7, 1947), the FCC attempted to assert a new policy of carefully reviewing stations' on-air performance when licenses come up for renewal. This had become necessary, the FCC argued, because stations were not fulfilling programming promises made on original license applications. But as Anthony Smith wrote

> Since the publication of the Blue Book . . . the FCC has legislated on the question of fairness, on the rights of reply, and on ethical questions in advertising. It has tried to force more local programs to be made. It has pushed stations and networks into providing more coverage of news, and of better quality. But whenever it summons up the will to take far-reaching action, it is defeated either by its adversaries or by the gradual weakening of its will.[37]

Public criticism and exhortation have proved to be feeble instruments for change because, as Smith explained

> The system whose heart is the FCC can approach its audience only along such lines. To attack the broadcasters for exercising their full energies within the system provided is merely to perplex them with inexplicable enmity. It is extremely difficult to try to change the nature of a competitive system by simply demanding self-denial or forbearance.[38]

In fact, the effect of the law has been to reduce government responsibility to policing the spectrum and regulating traffic so as to assure the freedom of the market. A free market system is the de facto communications objective of U.S. policy. What one would expect has come to pass: extraordinary expansion of the consumer marketplace through TV advertising, the fortune of Croesus for its network and station licensees, and the loss of a great educational opportunity for the public.

The 1934 Communications Act was a missed opportunity to moderate the force of the market and to structure the system in the public interest. By leaving such matters vague and indecisive, the act was an open invitation to the market to let practice set policy. No other country has permitted it to happen this way since. Maybe it happened because we were the first and lacked the experience to know that eventually the power of the media rivals the power of government itself. To all other Western countries and virtually all the free world, it was obvious that the public media were "more than instruments of *expression*, that they would become concentrations of social power, which rendered the process of regulation (which had to be undertaken by the state) inseparable from the duty of imposing forms and structures of social accountability."[39]

But in the U.S., TV's market accountability is to its customers (who are not to be confused with the audience)—to the advertiser, not the listener. So the measure of accountability is the rating, which answers the question, "how many?" not, "what do they want?" Nicholas Johnson, as FCC Commissioner, cautioned us not to "confuse the public interest with what interests the public."[40] Les Brown, formerly TV editor of the New York *Times* and *Variety,* has written, "This emphasis on the popularity of shows has made television appear to be democratic in its principles of program selection. In truth, programs of great popularity go off the air without regard for viewers' bereavement or because the people it reaches are not attractive to advertisers."[41]

Given the way market systems work, it was inevitable that television would become almost exclusively an entertainment vehicle. Its public-interest obligation is largely discharged through news programs that are more entertainment than enlightenment. This led David Brinkley once to remark that "if most of the people in this country are getting most of their news from television, they are getting damned little news." What is true of programs is also true of the advertising. Market-system dynamics determine *who* advertisers will be, *what* they advertise, and the *style* of execution. The astronomic cost of television favors big advertisers. Only broadly distributed and widely consumed products with generous margins between cost and selling price can afford the ongoing TV investment. The ultimate justification is the building of a strong proprietary brand name. Many vital categories of food products (e.g., fresh fruits and vegetables, fresh fish and poultry) are immediately eliminated because their low margin of profit cannot generate the funds. Thus, the frivolity of TV program fare is matched by the frivolity of the foods that can afford to advertise there. Even the style and content of advertising has been shaped by the environment of the medium. While advertising, believe it or not, has grown more responsible over the years, it has also become more humorous, less hard, more involved with image and less with reality, more with mood and manner than with value—in short, more of a piece with the entertainment that it seeks to interrupt with minimum pain and maximum pleasure.

What more could we expect? Who is to blame? The licensee, the advertiser, the programmer? The market system is a kind of anonymous dictatorship. With no one in charge, the entrenched interests it has spawned are naturally eager to preserve the status quo. But it is the system, not its licensees, that needs disciplining so that it can be operated in a fashion to reflect more accurately what we originally intended for it.

The public interest and public concerns like health education deserve a mandatory share of TV time. Social responsibility in television is a philanthropy of the licensee. It has not worked well and gives no promise of working better in the future. The result is that health education and other social concerns are badly neglected. This, as one social critic has noted, has had a deleterious effect

> Since television viewing occupies more time of Americans than any other single activity, and since it has taken the place of many of the learning experiences of the young people of an earlier period, its potential for constructive education should be developed and exploited. At present, most commercial television appears to distract young people from educational activities or to result in their learning things that conflict with accepted educational goals.[42]

The concept of TV as an extension of the classroom is eminently preferable to that of the classroom as an extension of TV. TV's entertainment vogue is finding sardonic mimicry in pedagogical style. Teachers confess a need to be more entertaining to engage student interest, to borrow fun and entertainment devices from TV that have no integral connection with subject matter. The degrading effect on educational quality and learning is broadly acknowledged.

Even in its demand on students' time, TV preempts the school. The average youngster between 12 and 17 spends about 1,300 hours a year with TV as compared to about 1,100 hours in school.[43] Cutting off the set is one desperate personal solution. A proper social-policy solution is to control what's on the set: if the child is transferring from school to set, let's move the school with the child. This means mandatory share of air by returning to public ownership through legislative mandate some stipulated portion of the schedule.

The 1969 White House Conference on Food, Nutrition and Health made such a recommendation. It urged that 10 percent of all radio and TV time be set aside from commercial broadcasting. This Time Bank, as I chose to call it soon after in 1970, could be a reserve for public service campaigns. It could be administered by a special public corporation established by Congress and independent of any political control. Under most social legislation there usually is a mandatory provision for information and education activities. This calls for a budgetary appropriation that is never enough to do the job right. There is rarely more than a dollop for mass media, except where military recruitment is concerned.

But with the Time Bank, there would be time on deposit, not dependent on licensee largess or imperilled by some station executive's whim. The executive branch would indicate in its budget an estimate of how much radio and TV time is required to do a proper job of delivering vital health education to the American public. There would be no need for penny pinching because no money is actually required. Once approved, this Time Bank draft would be at the disposal of the responsible agency to exchange for station and network time. Certain safeguards would protect stations against unreasonable losses. The Time Bank would have to be free of political control. Local communities would be assured of some share of the Time Bank's reserve for local public and private campaigns. The Time Bank would bring to health education the status and the prominence it deserves on the airwaves of the country.[44] In 1983, the dollar value of TV advertising amounted to $8 billion or about 25 percent of all national advertising. If 10 percent of this time were available to mandatory public use, it would be worth $800 million. And if health education were to receive 10 percent of this, or $80 million—only 1 percent of the grand total—it would rank among the 100 major advertisers.*

This would leave the free market system inviolate but under well-defined restrictions to protect the public interest. If we had but had the foresight to see it, the original legislation could have accomplished this by partial licensing of the air for commercial use. This would have been consistent with public policy in all other sectors of our national life, such as land use, our national seashores, our waterways, personal and business incomes, and even our manpower in times of threats to our national security. The principle of public claim to a share of our property, our income, our time, and our service is deeply embedded in our national purpose and integral to the policy of free enterprise and its system of a free market. The system could not survive without it. Restricted access to space and time is an integral support of our system and not, as shortsighted exponents of expediency insist, the instrument of its demolition.

---

*Public television is not an alternative, for as Herbert Schiller has pointed out, "The illusion of informational choice is more persuasive in the United States than anywhere else in the world. The illusion is sustained by a willingness . . . to mistake *abundance of media for diversity of content.*"[45] PBS is an addition to, not a change in, the system.

In May 1984, the Supreme Court upheld Hawaii's Land Reform Act of 1967, which enabled the state to invoke its power of eminent domain to break up large estates and transfer land ownership to tenants.[46] The constitution insists on just compensation for such an action and the Supreme Court decision was hardly radical. There is ample precedent for it and the Court had little trouble coming to an 8 to 0 vote. Recapturing 10 percent of U.S. radio and TV air time would be consistent with the principle of eminent domain, especially where the public interest is involved. Our concept of national security embraces the health and education of our people. If we can but accept the principle of the social marketing of health and education and the indispensability of the public media, then for that purpose we shall have no difficulty in accepting the need for mandatory public reserves of our air as we do of our land and our natural and human resources. In France, the prime minister fixes a quota for public service access to television and radio every six months. This amounts to about 90 minutes on each of two of the three TV channels. Health education is assigned about one-third of this quota.

The proposal for accepting such a commitment has even come from the industry. On November 16, 1971, the New York *Times* reported

> The National Broadcasting Company has expressed fear that the stability of radio and television is threatened by challenges from citizen groups and has proposed reluctantly that the Federal Government adopt a quantitative standard in reviewing licenses. Any licensee of a television station who devotes 10 to 12% of his program schedule to non-entertainment material should be presumed to have reached a performance level entitling him to retain his frequency, NBC said.[47]

The judicial history of the issue makes clear that absolute right either to all the air or to total control over content has not been absolutely reserved to the licensee. What is clear is that the law has not made it clear or that the law could do so. No legislation has ever attempted to clarify the situation, although there is solid judicial opinion to justify the effort. Supreme Court Justice Felix Frankfurter, in the majority opinion that forced NBC to divest itself of one of its two radio networks in 1943, declared

> The Act itself established that the Commission's powers are not limited to the engineering and technical aspects of regulation of radio communication. Yet, we are asked to regard the Commission as a kind of traffic officer, policing the wavelengths to prevent stations from interfering with each other. But the Act does not restrict the Commission merely to supervision of the traffic. It puts upon the Commission the burden of determining the composition of that traffic.[48]

Three years after its famous *Blue Book,* the FCC issued a *Report on Editorializing by Broadcast Licensees,* which is generally considered to be the first articulation of the Fairness Doctrine. It directed licensees to operate in the public interest through reasonable coverage of important controversial public issues and to provide fair and reasonable opportunity for opposing viewpoints. While principle was again reaffirmed, stipulated performance standards as to structure and air share were deliberately avoided. We must assume that political inhibition, not legal prohibition, prompted such evasiveness.

When the Fairness Doctrine was finally established in the famous Red Lion landmark case before the Supreme Court in 1969, some of the key language of that decision opened up even greater possibilities for the future. Justice Byron R. White, who wrote the majority opinion, said

> When there are substantially more individuals who want to broadcast than there are frequencies to allocate, it is idle to posit an unabridgeable First Amendment right to broadcast comparable to the right of every individual to speak, write or publish. . . . By the same token, as far as the First Amendment is concerned, those who are licensed stand no better than those to whom licenses are refused. A license permits broadcasting, but the license has no constitutional right to be the one who holds the license or to monopolize a radio frequency to the exclusion of his fellow citizens. There is nothing in the First Amendment which prevents the government from requiring the licensee to share his frequency with others and to conduct himself as a proxy or fiduciary with obligations to present those views and voices which are representative of his community and which would otherwise by necessity be barred from the airwaves.[49]

The opinion also reaffirmed that "it is the right of the viewers and listeners, not the right of the broadcasters which is paramount."

When the tobacco industry invoked the First Amendment against the FCC ruling in the historic Banzhaf case before the U.S. Court of Appeals, Justice Bazelon's decision rejected its claim declaring: "Some utterances fall outside the pale of First Amendment concern. . . . promoting the sale of a product is not ordinarily associated with any of the interests the First Amendment seeks to protect."[50] Bazelon went on to say that more than First Amendment issues were at stake. On a key question of "public interest versus public health," he was unequivocal: "Whatever else it may mean, however, we think the public interest indisputably means the public health . . . the power to protect the public health lies at the heart of the state's political power. . . . Public health has in effect become a kind of basic law."[51] The Supreme Court subsequently permitted the Bazelon decision to prevail by refusing to review it. In pinning responsibility on the media, these decisions made a major contribution to clarifying the public policy issue involved.

But regulatory agencies proceeded to ignore it. The FTC has in the past unsuccessfully proposed remedial actions, such as "affirmative nutritional disclosure," and presumed these to be the obligation of the advertiser, not the medium. A regulatory philosophy that holds the renter liable for an owner's responsibility obfuscates the issue and diverts attention from the problem. Advertisers can be held responsible for advertising trespass; the medium must be held accountable for the medium. If the FTC has no authority to deal with the media problem as a media problem, then converting it into an advertising problem over which it has authority is a low form of political forgery. Certain aspects are clearly advertiser responsibility: the content of the advertising and health risks in our foods. But the issue of access requires new structures like the Time Bank to bring the system into conformity with policy. These are not advertiser issues. They are media issues and ought to be addressed as such.

Reserving parts of the broadcast schedule for public use obviously has profit implications for licensees who may vigorously object that curtailing time for sale will reduce their income. But an examination of historic revenues of the industry produces little reason for concern. TV station and network profits are extraordinary whether measured by return on investment or as a percentage of sales. Smith observed

> By the middle of the 1950s, the highly profitable nature of the new television medium was already clear. The right to transmit, given away by the FCC, became an extremely valuable fixed asset of the fortunate bidder, who could sell his holdings on the market as if the public resource element of the station were a wholly-owned investment. Stations rocketed in value by ten times the actual amount of cash invested in them. A new television station was transformed artificially and overnight into an extremely large block of capital from a small one.[52]

Nicholas Johnson, an ex-FCC commissioner, once declared

> A broadcasting license has, understandably, been characterized as a "license to print money." There is no question about the financial ability of this industry to provide the American people what the National Association of Broadcasters characterized in the early days as a "considerable proportion of programs devoted to . . . concern with human betterment." . . . Not only has the industry failed miserably in its great opportunity, and obligation, to contribute to "human betterment," it has actually done great harm.[53]

What are the facts as reported by the FCC in its last annual financial review of the television industry in 1977?

1. Total broadcast pretax profits for station and networks grew from $492,900,000 in 1966 to $1,250,000,000 in 1976, a 150-percent increase.
2. Pretax profits in 1976 represented approximately a 68-percent return on

original cost of investment accumulated to that year but more than a 152 percent on the depreciated investment!

3. Over the five-year period, 1971 to 1976, TV networks alone increased their earnings by 192 percent as compared to all corporation earnings, which increased only 89 percent.[54]*

Few businesses aspire to, let alone achieve, such returns. A reduction in such extraordinary profits would be a hardship only in the light of historic earnings, but not on the basis of reasonable profit expectations. No other enterprise licensed to operate a public trust can demonstrate such spectacular profit performance nor, as in the case of public utilities, would it be permitted to do so.

Opponents of the Time Bank may also cite the limited supply of commercial time and the rising demand for more time. But licensees have the legal obligation to provide for the public interest and if they are already doing so satisfactorily, then the proposal is merely a formality for the fact. If not, then what justification can there be for opposing the arrangement? It is specious to insist that time slots are scarce, for how can networks and licensees explain the abundance of station and network "promo" announcements every night and in all time periods for their forthcoming programs? It has been estimated that as many as 300 are telecast by each network weekly without counting those aired locally. Between 1977 and 1983 alone, the total number of commercial announcements on the networks increased from 3,743 to 4,485 in an average week. This is an increase of 20 percent in actual number of commercials in six years.[55] Thus, the number of commercial announcements on the networks is increasing at a rate in excess of 3 percent per year, or about 10 percent over a three-year period. Such an increase alone could have put the Time Bank into operation if the number of commercial announcements had been frozen in 1980. Again, this takes no account of the increases in announcements on local stations, which is difficult to assess.

Hidden even behind these figures is the real proliferation of commercial announcements that occurred more than a decade ago when the industry converted from 60-second to 30-second message lengths. Today, almost 90 percent of all announcements are the shorter length, thus almost doubling their number. And close to 10 percent of the announce-

---

*While industry profitability figures are available for several years beyond 1976 by company, the data for segregated TV operations have not been available from the FCC since 1977. The FCC no longer requires the TV networks and stations to submit annual profit-and-loss statements. Consequently, no comparable figures exist for the early 1980s. However, there is no reason to assume that the historically high profitability of the TV industry has diminished to any appreciable extent.

ments on the air today are piggybacks, announcements for two or more often unrelated products.

The alternative to the Time Bank is for the government to pay for access, which it has been compelled to do when it wants to assure the effective delivery of its announcements and to avoid the uncertainties of public service time. In 1982, the U.S. government ranked number 29 among the top 100 advertisers, with a budget of $205.5 million, a sum greater than that spent by such marketing giants as Bristol-Myers (number 30), Dart & Kraft (number 31), Pillsbury (number 36), Gillette (number 37), General Electric (number 40), Kellogg (number 43), Campbell soup (number 52), Revlon (number 56), and Nestlé (number 57), among many others.[56] Most of the U.S. expenditure was for recruitment campaigns for the military services. Other radio and TV advertising activity by the government in behalf of health campaigns (e.g., hypertension, food and nutrition) of the Department of Health and Human Services and USDA is almost entirely public service. Naturally, they suffer the same fate as all PSAs—erratic scheduling in low audience time periods.

When the public pays for access to its own airwaves, then its government is fundamentally skirting the central issue of policy. For the underlying premise is, of course, that the use of the airwaves is as essential to the promotion of proper health and nutrition habits as they have been for products and practices of more dubious value. The premise has been proved beyond a doubt by social marketing projects over radio and television in the Philippines, Ecuador, Nicaragua, and the Dominican Republic, among other countries[57] (see Chapter 10).

To breed freedom and strength in a people requires policies of openness, of which the most important may be the right to the power of knowledge, the right to put that knowledge constructively to work for one's self, which is to say for one's role in society, and the right to the tools to make it happen. Social marketing supports enterprises to strengthen the capacity of people to be the custodians of their own health, to be armed with the self-confidence and self-reliance that are, finally, the only true defense against the wrong, the misleading, and the deceptive.

It has been said

> A society based upon the sum of its peoples' capacity is a democracy. . . . A service society based upon the "humanistic" ideology of service is sowing the seeds of tyranny. It teaches our people that they will be better because someone else knows better. A nation of clients is fertile ground for totalitarianism. In a society of clients, our problems are understood as technical issues resolved by the good works of elite professional service. In a nation of citizens, our problems are understood as political issues dealt with by the good work of people who have the capacity and competence to make a human community.[58]

The Problem of Access in Developing Countries

While the United States presents a far more complicated access problem, the situation is essentially the same in most countries of the Third
World. In those permitting private operations, commercial stations generally have no stipulated obligation to social marketing programs. They,
too, are licensed to operate in the public interest but the definition of that
obligation is typically vague. There are exceptions like Brazil and
Ecuador, which for years have required licensees to reserve a fixed
number of hours for public service, or Mexico, where since the late 1960s
the law obliges licensees to set aside 12.5 percent of their time. Some ten
years later, though, Mexico's law has yet to be enforced. Public interest
programs have, of course, been produced and some of them have been of
outstanding quality. Televisa's "Acompáñeme" ("Come Along with
Me"), a family planning series, is a first-rate example. But these have been
inaugurated and aired—and discontinued—at the licensee's discretion.

Pakistan offers another example of the difficulties facing social marketing programs even where broadcasting is a government monopoly. A
1975 government social marketing program for nutrition, helped by
USAID, was unable to obtain a free-time allocation from the Pakistan
Broadcasting Corporation (PBC). The PBC drew no distinction between
commercial advertisers and a social marketing campaign from an agency
of government. Both are required to pay. (The Population Planning
Council, another official body, had spent $130,000 to purchase radio time
during fiscal year 1973 to 1974.) The director of the Nutrition Planning and
Research Project was unable to obtain an exception from this policy. The
recommendation of the USAID consultants was not to support the project
on that basis.[59] When time was made available by PBC, it was usually for a
one-time, 15-minute or half-hour feature program not unlike a U.S. TV
special.

In countries where a dual commercial/governmental system exists,
the commercial operation invariably commands the major share of audience. Because of its revenue stream from advertising, the commercial stations are able to purchase the reruns of popular American programs. Despite the cultural gap, these programs attract huge audiences relegating
governmental channels and their inferior offerings to a minor role. The
irony is that even when educational programs are given allocations on
such governmental channels, their audience reach is severely limited.
Only motivated viewers are likely to make the effort to tune in the programs, leaving the really needy populations unreached.

Agricultural development specialists decry the paucity of appropriate programming for rural populations.

> Rural broadcasting seldom, if ever, gets more than a fraction of total air time. . . . A survey a few years ago showed that in most countries it got from 1% to 5% of broadcasting time. An FAO consultant recently visited four African countries to find . . . that in one country with well-developed broadcasting services and 90% of the population living in rural areas, only 1.22% of air time is given to rural broadcasting. The average of the four countries was 1.7%.[60]

But the problem is no different in urban areas. Radio and TV fare is predominantly entertainment and both rural and urban audiences have been homogenized by it. The charge is justified that there is a poverty of farm-oriented programming—farm forums, agricultural news—but it is also true that urban audiences are being offered little of relevance to their concerns and problems.

This lack of opportunity for educational use of the mass media is one of the serious constraints to social marketing. Media policy in most of the countries, except where broadcasting is state operated, follows the U.S. model and is anchored in a high-sounding public interest but without specific obligations as to subject matter or share of air. The consequence is that programming tends to drift away from true public interest imperatives to the lowest common denominator of entertainment for the general public in line with the exploitation of the airwaves by the commercial marketplace.

Programming, as in the United States, is fashioned to suit the needs of advertisers rather than audiences so as to attract the maximum number of potential consumers for the products hawked. Inevitably, this means preference for those with economic means and in the Third World this translates into urban audiences. It also decrees preemption of the best time periods for these purposes, leaving educational offerings to compete for the little that is left. That means time periods when audiences are smallest. Moreover, because rural people of developing countries are outside the cash economy, many of these stations restrict their power output to metropolitan areas. Government-operated channels that aim to make up the difference invariably fail to do so because of poor program quality, whether directed toward urban or rural audiences. In some parts of Central Java, Indonesia, where only the government radio service is available, investigators working for the Nutrition Improvement Program found that local radio listenership was so low (and, consequently, radio ownership, as well) that other means of communication had to be employed despite the media strategy to give radio the key role.[61]

Such a situation dramatizes once again the need for a media strategy that enables social marketing messages to reach its primary target populations en masse. Radio schools conducted in Honduras have been shown to benefit those among the *campesino* target audience who were already better off.[62] Others have found a similar effect among the audiences of "Sesame Street" in the United States.[63] This speaks for the reach-and-frequency format of short messages inserted among carefully selected popular programs and the need for a Time Bank, whether in Pakistan, Brazil, Kenya or the United States. Without some version of a Time Bank, social marketing goals will be thwarted by what we may refer to as the St. Matthew effect: "To him who hath shall be given; to him who hath not shall be taken away even that which he hath." The use of the mass media, unless redirected toward more equitable employment, can ironically widen the gap between rich and poor.

Notes

1. *Space Communications: Increasing U.N. Responsiveness to the Problems of Mankind,* a special report, National Policy Panel, United Nations Association of the U.S., May 1971, p. 13.

2. Osnos, P., "Britain Still Rules the Waves," the Manchester *Guardian Weekly,* August 28, 1983, p. 16.

3. Roy, P., Fliegel, F.C., Kivlin, J.E., Sen, L.K., *Agricultural Innovations Among Indian Farmers.* National Institute of Community Development, Hyderabad, 1968, p. 8.

4. Arbitron Ratings/TV, Universe Estimate Summary, 1983–1984, p. 3.

5. Ibid.

6. NTI/NAD (Nielsen Target Information/National Audience Delivery), 11/82; 2/83; 5/83; 7/83.

7. A.C. Nielsen, Estimates of U.S. TV Households, 1983–84.

8. NTI (Nielsen Target Information) Buying Guide, fourth quarter, 1983.

9. Miller, D.T., citing a study by the Columbia Broadcasting System in "The Only Truly Mass Medium Remaining Today: Its Role in Our Society," a paper presented for the Mass Communications Lecture Series, Cornell University, May 5, 1971, published as Communication Arts Bulletin No. 12.

10. Gatherer, A.; Parfit, J.; Porter, E., et al., *Is Health Education Effective?* London: Health Education Council, 1979.

11. Flay, B.R., DiTecco, D., Schlegel, R.P., "Mass Media in Health Promotion: An Analysis Using an Extended Information-Processing Model," *Health Education Quarterly,* 7/1980/2, pp. 127–147.

12. Koskela, K., Puska, P., Tuomilehto, J., "The North Karelia Project: A First Evaluation," *International Journal of Health Education,* 19/1976, pp. 59–66.

13. Farguhar, J.W., Maccoby, N., Wood, P.D., et al., "Community Education for Cardiovascular Health," *Lancet,* 4/1977, pp. 1192–1195.

14. Manoff International Inc., *Project Description: Nutrition Education and Behavior Change Component of the Indonesian Nutrition Improvement Program,* Manoff International, New York, 1983.

15. Schellstede, W.P., Ciszewski, R.L., "Social Marketing of Contraceptives in Bangladesh," *Studies in Family Planning,* the Population Council, Vol. 15, No. 1, January/February 1984.

16. Cooke, T.M., Romweber, S.T., "Radio Nutrition Education—Using The Advertising Technique To Reach Rural Families: Philippines and Nicaragua," final report, December 1977. Manoff International Inc. was engaged as technical consultants to this project, which was supported by the Office of Nutrition, Technical Assistance Bureau, Agency for International Development, Washington, D.C.

17. McCron, R., Budd, J., "The Role of the Mass Media in Health Education: An Analysis," in *Health Education by Television and Radio* (Ed. M. Meyer), K.G. Saur, Munich, 1981.

18. Bandura, A., "Social Learning Theory of Identifactory Processes," in *Handbook of Socialization Theory and Research* (Ed. D.A. Goslin), Rand McNally, Chicago, 1969, pp. 213–262.

19. Liebert, R.M., Neale, J.M., Davidson, E.S., *The Early Window: Effects of Television on Children and Youth,* Pergamon Press, New York, 1973.

20. Ford, A.S., Ford, W.S., "The Need for Cooperative Health Education: Some Survey Findings," *International Journal of Health Education,* 24/2, pp. 83–84.

21. Kaufman, L., "Prime-Time Nutrition," *Journal of Communication,* Summer 1980, Vol. 30, No. 3, pp. 37–46.

22. Collins, G., "Children, Reading and the Computer Age," the New York *Times,* September 5, 1983. p. 29.

23. Goldsmith, B., "The Meaning of Celebrity," the New York *Times Magazine,* December 4, 1983, p. 75.

24. Aronson, V., Harvard School of Public Health, Boston, Massachusetts, *New England Journal of Medicine,* April 7, 1983, p. 848.

25. "Swimming and Walking Top Activities in Poll," the New York *Times,* April 29, 1984, p. 38.

26. Mata, L., remarks made at a Symposium on "The Challenge of Food and Nutrition in the Promotion of Health and National Development," October 24–27, 1983, Caracas, Venezuela, the Cavendes Foundation for Nutrition and Health.

27. Zaltman, G., Hingson, R., Allwood, J., "The Impact of Education and of Mass Media Exposure on Child Feeding in Costa Rica," *International Journal of Health Education,* 13/1970/3.

28. Chaffee, S., Ward, S.L., Tipton, L.P., "Mass Communication and Political Socialization," *Journalism Quarterly,* 47/1970/4, pp. 647–659.

29. Richman, L., Urban, D., "Health Education Through Television. Some Theoretical Applications," *International Journal of Health Education,* 21/1978/1.

30. McCron, R., Budd, J., op. cit.

31. Ibid.

32. French, J.R.P., Raven, B.H., "The Bases of Social Power," in *Group Dynamics,* (Eds. Cartwright, Zander), Tavistock, London, 1969.

33. Kline, F.H., Pavlik, J.V., "Adolescent Health Acquisition from the Broadcast Media: An Overview," *Health Education by Television and Radio,* (Ed. M. Meyer), K.G. Saur, Munich, 1981.

34. Smith, F.A., et al., "Health Information During a Week of Television," *New England Journal of Medicine,* March 9, 1972.

35. Friendly, F., *The Good Guys, The Bad Guys and the First Amendment,* Random House, New York, 1975, p. 16.

36. Johnson, Nicholas, as cited by Harry S. Ashmore, *Fear in the Air,* W.W. Norton, New York, 1973, p. 136.

37. Smith, A., "American Television," *Daedalus,* Winter, 1978, pp. 201–202.

38. Ibid.

39. Ibid., p. 199.

40. Ashmore, H.S. *Fear in the Air,* W.W. Norton, New York, 1973, p. 139.

41. Brown, L., *Television,* Harcourt Brace Jovanovich, New York, 1971, pp. 59–60.

42. Tyler, R., "Learning in America," *Center Magazine,* November/December 1977.

43. A.C. Nielsen Company, November 1983.

44. Manoff, R.K., "You May Be Teaching Nutrition—But Are They Learning," presented to the American Diatetic Association, fifty-seventh annual meeting, Philadelphia, Pennsylvania, October 10, 1974.

45. Schiller, H.I., *The Mind Managers,* Beacon Press, Boston, 1973, p. 19.

46. "Eminent Sense on Eminent Domain," an editorial, the New York *Times,* June 1, 1984.

47. Gould, J., in his television column, the New York *Times,* November 16, 1971.

48. United States Supreme Court, *National Broadcasting Company* v. *U.S.* (1943).

49. United States Supreme Court. *Red Lion Broadcasting, Inc.* v. *Federal Communications Commission,* 395 U.S. 367, May 9, 1969.

50. Bazelon, D.L., *U.S. Court of Appeals, Banzhaf* v. *FCC,* 405 F.2d 1082, 1099 (1968).

51. Ibid.

52. Smith, A., op. cit., p. 204.

53. Johnson, N., as cited by H.S. Ashmore, op. cit., pp. 138–139.

54. "Television: A Gold Mine," *U.S. News and World Report,* quoting U.S. Department of Commerce reports, February 7, 1977.

55. *Research Department Report on Network TV Commercial Activity,* TV Bureau of Advertising, 1983.

56. "Top 100 Leading Advertisers," *Advertising Age,* September 8, 1983.

57. Manoff International Inc., "Radio Nutrition Education—A Test of the Advertising Technique: Philippines and Nicaragua Final Report," December 1977; "Mass Media and Nutrition Education: Ecuador," 1975; "Mass Media and Nutrition Education: Report of Assessment Visit to Pakistan," December 9–21, 1974; "Final Report on Nutrition Education Strategy: Dominican Republic," August 1977.

58. McKnight, J.L., "Good Work, Good Works," the New York *Times,* November 16, 1977.

59. Manoff International Inc., "Report of Assessment Visit to Pakistan," Manoff International, USAID consultants, March 5, 1975.

60. Fraser, C., "Adapting Communication Technology for Rural Development," *Ceres,* FAO, Rome, Italy, September 10, 1983, No. 95, p. 23.

61. Manoff International Inc., "Project Description: Nutrition Education and Behavior Change Component of the Indonesian Nutrition Improvement Program," Manoff International, New York 10022, 1983.

62. White, R., "Mass Communications and the Popular Promotion Strategy of Rural Development in Honduras,"In *Radio for Education and Development,* (Editors P. Spain, D. Jamison, E. McAnany) World Bank working paper 266, Washington, D.C., 1977.

63. Cook, T. et al., *Sesame Street Revisited.* Russell Sage Foundation, New York, 1975.

Part II

Putting Social Marketing to Work

6

Developing the Social Marketing Plan

What we know of Thales of Miletus, one of the seven sages, suggests that he may have been among the first in the line of the great Greek philosophers. An avid student of celestial events, he predicted within a year the solar eclipse of May 28, 585 B.C. But he was also a worldly man. In divining the relationship between the movement of heavenly bodies and changes in climate, he may have been the father of weather forecasting. Convinced by his observations of an impending drought, he craftily set about cornering the olive market in advance and made a killing. But genius can also be blinding. Obsessed with the mysteries of the skies, he could forego no opportunity to unravel them. Out walking one day, head cocked back and eyes focused heavenward in customary fashion, he stumbled into a well and was drowned. This mundane end to a brilliant life posits a moral even for the less gifted: when you reach for the stars, you'd better look where you're going.

The biggest pitfalls in organizing a social marketing project are the unbridged gaps with community organizations, whose cooperation can spell the difference between success and failure. This is not only operationally sound; it is also a political necessity. If they are denied participation in planning, they are not likely to support the program and, in fact, may obstruct it if only through sheer indifference.

A Collaborative Effort for Consensus Building

The participation offered collaborators is a matter of judgment and diplomacy. Clearly, no project can run without single-minded manage-

99

ment able to make operating decisions and execute them expeditiously. An unwieldy governing body, given more to debate than to action, will paralyze an enterprise from the start. Skillful handling is needed in arranging for representation, yet avoid having it hobble action capability. A board of advisers or directors affords such representation provided that a smaller executive committee is delegated authority for policy decisions required by managers of the project. Management authority must be uncompromised, for in the final analysis it is effective management that will reconcile differences of opinion and neutralize conflict. It will catalyze support even from quarters that at first appeared hostile.

The primary goal of collaboration is consensus building. The question of what can or cannot be said in messages about high-sodium consumption or dietary cholesterol must be resolved before message design can be undertaken. Lack of consensus means that conflicting messages will be directed to the same target populations. Minimizing message dissonance is one of the prime requisites of social marketing.

When products are involved (e.g., contraceptives, ORT salts, immunization, supplementary foods), planning may have to embrace private sector distribution collaboration under government subsidy. However, these should not conflict with normal private sector sales or with free distribution through the health care system All three should be complementary—designed to serve distinct population segments by product and price strategies that will, together, make the product more broadly available. Philip D. Harvey, one of the pioneers in contraceptive social marketing, defined social marketing of contraceptives as "a method of providing family planning services by selling highly subsidized contraceptives in programs designed to reach the maximum possible number of people through preexisting commercial networks backed by mass media (or equivalent) advertising."[1]

While contraceptive social marketing programs cannot serve those who are entirely outside the cash economy they can reach the poor of most Third World countries. Schellstede and Ciszewski offered this profile

> The typical buyer of Raja (the subsidized condom in the Bangladesh social marketing program) is a man about 27 years old, married for about four years and the father of two or three children. He works outdoors and earns less than $25.00 per month. He has had little schooling and probably is not functionally literate.[2]

This illustrates the strategic difference between commercial and social product marketing. Commercial marketing is competitive, concerned first with the battle for share-of-market and only secondarily with market expansion. Social marketing is complementary. Its only objective is market expansion.

Organization requirements of collaboration will depend on the level at which it is planned. At the national level, emphasis is on policy—selecting priorities, goals, objectives, and strategies. At the middle level, the focus is on management—planning and executing staffing patterns, training programs, control of budgetary expenditures, delegation of operating responsibilities. At the local level it is on community participation in determining the special aspects of the problem, the attributes of target groups, the solution, and the appropriate technical supports. The differing demands at each level dictate organization and planning needs.

At the state or national level, collaboration aims at reconciling the interests of independent policy-making bodies. At the community level, collaboration is sought among related operating programs. Sometimes the collaboration is hampered by political differences that are difficult to resolve. The unsuccessful effort to establish the Network for Better Nutrition (NBN) in the United States is a case in point.* On the other hand, opposition from religious groups to family planning programs in the Third World has begun to abate. The combination of population pressures, persistent advocacy, and a willingness of advocates to accept moderate initial objectives gradually builds consensus. Once such programs get started under official support, their expansion is inevitable. Growing programs in Mexico, Bangladesh, Brazil, and Indonesia are a testament to this approach.

Research is an effective means for achieving consensus. It offers a nonpartisan basis for arbitrating differences of opinion. Even where local groups are committed to predetermined directions, research can be effective in persuading a change of priorities. In Scotts Bluff, Nebraska, the organizers of what was to become the Community Health Coalition initiated a telephone survey of health-risk factors and used the findings as the agenda for a two-day organizing workshop.[3] The result was consensus on long-term objectives and a decision to develop strategies and plans. Continuing liaison with key community leaders led to the formation of the coalition, in which eventually 50 people became involved. Some 20 objectives were agreed on and the program was finally launched 14 months later.

Patience, perseverance, and painstaking groundwork are indispensable to building a collaboration. There is no way to avoid the investment

---

*The NBN is a defunct group. Initiated by FTC officials, the NBN comprised representatives of government, private industry, the health and nutrition professions, and the public. An experiment in volunteerism urged by the Reagan administration, it foundered when the White House withheld support and the USDA withdrew presumably under pressure from some sections of the food industry (see "The Role of the Private Sector" later in this chapter).

of getting a commitment from a group of well-known individuals willing to take leadership and to persuade others to set aside professional jealousies and turf protectionism for a common effort and of carrying out a major organizing activity, like a research project, to bring participants to a shared point of view on directions. Research is invariably appealing and few groups have the means to fund it on their own. Subsequent meetings provide a forum to explore the research findings and to move toward consensus on issues and strategies. But it is vital that all participants are involved at each stage. They represent resources too valuable to lose.

Identifying the Decision Makers

The real decision-making authorities are not always the portfolio officials. Knowing who they are in advance saves time, effort, morale, and perhaps the program, itself. Too often programs are developed with officials of little authority and less standing with other branches of government. The result is that such programs have difficulty in obtaining interagency cooperation. This is also true of the community at large, where enlistment of community leaders of standing and authority is essential.

A vaccination drive in Egypt against cholera in the summer of 1983 was launched on an emergency basis after 400 cases broke out in two neighboring villages of Cairo. What should have begun as a program far in advance of the crisis became a crash effort marked by confusion and discoordination. Blame was placed by one of the local Arabic newspapers on "governors and high-ranking officials" who presumably had "enormous facilities and funds" to avert the crisis but who could not be "reached" by the health professionals on the firing line.[4]

There are times when needed decisions are outside the authority of those immediately in charge. Halfdan Mahler, the director-general of the World Health Organization, declared that

> We must fight governments by bringing help from the soft underbelly of the Ministry of Health to a much more aggressive planning level in the Finance Ministry and the Planning Ministry making nutrition, for instance, important to the Ministry of Agriculture or making water or sanitation important to the Ministry of Public Works.[5]

Revelians Tuluhungwa, chief of Project Support Information at UNICEF, suggested that health messages necessary to the poorer communities may be redundant for the middle and upper classes. Unless there is a commitment to such a redundancy, he said, the advantages of mass media communications may be denied the poor. Most messages on the mass media are directed at the affluent, whose resources power the marketplace especially in the Third World. Without such a commitment, the communications gap between rich and poor and, by extension, the difference in health status will widen.[6] The Health Ministry may be in charge but the program requires the cooperation of those with authority over the media.

U.S. Secretary of Agriculture John R. Block was reported by the New York *Times* of August 30, 1982, as saying: "I am not so sure the government needs to get so deeply into telling people what they should or should not eat." When asked what USDA nutrition education will consist of in the future, John Bode, deputy assistant secretary for Food and Consumer Services, added

> It will be timely and accurate based on sound scientific evidence. We are not going to launch an aggressive campaign to instruct the public on how to eat. That is less important than providing information on nutrition. I know the distinction may seem subtle at first glance. What we are not going to do is make a national dietary prescription. That is the role for professional nutritionists.

Another official, a veteran within the department who would speak only anonymously, also declared: "Now, all of a sudden we're not telling people anything. This administration is giving out nutrition information but no analysis. It won't help people decide whether to eat butter or margarine or whether to drink skim milk or whole milk." A government's position on any issue depends on the official one approaches. But what the government will eventually do about it will be decided at the center of power, which had better be identified early on.

The Resources Needed

Table 6.1 depicts the planning stages of social marketing. The necessary resources are a research facility, the mass media, media professionals capable of analyzing and planning their use, marketing experts, creative people for message design, and materials production specialists. This array of services need not have a paralyzing effect on health professionals unfamiliar with the world of marketing. They will be found in almost every major city of the world and the caliber will be satisfactory to meet social marketing's needs. In New Mexico, a nutrition education campaign was without funds to employ a local commercial studio to produce TV

Table 6.1.   Process for Developing Social Marketing Program

I. DEVELOP STRATEGY

A. ACTIVITIES:

Given	Identification of Objectives / Definition of Strategy Components	Strategy Formulation
General Goals	The problem	Develop specific strategies for each component:
	Objectives	
General Target Groups	Target groups (segments)	• Messages
		• Target groups
	The proposed behavior change	• Research (method of tracking success of program)
	Resistance points	
	Media systems	*Media:* Delivery systems for information for each objective for each target group
	The product	*Product:* Characteristics, benefits, name, pricing, packaging, promotion
	Distribution systems	*Distribution:* Integration with health clinics, pharmacies, public and private service and commodity distribution centers, retailers
	• Messages	
	• Products	

B. RESOURCES:

Review:
• existing studies

• feedback from ongoing programs

Conduct:
qualitative investigation followed by quantitative studies

Analyze:
all data and information for written situation review

Table 6.1. (continued)

II. IMPLEMENT STRATEGY			III. ASSESS STRATEGY
A. ACTIVITIES:			**A. ACTIVITIES:**
Production of Draft Materials	**Testing Messages, Concepts and Materials**	**Inaugurate Program**	**Periodic Evaluation**
Messages for different materials and media	Authorities Target audiences	Finalize social marketing plan Produce materials Execute media plan (reach, frequency, continuity, coverage area) Coordinate with other programs Train Field personnel	Feed results back to project managers Determine strengths and weaknesses Revise program accordingly Assess cost-effectiveness
Product packaging, promotion and sales materials	Target audiences	Execute sales and distribution plan (sales training, meetings)	Product sales
B. RESOURCES:			**B. RESOURCES:**
In-house production Advertising agencies Contract out; other arrangements	Groups or "in-depth" individual interviews to test • Messages: for comprehension, cultural relevance, practicality, emotional appeal, memorability • Product: for performance, packaging, pricing, name		• Tracking Studies (KAP) - qualitative and quantitative • Observation by supervisors • Reporting by field workers • Monitoring of media • Wholesale and retail audits of product sales

messages. The son of one of the project participants, a film student at the University of California at Los Angeles, was recruited for the job. Assisted by a classmate and using equipment borrowed from the university, the young man filmed the series of six messages for the cost of film stock, processing, and a car rental.

The Step-by-Step Process

This is a summary discussion of the various steps involved in developing the social marketing plan along with the resources (tools, techniques, or methods) required to implement them as outlined in Table 6.1. The sequential steps are grouped into three broad phases of activity: strategy development; strategy implementation; and strategy assessment.

The preparation of a social marketing plan is the purpose and outcome of the strategy development and implementation phases. It is the responsibility of campaign management and delegated to those charged with the social marketing function. Table 6.1 is, in essence, an outline of what goes into the marketing plan. What follows is an elaboration of the indicated elements to clarify the tasks involved.

Strategy Development

Activities

Defining the problem and setting objectives. To prevent a divergence in the perception of a problem between program planners and the target audience, it is necessary to define it from the consumer's viewpoint. And as we have demonstrated, this must be done from the beginning, and with the kind of research that will persuade the authorities to accept this redefinition.

Similarly, the objectives of a program postulated by authorities may be too broad, too vague, too unrealistic, or "off-target." Ideally, the objective should be stated in quantitative terms: required input, desired output, and a time frame. Projects have been adjudged failures when in fact they were flawed from the start by unrealistic objectives.

Identifying the target audience. There are very few social marketing programs that are directed at a single, homogeneous target audience, as we have demonstrated with our Indonesian example. In addition to segmentation of our primary target audience, the typical situation also involves target differentiation of secondary and, perhaps, even tertiary target audiences. The assessment of their relative importance is critical to decisions affecting subsequent marketing activities and allocation of program resources. Even given the same problem, the relative importance of audiences may vary from program to program and country to country. For example: while women may be assumed to represent the primary target audience for sales of the OC (oral contraceptive) pill, this assumption would not hold true in Bangladesh where men are responsible for 93 percent of all retail purchases and are, therefore, the primary buyers of virtually all products, including female undergarments and OC pills.[7]

Examples of secondary target audiences include those with influence over the actions and attitudes of the primary audience like respected relatives (wife's mother-in-law, in many societies), teachers, doctors, midwives, etc. Tertiary target audiences might embrace opinion leaders, government officials, the religious establishment, retailers, etc.

Defining the proposed behavior change.   Every social marketing project has as its desired end the adoption of a new behavioral mode on the part of the target audience, whether a change in dietary practice, in breast-feeding practice, contraception, or health practices. Defining the behavior change precisely is another critical dimension of strategy development that is often neglected. This neglect often leads to well-meaning but ineffective sloganeering campaigns like "Eat a Balanced Diet" or "Breast is Best."

Identifying the resistance points.   *Resistance points* are the inhibitors militating against adoption of the desired behavioral change. They may be of social, cultural, economic, or religious origin, or the product of ignorance. Within the same society, they may differ from stratum to stratum, from urban to rural areas, and between the sexes. Thus, different target audiences will have different *resistance points.* The social marketing approach demands their acknowledgment, evaluates their relative strengths within each target audience and its segments, and develops and tests appropriate strategies for overcoming them.

Assessing media availability.   At the earliest possible stage, parameters of the various mass media available in the country are determined: their overall penetration; their reach of the target audience segments;

their national, regional, or local coverage; their policies with respect to public service; their costs if public service time is unavailable. In many LDCs much of this information is either unavailable, of doubtful accuracy; or badly out of date. A media data bank can be developed by adding questions on media exposure (listening, reading, and viewing habits) to other ongoing research projects.

To develop an effective media plan in the strategy implementation phase, it will be necessary to know how target audiences relate to the available media, the media they rely on for information, how often and when they read, listen, or view, the most popular radio/TV programs. In LDCs literacy levels need to be ascertained. (See special discussion of media in Chapter 8).

Designing the product.   The need for a product grows out of problem and target audience analysis. Product is thus a strategic response to the problem—a key element of the solution. Contraceptives, ORS packets, vaccines, vitamin A capsules, and iron pills are product strategies designed to solve health problems. But breastmilk, homemade enriched weaning foods, and home prepared ORS are also products, though they need not be obtained commercially or through government distribution schemes. From a social marketing point of view, the distinction as to source of supply is almost irrelevant. The challenge is the same so long as the "product," regardless of its source, represents an innovative item to the consumer or requires the adoption of a new behavior. Once again, consumer perceptions are fundamental and are to be taken into account in deciding product form, presentation, and the components of the campaigns to win their acceptance: product composition, appearance, method of use, name, packaging, price, and promotion. In a food, obviously, taste and "mouthfeel" are important.

Choosing distribution systems.   Organizational networking will multiply the impact of media systems for messages (radio, TV, the press, billboards, the health care system, and so forth). This means collaboration with private voluntary organizations (PVOs), religious organizations, school systems, and others that are active in health-related activities. Such collaboration adds extra dimensions of effort and assures message harmony with the public. This should be arranged from the start so that the collaboration builds as the program unfolds.

Selecting commercial distribution systems for products requires the help of the private sector. Familiarity with local food and drug marketing patterns is essential so that appropriate firms may be chosen for products. Criteria for this selection will include the firm's current product line (for compatibility), classes of retail trade served and retail areas covered (target audience reach), frequency of coverage, reputation in the market, the standing of its products and price ranges, and promotion capabilities. (See discussion on role of the private sector later in this chapter.)

For each product to be marketed, the marketing plan should also contain a volume base and spending plan. The latter is a quantitative statement of the sales objective (in units and monetary terms) and the proposed expenditure required to realize the objective. The marketing plan format also calls for a situation review and an analysis of competitive activity and spending (if appropriate and/or available).

Resources

Both primary and secondary research are utilized for input during the strategy development phase. This calls for review and, if necessary, reanalysis of previous studies and feedback information from ongoing programs to expand knowledge of the relevant issues, to learn from past mistakes, and to prevent duplication of research effort. This review invariably suggests ways in which additional research will prove fruitful.

Most important, however, is reliance on primary research among the target audience. At this stage, qualitative, as opposed to quantitative, studies produce more insights into why people think and behave as they do. The traditional KAP-type of study typically describes behavior; qualitative research seeks the reasons for behavior through loosely structured "open-ended" questions, in-depth probing of responses, indirect questioning, and the use of projective techniques.

It is necessary to be open-minded about qualitative research techniques. Focus groups may not be useable in countries where, for example, cultural inhibitions make discussion of family planning issues difficult. Individual in-depth interviews produce equally good results, albeit at a somewhat higher cost per unit of data.

Projective techniques are useful when dealing with such delicate and sensitive matters as individual attitudes toward contraception. They are powerful tools used to overcome reluctance in discussing feelings of an intensely private nature, whether within a group environment or in individual interviews. For example, in several countries Manoff International has used the photo-sort technique by which respondents are shown a series of photographs of individuals from different population strata and asked to sort the photos into two groups: people they feel would practice family planning and those they feel would not. They are next asked to select the persons most likely and least likely to practice family planning and to give reasons for their choices. Finally, they are asked to select the photo of the one person most like themselves. In this manner, we were able to ascertain the respondents' feelings about their position in the spectrum, ranging from rejection to indifference to acceptance of family planning. All the information gleaned from secondary sources and the qualitative research is then analyzed, and a written situation review is prepared. This document forms the basis for the subsequent strategy formulation activities.

Expertise in qualitative research and the application of projective techniques can be found among private sector research firms. Where in some countries that is not the case, consultant specialists are used to train the management, professional, and field research staffs of local organizations. The required degree of competence and comfort in their application can be attained in a surprisingly short time. This represents a transfer of qualitative research technology that benefits the future research needs of public and private sector organizations.

At times it has been advantageous to assist in the creation of new research organizations in countries where firms are unable to handle the volume of research activity required. In those instances, fledgling organizations are provided with requisite technical training and counseling on business management as well.

Strategy Formulation

Specific written strategies are formulated for every component of the social marketing program. Wherever feasible, alternative strategies are developed, reviewed, and evaluated, and the most promising strategy is then incorporated into the marketing plan. Written strategy statements are prepared in the following areas:

Messages.   What is the principal point we want to communicate to the target audience? What, if any, are the subordinate points? What are the mandatory considerations to be incorporated? What is the tonality (or tone of voice) we wish to use with the target audience?

Target audiences and segments.   For whom is this message intended? Men, women, others? What age brackets? Urban or rural? Socioeconomic status? What segments of each primary group? What secondary and tertiary groups?

Media.   What media and media mix will we use? What is the rationale for each medium? What proportion of the target audiences do we want to reach? With what frequency? How much continuity do we need (or how much continuity can we afford) or should messages (and advertising) be pulsed (delivered in waves over time)?

Product.   For each product in the product mix, the following must be delineated: consumer target groups; physical characteristics; consumer benefit(s); name; pricing; packaging; promotion strategy; and distribution channels.

Research.   What continuing formative (process) research is required for tracking the operation of the program? What summative (impact) research will be used to measure results?

Integration with other ongoing activities.   What strategies will be used to integrate the program with other programs being conducted by the government or by NGOs? What provisions will be made for collaboration with health centers, pharmacies, public and private service and commodity distribution centers, wholesalers and retailers?

Strategy Implementation

Activities

Acceptance of the first phase, marketing plan development, means that execution of its components may proceed. This involves four steps: preparation of draft or prototype materials; materials testing; final production; and program inauguration.

Preparation of prototype materials

•*Messages.* Prototype messages are developed for each medium. Frequently, this involves pretesting alternate messages to help select the strongest of the alternatives (see Chapter 9 on Message Design).
•*Product.*

Name/logo. A list of possible brand names and/or a logotype (logo) are developed. Normally, names should bear some relevance to the products but this will depend mostly on creative judgment.

Meaningless names have been attached to products that proved to be eminent successes. It is doubtful that the names had much to do with the success. It is more likely that sound products and successful marketing ventures make the names prominent, not vice versa.

Packaging. Alternative package designs are created for subsequent testing and evaluation. Single unit, multiple packs, and dispenser packages are typically developed at this stage, though not necessarily for simultaneous entry. Sometimes it is better to introduce additional package extensions *ad seriatim.*

Pricing. Various proposed price points are developed, taking into account the income levels of the target population, prices of commercial products (if these are a factor in the market), trade discount practices, distribution costs, and cost recovery considerations.

Promotion and sales materials. Alternative point-of-sale materials (posters, literature, store signs, calendars, or other give-aways) are created once brand name, logo, and packaging have been determined. Trade discounts are important trade promotion devices (dealer-loading, retail features).

Materials testing.   Prototype messages are tested among samples of the target audiences. In the Third World production costs tend to be minimal by U.S. standards so it is possible to test fairly comprehensive versions of materials (except for films). Thus, press ads are tested with type and illustrations in place, radio scripts are recorded on cassettes with professional voices, music and sound effects are played for respondents on portable cassette recorders. For TV or cinema, tightly drawn storyboards can be used sometimes in conjunction with recorded dialogue. Messages are tested for comprehension, cultural relevance, practicality, emotional appeal, persuasiveness, and memorability. (see the special role of research later in this chapter.)

In the United States there are many testing services available, with varying methodologies and sworn supporters. None is faultless though all are interesting and helpful. The research approach, once again, is almost always qualitative and suitable for most countries; questions are indirect (e.g. "how would your friend react if she heard this message?") and open-ended. Extensive probing is utilized to get at the reasons behind respondents' reactions and to uncover any negatives, ambiguities, or other barriers to effective communications that may have inadvertently been incorporated into the message.

A qualitative technique yields a wealth of diagnostic insights that are subsequently useful to writers and artists if revisions are indicated. Revised materials can be retested, but at some point the judgment must be made that diminishing returns do not warrant further test investment.

Brand name, logo, and packaging alternatives for the product are tested among the target audience either in the field (taste tests) or through sample "drops" for in-home usage. After a predetermined sampling period, homes are revisited for interviews with consumers about the product's performance, consumer likes and dislikes, competitive comparisons, clarity of instructional material, compliance with product directions, and "willingness to buy" at the alternative price points.

Point-of-sale promotional materials are tested among samples of consumers and retailers. Testing determines retailer likes and dislikes of content, whether the material is of the proper size for the average outlet, and how long it is likely to be kept on display. It also helps develop an estimate of retailers "likely to use." Sales and discount policies are "tried out" on sales representatives and selected individuals in the trade for probable acceptability.

Final production. Once tested and revised the materials are presented along with relevant research support to the appropriate officials for approval. Positive test results almost always help in resolving conflicts of opinion and judgment among responsible authorities. Final production follows in accordance with the marketing plan estimates of the quantities required together with the requisite cost data.

While the foregoing activities are unfolding, a detailed media plan has been in process for each product and is presented for review by project management. In accordance with the media strategy statement, the media plan specifies the media mix, the desired reach and frequency goals for each target audience and segment, national versus regional versus local coverage, pulsing versus uninterrupted continuity, heavy-up periods for seasonal and promotional reasons, cost estimates, and other strategic considerations.

Program inauguration. Advance planning is required to plan meetings for announcing the program to governmental, NGO, and PVO organizations with whom coordination of effort is deemed desirable or necessary and for presenting product sales and distribution programs to wholesalers and/or retailers.

In establishing the launch data, project management must take into consideration such factors as: the time required to train health workers at all levels and, in connection with the products, the sales forces of commercial distributing firms; the time required to produce packaging, advertising, and promotional materials; the time required to achieve a predetermined level of effective product distribution at retail. Whether media are to be paid or not arrangements should be completed for time and space, to negotiate for the most preferred time periods or position in publications, to select prime sites for billboards (hoardings) and to conclude all matters specified in the media plan (see following section on the role of the advertising agency).

Resources

Preparation of prototype and final materials.   Most governments have their own printing and film production facilities, although these may not always be the best sources of supply. Program planners should develop others from among local printers, film producers, art services, and advertising agencies whose special capabilities for various needs ought to be assessed. This diversification of supply will afford higher standards of quality and creativity. Even among university communications departments can be found the requisite talent for many projects. These young aspirants are always eagerly seeking opportunities for employment, often on a *pro bono* basis.

Materials testing.   Testing can usually be handled by the same organizations employed for the various research projects of the strategy formulation stage. They will have become adept in the application of qualitative research methodology but will require additional training in the probing techniques utilized in test studies and in in-home tests with products. Depending on local circumstances either focus groups or individual in-depth interviews with samples of the target audience would be utilized.

Strategy Assessment

Activities

It is convenient to distinguish between two types of assessment activities: *Process evaluation.* Are we on the right track? What are the strengths and weaknesses of the program? What strategic or tactical changes are indicated? *Summative (impact) evaluation.* Is the program meeting its output objectives? How cost-effective is it?

Process evaluation.   As the name implies, process evaluation is conducted at periodic intervals during program operation. Since marketing plans typically employ a one-year time frame, process evaluation studies should be conducted two to four times a year. They tend to be small in scale and are designed to furnish rapid feedback to project management. Process evaluation studies are conducted among consumers and retailers as well as media systems, and are designed to provide information in the following areas:

●*Consumer research.*
KAP (Knowledge, Attitude, Practice).
message awareness
message recall
message comprehension
behavior adoption

Product.
product trial, repeat, and current usage
reasons for nontrial or nonrepeat
intention to try product in future
product satisfaction/dissatisfaction
specific focus on key issues; i.e., price, availability, and packaging convenience.

●*Distribution research (education materials or product).*
Education materials.
available at key points (MCHs, schools, etc.)
supply problems
health workers' reactions
target audience reactions
need for revision/replacement
future need

Product.
stocked or out of stock
supply problems
frequency of salesperson's visits
product display
pricing
point-of-sale material display
perceived level of consumer demand
competitive situation

●*Media Research.*
Are mass media systems performing according to plan (reach, frequency, continuity with target audience)?

Are other media systems performing according to plan (government departments, community groups)?

Process evaluation pinpoints weaknesses in the strategic plan and enables prompt corrective action while the project is in operation. For example, low consumer awareness might dictate a change in media strategy or message design. With products, high consumer trial rates but low repeat usage could indicate product/pricing problems or need for strategic redirection of advertising. High out-of-stock situations at retail could signal inadequate dealerloading or poor pattern of salesperson's visits.

But process evaluation can also be invaluable for identifying new opportunities—the chance for more effective new appeals or, with products, variations in package sizes, usage instructions, pricing, or formulation. Periodic sales audits at the wholesale or retail level must also be conducted to determine trends in share of market.

Finally, a mechanism must be developed for periodic monitoring of mass media activity. Are messages broadcast at the time and with the frequency contracted for? Are press ads positioned and sized according to specifications?

Summative evaluation. The traditional approach to evaluating the effectiveness of a program over an extended period of time is to conduct large-scale quantitative studies of the KAP type. A baseline study is conducted prior to program launch with follow-up studies conducted at anywhere from 6 to 24-month intervals. By rigorous adherence to a well-designed sampling plan and to well-defined data collection procedures, wave-to-wave comparability is achieved and, thus, long-term trends can be determined with a relatively high level of confidence. Some subjects, like family planning, pose difficulties. The highly structured, close-ended format employed in KAP studies does not permit meaningful measurement of attitudes toward family planning. The intimate nature of the subject requires the use of indirect, probing techniques not usually employed in quantitative studies. But qualitative techniques can be combined with quantitative tracking studies. Field investigators, coders, editors, and research-firm management personnel can be trained in the complexities of multistage probing, code construction, and other skills.

Large-scale evaluation studies can also be used to provide project management with detailed media exposure data for various demographic segments of the country's population where this information was not directly available from other sources.

Resources

The basic research design for both process and summative evaluations can be developed through the same resources used for studies of the preparatory (formative) stage. In fact, the ground covered is essentially the same and the probing is intended to assess the decisions based on earlier insights. The summative evaluation seeks a measure of progress toward objectives and the identity of contributing circumstances. University research groups, commercial research firms, and the research departments of advertising agencies are among the likely resources for these tasks.

The monitoring of the mass media and other message delivery systems usually has to be tailored to situations. In some, media monitoring systems already exist. Where this is not the case effective mechanisms, such as corps of at-home elderly or invalids, can be initiated for monitoring radio and TV announcements. These have proved useful in the Philippines, Nicaragua, Ecuador, and elsewhere. Many countries require radio and TV stations to maintain public logs and regular inspection of these records offers a feasible means of checking on mass media performance. The effectiveness of collaborating organizations as delivery systems for the same messages can be measured in the course of the process evaluation by the questions aimed at identifying the source of message awareness among the knowledgeable. Organization affiliations are determined and matched with KAP results.

The foregoing description of the social marketing planning process deserves elaboration with respect to the special roles played by an advertising agency, research, the mass media, message design, and private sector involvement.

The Role of the Advertising Agency

Ordinarily, the ideal resource is an advertising agency. The reasons are evident from Figure 6.1, which maps the flow of work through a typical agency. The resemblance to the social marketing process should come as no surprise since social marketing is the adaptation of modern marketing disciplines to social programs. The modern advertising agency is the embodiment of these disciplines. But no agency, no matter how big, has every facility in house. Certain special services are subcontracted. The advantage of an agency is the availability of every needed service from the one source, obviating a multiplicity of arrangements and the extra time and administration demands they entail.

Figure 6.1. Advertising Agency Process for Developing Marketing/Advertising Program

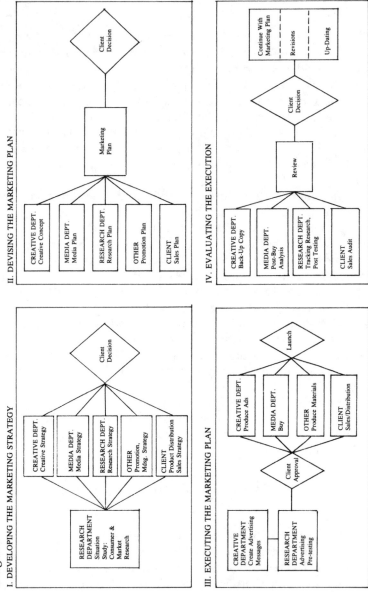

I. DEVELOPING THE MARKETING STRATEGY

RESEARCH DEPARTMENT Situation Study: Consumer & Market Research

CREATIVE DEPT. Creative Strategy
MEDIA DEPT. Media Strategy
RESEARCH DEPT. Research Strategy
OTHER Promotion, Mdsg. Strategy
CLIENT Product Distribution Sales Strategy

Client Decision

II. DEVISING THE MARKETING PLAN

CREATIVE DEPT. Creative Concept
MEDIA DEPT. Media Plan
RESEARCH DEPT. Research Plan
OTHER Promotion Plan
CLIENT Sales Plan

Marketing Plan

Client Decision

III. EXECUTING THE MARKETING PLAN

CREATIVE DEPARTMENT Create Advertising Messages
RESEARCH DEPARTMENT Advertising Pre-testing

Client Approval

CREATIVE DEPT. Produce Ads
MEDIA DEPT. Buy
OTHER Produce Materials
CLIENT Sales/Distribution

Launch

IV. EVALUATING THE EXECUTION

CREATIVE DEPT. Back-Up Copy
MEDIA DEPT. Post-Buy Analysis
RESEARCH DEPT. Tracking Research, Post Testing
CLIENT Sales Audit

Review

Client Decision

Continue With Marketing Plan
Revisions
Up-Dating

118

Traditionally, health professionals have been reluctant to enter the disdained environment of an advertising agency. Theirs is a popular misconception about advertising agencies, the kind of people who staff them, and the nature of the services they perform. Advertising agencies, like the mass media, are not the exclusive minions of their commercial clients. People working in agencies, like their fellow citizens outside, enjoy opportunities to apply their skills and experience to social projects. In fact, they have a long history of doing so through organizations like the Advertising Council. However, most of these have been *pro bono publico* advertising efforts executed without the full range of marketing services paying clients receive. This is primarily because of the inexperience of noncommercial clients, who are typically unfamiliar with all the services an agency has to offer. Even if they were to know, most would be unsure of what to ask for. But making ads and placing them with the media are only the final stages of a lengthy process of research, study, analysis, and strategic marketing decision making that the modern advertising agency is equipped to deal with.

The process begins with the research department, which has responsibility for analyzing all available information about the product or service and identifying areas for further inquiry. It unfolds under the direction of an account executive, the agency liaison with the client and the manager of the account. The analysis involves recourse to all sources of market and consumer information and produces a situation study, a total review of all facts and circumstances ending with recommendations for further study where gaps exist.

The situation study is the basic reference for all the service departments (research, media, creative, merchandising, promotion, materials production). The findings are examined by the group for implications regarding target audience(s), market segmentation, the product (price, sizes, packaging), product positioning, buying incentives, competition, distribution and other trade factors, sales and market trend data, promotion patterns (consumer couponing, discounts), market structure constraints (laws, regulations), and category advertising levels.

The procedure would be the same were no product involved. Market research for a breast-feeding promotion campaign, for example, would seek to define the parameters of the breast-feeding market. It would probe for some measure of the prevalence of the practice among new mothers, the trend, duration, and extent of mixed feeding. It would assemble data on competitive products and practices—the size of the breast milk substitute market, the trend of sales, the distribution systems, seasonal and geographic patterns, advertising and sales promotion practices and expenditures, and advertising and promotion strategies and claims. It would examine the market for conditions that militate against breast-feeding—hospital practices, the need for social policies in behalf of nursing mothers who work outside the home, and for restricting commercial marketing practices detrimental to breast-feeding. It would explore the availability of support programs in the community to identify opportunities for collaboration. In toto, the aim is to identify the dimensions of the problem, the array of opposing forces and their strategies, the manner of their deployment, and the likely sources of support.

Consumer research for the campaign would focus on constructing the demographic and psychographic profile of the target audience. The nursing mother is the primary concern but she must be differentiated in ways that can make significant strategy differences. In which segments of the nursing mother universe is the decline in breast-feeding most severe? In which is breast-feeding duration insufficient? Is breast-feeding's decline related to ignorance, indifference, life-style, fear and anxiety, or to external influences—the hospital, the obstetrician or pediatrician, the commercial marketplace? The answers enable planners to perceive segmentations of the primary target audience (by socioeconomic group and work status) and to identify others—the medical profession, the government—who should not be ignored. They should also produce insights into the cultural and psychological resistance points that block breast-feeding among new mothers and into such pertinent behavioral factors as media habits. What are their favorite media? Which are the popular TV and radio programs? What are their reading, listening, and watching patterns?

When the sale and promotion of a product are involved, the agency will join with the client in examining its position in the market. New products entail a new research process—consumer panels to test for acceptability (performance, price) against alternatives as well as package and label studies with consumers and the trade, including on-shelf tests. Even with existing products, research is necessary to monitor consumer experience—likes and dislikes, usage patterns—vis-à-vis the competition. With personal products like contraceptives, research is difficult and the methods and questioning must be sensitively designed.

In Haiti, a costly decision about the condom offered in the government's program could have been avoided. Officials chose a colored condom and not until disappointing results led to a consumer study was it revealed that the strong preference among users was for the clear type.[8] Highly rewarding focus group sessions were an important element in a well-regarded family planning study conducted in Mexico in 1978. In all, 44 separate sessions were organized with sample groups differentiated by age, sex, marital status, socioeconomic status, residence, and by use or nonuse of contraceptives. Similar work was done successfully in the late 1970s in Indonesia and more recently in Bangladesh in 1983.[9]

The media department needs these inputs for strategic decisions regarding media and the most cost-effective use to make of them—the specific magazines or TV time periods and the necessary reach, frequency, and continuity levels. Factors weighed include competitive activity, the maturity of the product category, the nature of the client's product (e.g., the competitive superiority of breast milk to artificial milks), and the budget, among others. The media strategy is necessary before the creative work of designing messages can begin.

The creative department now knows the media for which it must design the advertising. From its exploration of the situation study, it has developed the elements of the creative strategy—the buying incentive, the consumer benefits, the reasons why, the "feelings that," the concepts to combat *resistance points,* the special environment (tonality) of the advertising, and the casting of models and/or performers. If consumer promotion and publicity are to be elements of the marketing mix, representatives of those agency services will submit proposed strategies for such activities.

None of this is poured in concrete. The account group will discuss and debate—most often at high fever and pitch—until consensus is achieved, either by accommodation and compromise or management/client fiat. The account executive's role is to move the project along, mollifying anguish and reconciling differences. The process, though painful, is essential because the resultant strategies are the mandatory rules of the venture. Once decided on, they must be inviolable and all subsequent work must be scrutinized in their light. They are, at one and the same time, insurance that the project remains on track and that each department's independence within the stated parameters is secure against interference.

Once strategies have been agreed to and approved (perhaps, by an agency review board), they are incorporated together with the original situation study, the findings of the research, the sales objectives, the media plans, the advertising materials, and the budget into the marketing plan.

The unfolding of the marketing plan can be interrupted for any number of reasons. The research department may need additional research and, if the client agrees, strategy development will have to wait. Advertising is not always predestined. The situation study may reveal circumstances, confirmed later by further research and analysis, that militate against an advertising strategy in favor of consumer price promotion, discounts to the trade, or even a redesign of the product itself. Surprising though it may seem, agencies have been known to recommend against advertising given such circumstances.

It becomes clear that the agency is a planning and development entity. When ready to execute plans the agency relies mainly on outside suppliers. The research department will design the research studies, including questionnaires and protocols, but outside research organizations will be engaged to conduct the interviewing and the preliminary analysis of results. The final research report will be a joint effort.

The creative department will prepare rough copy and layouts of ads. For TV commercials, these will be storyboards—schematic individual drawings indicating the cinematic sequences, each keyed to portions of the audio script and desired camera moves; for radio, only scripts with audio cues and instructions are necessary. Music is sometimes scored in-house but most often by an outside music contractor. Casting may be done jointly by the agency and an outside director or by a casting company. In all cases, finished execution is farmed out. Print ads are designed by agency art directors and given to outside typesetters. Photographers and art studios are selected to produce final art. A TV production firm or a recording studio for radio is engaged to handle final production. Agency art directors, writers, and producers supervise this production.

The research department will be called on again for pretesting advertising. Pretesting can be an expensive exercise. Where budgets are small (or client and agency egos are big), it is frequently not resorted to and advertising will be used untested. Also, once a campaign has been measured and passes muster, new executions of the same strategy, copy, and graphics are frequently assumed not to need further testing (see "The Special Role of Research in Social Marketing" in this chapter).

The media department executes its plan through media representatives of the networks, local TV and radio stations, and the magazines and newspapers. These reps present availabilities in accordance with specifications—the target audience, reach, frequency, continuity, and budget. Magazine and newspaper selections are made by comparing readership profiles and cost-per-thousand efficiency (see Chapter 8—"Using the Mass Media for Social Marketing"). The use of outside suppliers has an economic and professional rationale. No agency could afford to staff such diverse talent on a full-time basis.

Traditionally, agency compensation has come from a 15-percent commission paid by the media, except for certain special services arranged for which clients pay supplementary fees. This system, long under attack as irrelevant and open to abuse, is a vestige of the day (long before radio and TV) when the first advertising agents were space salesmen for newspapers and magazines. The more enterprising of them came to realize that sales of space depended on creating an advertising idea, selling it, and, finally, arranging to produce it. From these modest origins of the advertising agent, and with the explosive advent of radio, TV, and modern marketing techniques, have emerged the advertising agency and the proliferation of its marketing services. Though the making of ads is still its primary responsibility, the agency of today is a highly sophisticated organization staffed with professionals from every marketing discipline. The business still comprises thousands of smaller firms without these elaborate services, but they serve smaller advertisers whose budgets are neither big enough to interest the full-service agency nor to warrant its services. The latter, organized for major marketers, have become their indispensable partners in today's highly competitive struggle for share-of-market. Marketing is the new battleground and advertising, with its clash of claim and counterclaim, its major weapon.

Today, agency compensation patterns are varied. The media commission system still predominates but for very big accounts it is usually less than the traditional 15 percent. Fee arrangements between agency and client are replacing the commission system, because they free the agency from the temptations inherent in a dependence on media spending and acknowledge the relationship between service and compensation.

In all countries, it is customary for advertising agencies to engage in public service efforts on a *pro bono publico* basis. In the large industrial nations, local advertising councils have been set up jointly by agencies, advertisers, and the media for this purpose. There is more demand, however, than can be satisfied, so it is not uncommon for agencies to volunteer when solicited for their services directly. However, one should have no illusions about what to expect of them. Agencies cannot afford to provide a full range of service without compensation. They may be willing to create ads gratis but will expect to be compensated for research, testing, and the like, as well as for out-of-pocket costs for art, photography, typesetting, engravings, and TV and radio production. Under such an arrangement, the agency may also agree to aid in obtaining public service time from local media or, if there is a budget for media, to negotiate deep discounts on a net basis (i.e., forego traditional commissions).

With experience, it is possible eventually to go in-house for these services, to arrange for them directly with local research organizations, the media, and the TV and radio directors and producers on an a la carte basis. This is an ambitious undertaking that commercial marketers try from time to time, usually with disappointing results. The economies prove illusory and the coordination, so conveniently managed by an agency, can become a burdensome chore.

The Savings Bond division of the U.S. Treasury early in 1984 decided it had had enough of voluntary assistance. After 42 years as the premiere public service client of the Advertising Council, its officials concluded that they "would get better results if they pay their own agency to produce the campaign" and handle placement of the materials with the media.[10] The intention was to continue soliciting the media for public service time and space but they believed that an agency could do a better job of it. Robert Keim, the council president, agreed that agencies are better for an aggressive, product-oriented sales effort. This should not necessarily discourage other social marketing ventures from seeking voluntary assistance if they can get it. After 42 years, if circumstances require it, they, too, might want to consider a change for the better.

The Special Role of Research
in Social Marketing

The research techniques employed in social marketing are no different from those employed, generally, in the social sciences. The essential difference is in the uses to which they are put and the special insights searched for. Mostly, the difference is a matter of focus and emphasis.

The research goal is formative, process- rather than problem/solution-oriented. Obviously, social marketing also needs to audit how effectively solutions are resolving problems. But social marketing is even more concerned with evaluating the performance of every element to identify weaknesses or even failures in the process. Otherwise, impact evaluations can be misleading. We shall know that a program failed but we may never know why nor be able to trace the failure to its specific cause. Because of a flaw in one or more executional elements, the strategy may be rejected. An outbreak of botulism in a poorly operated food plant would not lead us to reject canning as a food preservation strategy. We trace such failures to the cause and eliminate it.

In social marketing, emphasis is on refining our appreciation of why things happen and how. We accept the need to measure the what and the extent of its change but only after we uncover the means for interpreting why and how it happened. Research is a diagnostic tool, not merely a measuring rod. Though the goal of social marketing strategies is to solve health and human welfare problems, in the process we are determined to learn how to make these strategies work better. This is why research that helps produce fresh insights, free of preconceived notions and the constraints of past experience, is invaluable. In commercial marketing it takes the form of the focus group interview and its effectiveness has given it a prominence within the research community. Borrowed from the qualitative techniques of anthropology, it was largely overlooked by the other social sciences until recently. With the growing awareness of the ingenious uses commercial marketers have made of the focus group, it is being rediscovered in academic circles and references to it in the literature are now commonplace.

Qualitative research does not require the interviewing prowess of highly trained professionals. The perception is growing that a good deal of meaningful information can be derived through simple research tasks for which pararesearchers can be specifically trained in short periods of

time. This is the view of a group of 305 worldwide health education authorities expressed at the Technical Discussion at WHO's thirty-sixth
World Health Assembly

> Much can be done and should be done by the community itself in terms
> of simple inquiries and observations provided the people receive some
> training. . . . Community self-studies are more likely to take into account
> values and social concerns. . . . Members of the community . . . were also
> to have an opportunity to find or to seek solutions.[11]

But with the gathering acclaim for the focus group interview has
come the inevitable mythic distortions as to what it is and how it should
be conducted. What now imperils the technique is the inclination of an
enlarging priesthood to dogmatize it. This will have the regrettable effect
of rigidifying a technique notable for the pliability it offers a small
homogeneous group to exchange freely on a specific subject. The responsibility of the moderator or the facilitator (notice, not the interviewer) is to
let this exchange happen—neither to restrict nor direct it autocratically. It
is, in fact, not an interview at all but an interchange among the group. The
theory is that under such circumstances they are apt to unravel more of
the twists and turns in their attitudes than they would under direct inter-
rogation by an interviewer. Without such insights researchers are thrown
back onto opinion and conjecture and to negotiating differences among
themselves. But arbitration among the authorities is not a reliable basis for
decision making about the consumer mind. When authorities fall out,
only insight into the beliefs and perceptions of the target audience
through the target audience can reliably reconcile differences.

Qualitative research, like the focus group, aims either to modify or to
reject previous interpretations and to uncover the basis for making new
ones. Quantitative research—the standard technique of social science—is
most useful for quantifying the validity of this intelligence. The focus
group is conducted with discussion guidelines, not questionnaires, with
target audience samples of from 6 to 12 people. This optimal range has
now been seized upon by dogmatists as a minimum-maximum range.
This is unnecessarily arbitrary. Productive focus group sessions can be
managed when only three or four are available. In fact, the technique is
adaptable even to an exchange between two, though with some loss of
the spontaneity a larger group stimulates. But it is the quality of the interchange that is important and not the religious adherence to prescribed
conditions that may not always be available in the real world.

Growing popularity of the focus group has been fed by persistent dis-
enchantment with the limitations of the statistical intelligence of quantitative research imposed by the rigid structure of closed-ended questionnaires. More and more, the realization has grown that these studies sim-

ply represent an updating of answers to old questions when circumstances indicate a need to raise new ones. The difficulty is in ascertaining what those questions should be. The focus group with its loosely
structured approach has proved effective in uncovering these elusive
items.

The focus group and qualitative research are, in general, no substitutes for quantitative studies that have their own valuable but explicit applications. Whereas the focus group can uncover new questions, and reveal well-hidden attitudes and perceptions, only quantitative research
can help ascertain their significance as a community characteristic. It is
possible in highly structured traditional societies to bypass this quantification if the insights derived from the group are explicit and virtually un-
contradicted. Then the risk can be taken that in a homogeneous culture
the attitudes will be upheld.

General guidelines for conducting the focus group interview can be
summarized

1. Elaborate a question guide rather than a questionnaire, the guide to be
   used by the moderator in stimulating response and discussion.
2. Phrase the questions so that they will allow for more than merely yes-or-
   no answers and are directed more to what people do, how they feel, and
   what they think than to factual responses.
3. Listen to the answers, for the way things are said may be as important as
   the answers themselves in that nuances of expression, mood, and word
   choice may stimulate new directions for the exchange or reveal richer attitudinal information.
4. Formulate new questions stemming from the responses or, in a group
   discussion, to stimulate others to react.
5. In the face of reluctance or hesitation, employ the indirect device of a third
   person about whom the question is asked rather than of the respondent
   directly.
6. Tape record the entire session so that the exchange may be reviewed to
   capture gems of insight that can be overlooked during the session.

In the commercial marketing world, focus group sessions are usually
held in rooms where clients may sit behind one-way mirrors to monitor
the sessions. This also affords the opportunity to send into the session
new questions unexpectedly inspired by the proceedings.

The cultural sensitivity of the anthropological approach safeguards
against the mechanistic responses inevitable from the rigidly constructed
questionnaires of quantitative research. Moreover, if the answers are not
reliable because they are summoned from respondents' imperfect recall,
then ingenious statistical analysis can only make matters worse. The re-

sultant tables, cross tabs, regression and multivariate analyses, graphs, and charts bestow a legitimacy to dubious data. A largely counterfeit universe is being presented as the real world. Others have noted the shortcomings of the purely quantitative approach to research and analysis.[12]

One commercial marketing executive declared that his company will "proceed to quantitative research if qualitative results are mixed. However, the volatility of our marketplace limits the efficacy of large-scale, quantitative studies."[13] Zeltner noted that "there is an unsurprising emphasis on qualitative approaches in matters of advertising development and evaluation—and a notable preference for quantitative techniques in marketing and analysis."[14] He also quoted Norman Goluskin, president of the Smith/Greenland advertising agency in New York City, that his agency was firmly committed to qualitative research for "fresh insights which quantitative research failed to uncover. Numerical surveys are useful in confirming that which is known or at least hypothesized. Obviously we can't measure what we don't know."

The problem with research responses based on recall is well illustrated by Harry Balzer, vice president of the NPD Group, a Port Washington, New York, market research firm. "Nobody," he said, "likes to admit he likes junk food. Asking a candy eater if he eats a lot of candy is like asking an alcoholic if he drinks much. The problem . . . is that people don't always tell the truth and product and marketing decisions based on such inputs can often lead companies astray."[15] Perhaps it was not far-fetched for Joseph Weizenbaum, professor of Computer Science at MIT, to declare that because

> Graduates of MIT are required to pass a swimming exam . . . [and that since] . . . MIT graduates are disproportionately represented among the leaders of the American high technology industry, a simple-minded statistician would wrongly infer a cause and effect relationship between the ability to swim and managerial success.[16]

Product testing is a distinctive exercise to determine through consumer reaction at the premarketing stage the product's acceptability. Free samples are distributed to targeted homes and consumer reactions obtained in follow-up interviews. These may be monadic blind-product tests in which the product is not identified by brand name or dyadic or triadic trials in which the product is compared with one or two unidentified competitive brands. Tests are also conducted in which people are given taste samples and then interviewed for their reactions.

Another vital role of research is the pretesting of advertising to assure that concepts, products, and messages fulfill the intentions of their designers and harmonize with the perceptions and expectations of the target audience. However, pretesting cannot help program planners decide strategies. These are arrived at through situation investigation and analysis and are management, not consumer, decisions. But pretesting of concept, product, and message executions of a given strategy can reveal strengths and weaknesses not evident to the designers. It can help decide which execution produces the most impact on the target audience on the basis of

1. *Attention/Impact*—How well it captures the audience and keeps it engaged (intrusiveness, memorability)
2. *Persuasion*—How well it convinces, motivates, instills confidence (attitude shift, resistance resolution)
3. *Cultural acceptance*—How well it coincides with the cultural patterns and symbols of the audience (likes/dislikes, positives/negatives)
4. *Tonality*—How well it creates a compatible environment for audience and message (mood, emotion).

At best, pretesting procedures are imperfect. The most sophisticated of the techniques make ingenious efforts to replicate the real world. They come remarkably close but not close enough to provide ironclad guarantees of future performance. For one thing, they are all based on one-time exposure to messages intended for repetitive delivery. No way has yet been found to foretell reliably how much repetition (frequency) a message needs to complete its task. Too many variables are involved, not the least of which are ups and downs of psychological and social stress that differentiate individuals at any moment as well as the quality of the message design.

Message testing procedures will vary by medium. For the most part, the focus group can offer the most rewarding results. The inquiry can be made as wide ranging as desired, but in general, the objective should not be clouded with extraneous probings that may intrigue the researcher but frustrate both interviewer and respondent. It is best kept simple, focused, and direct. Experience in Third World countries confirms that pretesting of messages can be conducted by nonprofessionals with a minimum of training so long as the guidelines clearly set forth the need to know how well each element is received, comprehended, responded to, and believed; how promising, persuasive, and convincing is its effect; how closely it identifies with target audience psychology toward change, its view of the world, and emotional availability. The appropriate questions are put to the audience after it has been exposed to the message. In a focus group setting, the response to such questions is elaborated by interchange among the group. This helps minimize the inevitable bias implicit in an interrogatory relationship. Distortion of response to a direct question tends to refocus when it undergoes examination during a peer exchange.

Radio messages are prerecorded, preferably on cassettes, for playback before the group. Though often referred to as scratch tracks, these should contain all the elements of the finished production—sound effects, music, and professional actors. It should come as close to the actual radio-listening experience as possible. The objective is to identify elements of discordance—offensive language, inappropriate idiom, unresolved *resistance points,* and incredulity—that will need to be rectified.

TV messages impose some difficult choices. Obviously, production of test films or tapes is considerably more costly than audio recordings for radio. Storyboards—schematic frame-for-frame drawings or still photographs with dialogue indicated for each scene or a prerecorded sound track—are the least expensive, if not the most satisfying, alternative. Better still is the animatic, a filmed version of the storyboard that simulates camera movements and imparts a sense of motion. Even better but more expensive is to film or videotape the message on a minimum basis with regard to the acting, soundtrack, or editing.

Print messages (newspaper and magazine ads, posters, and pamphlets) can be tested from rough layouts or dummies. Drawings can be substituted for proposed photographs, although test shots are preferable. Polaroid photos blown up and cropped to desired size are useful. Text can be supplied by typewritten copy read separately or perhaps rendered to size for paste up in the design.

If an advertising agency is engaged, its research department can arrange and supervise the pretest. Outside research organizations without previous experience with such assignments may tend to overdesign the study. Pretesting can be worked out satisfactorily with the help of a consultant and the use of local students recruited for interviewing. In Bangladesh and Indonesia in recent years, highly satisfactory pretesting was accomplished this way for family planning and maternal/infant nutrition programs.[17] Local university students were hired and trained in the use of guidelines and put through pilot sessions with typical focus group gatherings. Guidelines were drawn up by the project officials and Manoff International consultants on the basis of necessary pretest criteria. Production of test materials was arranged through resources eventually used for the finished job.

In the United States and other developed countries, professional pretesting services of a high standard developed for the commercial marketing world are widely available. The captive audience method will usually recruit respondents by mail and invite them to attend a TV preview often at a converted movie theater. Before the screening, respondents complete a questionnaire dealing with their backgrounds, brand preferences, attitudes toward brands, and product usage patterns. They are then exposed to a typical TV program in which commercials have been inserted, including the test candidate. After the screening, certain portions of the questionnaire are readministered. The effectiveness of the test commercial is measured by comparing the shift in preference among the viewers as evidenced by their before-and-after responses. Respondents may be offered a sample of the brand preferred or even the prize of a year's supply in a subsequent drawing. They are permitted to change that choice after the performance, which ascertains the shift in brand preference. This technique is used by McCollum-Spielman & Co. Another firm, Audience Studies Inc. (ASI) augments this method with a composite moment-by-moment audience reaction profile in a graph form constructed from the readout of a meter hand-held by each respondent. Moreover, ASI also conducts a group discussion with several of the respondents after the screening session.

The in-home projector method (black box) takes a 16-mm projector into a sample of homes to screen a test commercial that may or may not be included/inserted within an entertainment film. The interview is given twice, once before the screening and again after in order to ascertain the shift in attitudes and preferences.

The recruited natural environment is usually conducted in the vicinity of a supermarket, drug store, or shopping center. After a screening interview, respondents are invited into a trailer to see a film including several test and control commercials on a simulated TV set. After the screening, respondents are given a packet of discount coupons to be used in the store for the purchase of product. Meanwhile, a matched group not exposed to this screening is given a similar packet of coupons. A comparison of redemptions between the two groups is used as a measure of the selling effectiveness of the test commercial. The interviews also provide an opportunity for collecting diagnostic data as an analysis of the performance of the test commercial elements. Those who prefer this method argue on behalf of its behavioral rather than purely attitudinal characteristics. Teleresearch is the outstanding firm for this method.

In addition, there are services that specialize in on-air or in-the-market testing, which involves airing the test commercial in a regular broadcast. Then, a random sample of respondents is selected and interviewed by telephone. Burke Marketing Research offers aided recall of sales messages 24 hours after airing but does not measure attitude change or motivation. Gallup and Robinson's "in view" is also a 24-hour recall measure on brand name registration, idea communication, persuasion, and favorable buying action.

Teleresearch and ASI also pretest radio commercials. The pretesting of outdoor materials—billboards and hoardings—often employ a tachistoscope (t-scope or eye-blink) for measuring reaction to alternative layouts for outdoor posters. This presumably provides a measure of how effectively proposed designs register brand name and key selling messages during the brief exposure.

Even though such intricate pretest procedures are unavailable to most of the world, they nevertheless illustrate the various pretesting possibilities. New ones appear every year. It is possible to experiment along similar lines almost anywhere. No costly infrastructure and inordinately expensive equipment are required. The effort is worthwhile. Testing reduces risks and enhances chances of success.

Even evaluation planning requires strategic thinking because without it criteria can sometimes prove irrelevant. Shall the communications effort be evaluated on the basis of communications objectives or of behavioral change goals? The responsibility of social marketers is to design and deliver messages to desired audiences. But they cannot judge whether the advocated behavior change is effective. They accept it as an article of faith from health authorities. When evaluation reveals indecisive results, is the message or the advocated behavior at fault? The program may have achieved its goals fully; a clearly understood, highly motivating message meeting every rigorous pretest is delivered with appropriate reach, frequency, continuity, and impact to its audience. Yet, the behavior change did not materialize; if it did no apparent improvement in health status was produced, recalling the old medical paradox— the operation was a success but the patient died. Family planning communications campaigns have not been notably successful in winning converts to the practice despite their high awareness and attitude impact. What is at fault—the campaign, the media, or the message design? Or is it the proposed behavior change? We know from the biomedical authorities that contraceptive devices work. But, like the Edsel automobile, does it fail to meet consumer expectations?

How shall we evaluate food supplementation programs? By anthropometric criteria or by other indicators such as increase in physical activity and a reduction in morbidity? UNICEF concluded after a review of the matter that "there is considerable doubt whether the benefit measured as physical growth and development is either the total benefit . . . or even the most important."[18] Children with the most severe malnutrition showed the most dramatic response to the extra feeding but apparently growth was not an outstanding result among all of them. UNICEF concluded that "the 'missing energy' may be producing unmeasured benefits [with] greater significance than growth per se." Yet many food supplementation programs, evaluated solely on the basis of growth, are threatened with cancellation when growth objectives fail to be met.

Flay wrote that "literally thousands of mass media health campaigns have been implemented since World War II but only a minority . . . have been reported in the literature and an even smaller number have been evaluated."[19] He and his colleagues examined hundreds and reported that most evaluations are flawed one way or another. Many fail to examine media patterns, either for appropriateness of message or audience or for reach, frequency, and continuity. Even more provide no analysis of appropriateness of message elements to the problem, the solution, and audience characteristics. Even if the evaluators were intent on such analyses, they would have been frustrated by the paucity of information regarding target audience values and perceptions, *resistance points,* and so forth. Rigorous formative research was the rare exception, making meaningful media and message decisions almost impossible.

In general, evaluation efforts have concentrated on measuring results of campaigns and not the quality of their planning, development, and execution. Gatherer et al. have reviewed, for the Health Education Council of England, evaluations of 49 health campaigns conducted within the preceding 15 years. The typical evaluation was a survey of a cross section of the public before and after the campaign.[20] There is virtually no evidence in any of these of an effort to assess the effectiveness of the campaign's components. Evaluation by results alone reveal what, if anything, was achieved. This can lead to a conclusion that the strategy is ineffectual when, in fact, the execution may have been at fault. Was it message design? An ineffective media plan?

Health education programs in schools fare little better. In a review of 27 school antidrug education efforts, most were found either inadequately evaluated or with evaluations ignored altogether. Only five met minimum evaluation standards. Only two gave some indications of success. The conclusion of the authors: "Schools have not been able to demonstrate that they are succeeding in preventing drug abuse."[21] Given this dismal assessment, is the conclusion justified that school drug education programs be discontinued? Current approaches may not be working because of conceptual or executional flaws. They need to be analyzed before they are summarily repudiated. Other reports indicate that school education programs have led to increased drug experimentation[22] and higher drinking rates.[23] Something is obviously wrong or missing in the content of instruction, the method, or the motivation. Could it be a factor beyond the control of the school—easy availability of drugs and alcohol in the nearby environment or their aggressive promotion through peer groups or local discos? A more elaborate evaluation of all such factors seems indicated. Analysis may suggest that the problem is beyond education and involves more complicated psychological or social constraints.

In social marketing, evaluation is ongoing from the start. It may be conveniently depicted in three stages:

Planning. Formative evaluation with qualitative research is employed to probe for popular perceptions. (Priorities? Any new questions? Previously unidentified attitudes or customs? Target audience *resistance points?*) It is also used for the testing of new behavioral concepts; acceptance of a new or modified product (where relevant), and messages.

Process. Ongoing evaluation is made of the efficacy of each component of the program—the messages, the media schedules, the performance of the collaboration, product usage acceptance, and competitive activity.

Progress. A summative assessment of impact on the probing, including changes in knowledge, attitude, and practice; effect on morbidity, mortality, and health status; and cost and effectiveness.

Planning relies mainly on the focus group technique or, as an alternative, in-depth personal interviews. Product or message concepts are tested by presentation in written or oral form with guidelines for discussion. Products are evaluated through in-home usage tests of samples with or without competitive products; consumer reactions are sought in callback interviews. Messages in draft form are exposed, played or exhibited, and tested in interviews with the audience.

The process stage involves a continuing audit of these elements with tracking studies at various time breaks in the program—six months or a year. Messages are posttested. (What has been the message impact—comprehension, conviction, and behavior change? Are pretest results confirmed? Are changes necessary?) Consumer acceptance and usage patterns are probed. Product distribution is monitored through selected networks. Analysis of media schedules is made (reach, frequency, continuity) (see Chapter 8). Collaborative performance, coordination and administration are monitored (message dissonance?).

Progress is mainly a quantitative question. Changes in knowledge, attitude, and practice are recorded through direct observation or self-reporting measures with comparisons against baseline data or preestablished health indicators. Sales audits of product movement through distribution networks are maintained. Relevant mortality, morbidity, and birth-rate data are collected. Awareness of the linkage of health programs to social and economic factors has not produced a commensurate appreciation of these factors in evaluation, which continues its narrow focus on biomedical impact. The social marketer may want to include a self-assessment: how well is he or she planning and executing tasks? One way to answer is PRISM, a social marketing technique that has proved helpful in the past.

The Pooled Rating Index for Social Marketing (PRISM)

Why a rating scale? Because it satisfies a craving for excellence, a human need for measurement, winning instead of losing. It also provides

an incentive to observe the rules of the game and to execute them profi-
ciently. The Pooled Rating Index for Social Marketing (PRISM) is calculated on the basis of the tasks required (Table 6.2). Note the approximately equal weight given each task merely for its inclusion in planning—
a meritorious award for not overlooking it. But execution is another matter. Here the relative values of one component versus another become
apparent.

Though arbitrary, these have not been casually assigned. They reflect the judgments based on two decades of experience in social marketing as to the relative importance of the tasks and the emphasis they
should receive. Thus, the highest PRISM executional score of 25 deems
the task of supreme importance. We have not attempted PRISM scores for
the case histories in Chapter 10. That would require far more intimate
knowledge of each than is available to outside parties. PRISM is not
meant to be a competitive rating system. It serves best for self-rating purposes by aspiring social marketers. Used this way it can be a valuable tool
for self-analysis and criticism as it has been for my colleagues and me. It
should be put to work almost like a check list from the start of the project,
not held in reserve until the end when it will be too late to alter decisions
once they have become deficits or, still worse, disasters.

Table 6.2. Pooled Rating Index for Social Marketing

Social Marketing Task	Planning PRISM: (Was it done?)	Execution PRISM: (How well?)
Situation study	1.00	10.00
Market review*	.27	2.00
Consumer analysis	.25	3.00
Media analysis	.25	3.00
Priorities review	.25	2.00
Formative evaluation	2.00	15.00
Target audience identity	.33	2.00
Concept test	.33	3.00
Product test*	.35	2.00
Benefits	.33	3.00

Resistance points	.33	3.00
Media habits	.33	2.00
Setting objectives	1.00	10.00
Setting strategies	2.00	15.00
Target audience	.33	2.00
Communications/Message	.33	4.00
Research	.33	2.00
Media	.33	3.00
Product*	.35	2.00
Sales/Distribution*	.35	2.00
Social marketing plan	3.00	25.00
Message design	.33	4.00
Message testing	.33	3.00
Media reach and frequency goals	.33	4.00
Media postanalysis	.33	3.00
Research design	.33	2.00
Community collaboration	.33	2.00
Product design*	.35	3.00
Sales/Distribution*	.35	2.00
Budget/Timetable	.33	2.00
Evaluation (process)	2.00	15.00
Message impact	.33	4.00
Media goals	.33	3.00
Product performance*	.35	3.00
Sales/Distribution efficiency*	.35	2.00
Community/Collaboration	.33	2.00
Budget/Timetable audits	.33	1.00
Evaluation (impact)	2.00	10.00
Baseline data	.25	1.00
Knowledge	.25	1.00
Attitude	.25	1.00
Practice	.25	2.00
Sales*	.27	2.00
Morbidity/Mortality	.25	2.00
Cost effectiveness	.25	1.00
Maximum PRISM score	12.00 ±	100.00 ±
Maximum PRISM* score	9.00 ±	80.00 ±

If no product is involved, eliminate PRISM credits and use Maximum PRISM scores as the base.

The Role of the Private Sector

A basic premise of social marketing is that every means be explored for message delivery and/or product on the basis of target audience analysis, trade practices, and media availabilities. Thus, in marketing oral rehydration salts (ORS), it is unlikely that the program should rely exclusively either on home preparation or the packaged product. All markets are segmented and neither version can ever hope to reach its maximum consumption potential with the target population. This is why the recent debate between UNICEF and WHO on home preparation versus the packet is academic.[24] In the field, both strategies will be necessary to appeal to different segments of the population. Even under the best distribution system, the packet is not likely to achieve universal stocking and availability. Nor is this the only issue. Which distribution systems should be used, the government health care system or commercial outlets? The answer, again, is that both have a role since the objective is to distribute the packet as broadly as possible.

In Bangladesh, the contraceptive social marketing program, with distribution through the *panwallas,* stalls, and the stockists of Bangladesh, is selling more condoms than the government is able to give away free through its health centers.[25] But the combination does better than either could alone. Contraceptives and ORT salts are not the only items with potential for private sector distribution. The U.S. food stamp program indirectly employs the retail food system for food supplement distribution to targeted needy populations. Food stamps are drafts on food supplies from commercial outlets instead of government-controlled distribution centers. The commercial world overlooks no means for delivering merchandise to the consumer whether or not it is a traditional channel. The aim is to move the goods to consumers. If it takes church organizations, school groups, postal systems, or a troop of girl scouts to do so, the commercial marketer will not hesitate to employ them if the wholesale retail system leaves market segments unserved.

The number of private sector retail outlets usually exceeds those available to the government through its health care system. Also, the private sector promotional support of distribution creates greater awareness than traditional government educational programs achieve in the same period of time. The social marketing techniques of advertising and promotion are essentially a trading of time for money, of telescoping the time for ideas or products to be accepted. The premise is that they accelerate the rate of consumer trial, adoption, and usage.

Most health care systems cannot provide total coverage. Their outlets, the maternal and child health centers, hospitals, and clinics, are too few and far between. Furthermore, important segments of the target population remain unmotivated. Typically, those underserved are the most needy for which innovative distribution schemes must be devised. When consumers do not come to the health center, then means must be found to bring the services and products of the health center to the people.

Though all countries have some outreach from health centers, very few have a health-worker-to-population ratio adequate to the task. China, with rigid control over its people, may be the notable exception. Almost two million barefoot doctors are assigned mainly to China's rural areas. Fewer than 200,000 work in the cities and towns. This is a ratio of roughly 1:600 health-workers-to-population. Added to this are three million health aides and birth attendants at the village or production team level. About 15 years ago, contraceptive distribution and education was broadened by resorting to this health worker network. Today, it is estimated that some five million cover a population of more than one billion, a ration of 1:200. No other country in the world even comes close to this kind of coverage.[26] Other countries must resort to different means. The social marketing of contraceptives in Bangladesh, India, and Sri Lanka is a good example of an effective alternative (see Chapter 10).

Involving the private sector in social marketing schemes is a task for social marketers experienced in commercial product distribution. This calls for arrangements with marketing organizations and their advertising agencies and placing the operation under the direction of an individual drawn from those sectors. Selecting a distribution system is an intricate procedure. Should distribution of ORS be exclusively with one distributor? Only an analysis of the retail outlets and the extent to which given distributors have access to them can provide the answer. An exclusive arrangement with one rarely provides maximum distribution. It is more likely to be achieved with a combination whose operations complement one another. This calls for analysis of sales route and territory coverage.

Once distribution has been decided, a sales plan is needed to establish pricing policies, dealer loading, in-store merchandising arrangements, sales promotion, and consumer advertising. Continuing sales surveillance of the effect of these arrangements through retail sales audits and share-of-market tracking ensures maintenance of distribution, as well as more shelf space and expansion to new outlets. It prevents out-of-stock conditions and ensures price level maintenance. Price to the consumer is a decisive factor. Subsidies are no guarantee that the desired retail price to the consumer will be maintained. It is not uncommon for dealers to pocket deep discounts as profit and price the product at a normal retail, thus defeating the pricing strategy. Prepricing the package is necessary to guarantee the desired price to the targeted consumer.

The participation of the private sector has broader possibilities. A decade or two ago, prevailing opinion among food processors was that nutrition won't sell. Emphasis on convenience foods with taste and pleasure appeal is changing. Witness the flood of new items designed to meet the rising demand for food values of nutrition and health. Borden's Wise Lite-Line snacks offers one-third less fat and fewer calories than Wise's regular snacks. Prince Superoni, self-styled "the smarter spaghetti," advertises "If Prince Superoni didn't taste so good, you might think it was a health food." It claims 70 percent more protein than regular spaghetti, no cholesterol, "lots of essential vitamins and minerals, is low in sodium and has practically no fat." Mazola Corn Oil: "a tablespoon of Mazola 100% pure corn oil is only 120 calories and a pat of Mazola margarine a mere 35 calories. Both are low in saturated fats and have no cholesterol." Fleischmann's Light Corn Oil spread counters: "25% less salt, 25% less fat, 25% less calories than regular margarine." Procter & Gamble reports it is at work on a "proposed calorie-free cooking oil that one day may make junk food into diet fare and flush cholesterol from the bloodstream."[27]

Safeway has had a Safeway Nutrition Awareness Program—SNAP for short: "to provide our consumers with more information to help them eat better" and a nutrition center in each store to disseminate nutrition information. Campbell's has brought out seven low-sodium soups. Kellogg's has put low-sodium Rice Krispies and Corn Flakes into its product line. Libby's has an entire 12-product line of no-salt vegetables. White Rock is brewing a low-salt beer. Del Monte has 14 canned vegetables that contain no added salt. Ralston Purina has removed 50 percent of the salt from Chicken of the Sea tuna and Star-Kist has gone it one better with 60 percent.[28]

None of this is accidental or beneficent. Food marketers rarely create market opportunities. They uncover them through surveillance of the changing marketplace. They know success comes to those who identify opportunities first and seize them. Only health and nutrition advocates with the assistance of government and the media can motivate consumers to make nutrition demands. When those demands register, industry responds with new products and new advertising appeals based on unexploited nutritional benefits. Meeting consumer demand is a food company's first charge. When it ignores or misreads the market, it pays dearly. The president of Campbell's has some frank things to say about flops with consumers. "Swanson's frozen dinners were wrong for adults," he said. "They served kiddy vegetables—peas and corn—when adults wanted things like broccoli, zucchini, and mushrooms. It took me to call Swanson's junk food to get people off their duffs."[29]

Consumer interest in nutrition also correlates with the shift in nutrition education from the old bland curriculum of the four food groups and the neutrality of nutrient instruction to the more pressing new priority of high-sodium, sugar, and fat consumption. One day the dietary guidelines may well be recognized as an historic stride in nutrition education as much for its strategy of focus-and-attack as for its instruction. This model of priority-focus-and-attack creates an enlarged partnership in which the private sector is willing to participate. In 1981, an effort was made to create such a partnership in response to the Reagan administration's call for volunteerism. The Network for Better Nutrition had among its sponsors industry representatives from General Foods, Quaker Oats, Safeway, ITT Continental Baking, advertising and communications professionals, government officials, and health and consumer groups. Its aim was to establish a network for public education. The focus was to resolve conflicting interpretations of key issues through consensus building. Priority food and nutrition problems were to be identified and assessments made of how well target populations were being served. The private sector took a leadership position from the start. Carol Tucker Foreman, former assistant secretary of USDA and formerly head of the Consumer Federation of America, was cochair with Richard Laster, executive vice president of General Foods. This partnership would have been deemed inconceivable in the adversary atmosphere that existed only a few years earlier. But the partnership failed almost before it got started. From USDA and the White House came legalistic objections that government officials could not officially participate in the policy affairs of a nongovernmental organization. Though these were quickly overcome by assigning government representatives ex officio advisory status, the issue was not resolved. The real reason was the administration's less aggressive attitude toward government's role in health and nutrition education. But here was a manifestation of industry's new willingness to participate in the kind of joint public effort that it had previously eschewed.

This new attitude also characterized a changed private sector attitude on the international scene. It was in marked contrast to milk companies' overmarketing of breast-milk substitutes or of drug companies' promotion of questionable products to Third World populations or of reluctance to offer much-needed ones. Some observers credit the pharmaceutical industry with improvement in the drug distribution system in The Gambia. Ten members of the Pharmaceutical Manufacturers Association (PMA) funded the effort so that, according to one reporter, "people who needed drugs most in the impoverished West African nation were able to get them" through a system of 12 regional health centers. As a result the PMA has undertaken plans to expand the idea to other countries.[30]

Such developments are a response to changed market circumstances. The world has raised its expectations of the private sector and managements, ever sensitive to their public images, have grown more responsive to social obligations. This suggests that a business partnership in behalf of social marketing projects is now a more realistic prospect. Ciba-Geigy, responding to the criticism that drug companies fail to serve Third World needs, has inaugurated Servepharm, a project to "produce 40 essential drugs . . . at a modest price and for a small profit."[31] These include drugs for schistosomiasis, a parasitic liver infection, and leprosy. Ciba-Geigy has also been working with UNICEF on ORT salts. Merck has been conducting research on products for Chagas' disease, a parasite-induced ailment widespread in Latin America and onchocerciasis, the river blindness scourge transmitted by a wormlike parasite in Africa.

In private discussions, executives of such companies freely state that this awakened interest in underserved markets is a result of criticism leveled at past marketing practices of overpricing, dumping, and indifference to local health requirements. Some sense of the significance of this turnabout can be gleaned from the economics involved. The head of the international division of the PMA, Jay Kingham, reveals that U.S. drug firms' return from sales in the Third World is less than half that on sales from the Western world.

This new willingness of the private sector offers previously undreamed of possibilities. A "No-Birth Bonus Scheme" established on three tea estates in India in 1971 offered women who worked there a five-rupee-a-month bonus if they agreed to have no more than three children and to space the second and third at least three years apart. If a pregnancy occurred a substantial portion of the accumulated bonus was canceled. The bonus incentive offered the prospect of having enough money one day to purchase land.[32] The bonus plan was funded by tax incentives from the government. By 1977 per-thousand-population birth rates on the participating tea estates fell to half of those for other estates, whose rates were approximately the same as for India as a whole. A group of international business organizations voluntarily proposed to UNICEF in 1983 the possibility of participation in that agency's programs in behalf of its Child Survival Revolution program.

The old view of the private sector as a monolithic antagonist to public health may need to be revised. Like every grouping of the human community, it is highly segmented. On that basis, individual approaches need to be tailored to each segment—a strategy of opposition when practices are wrongful and of collaboration when they are helpful.

Notes

1. Harvey, P.D., Population Services International, New York City, in a personal communication, March 1984.

2. Schellstede, W.P., Ciszewski, R.L., "Social Marketing of Contraceptives in Bangladesh," *Studies in Family Planning,* Vol. 15, No. 1, January/February 1984, p. 34.

3. Taylor, J., "Health Promotion Organization in the Community," *Focal Points,* 1984, No. 1, p. 11, Public Health Service, U.S. Department of Health and Human Services, Washington, D.C.

4. Miller, J., "Egypt Wins Another Summer Battle Against Cholera," the New York *Times,* July 10, 1983, p. 12.

5. Mahler, H. "Rescue Mission for Tomorrow's Health," *People,* Vol. 6, No. 2, London, 1979.

6. Tuluhungwa, R.N., "A Communications Strategy for Development?" *Health Education by Television and Radio* (Ed. M. Meyer), K.G. Saur, Munich, 1981.

7. Manoff International Inc., "The Bangladesh Motivational Family Planning Campaign," 1984 (unpublished report).

8. "Port-au-Prince Pharmacy Study," Porter and Novelli Associates, Washington, D.C., 1981.

9. Folch-Lyon, E., de la Macorra, L., Schearer, S.B., "Focus Group and Survey Research on Family Planning in Mexico," *Studies in Family Planning,* Vol. 11, No. 12, December 1981, Part 1, p. 409.

10. Snyder, D., "Ad Bond is Broken," *Advertising Age,* April 23, 1984, p. 3.

11. "New Policies for Health Education in Primary Health Care," report on the Technical Discussions, thirty-sixth World Health Assembly, A30 6/Technical Discussions for 5/83, WHO, Geneva, Switzerland, p. 13.

12. "Anker, R., Buvinic, M., Youssef, N.H., "Women's Roles and Population Trends in the Third World," ILO/Coor Helm, London, 1982.

13. Kerby, M. as quoted by Zeltner, H. in "Research Must Meet Greater Demands Than Ever," *Advertising Age,* August 15, 1983, p. M4.

14. Ibid.

15. Morris, B., "Study to Detect True Eating Habits of Junk Food Fans and the Health Food Ranks," the *Wall Street Journal,* February 3, 1984, p. 25.

16. Giesbert, F-O., "The Computer Fallacy," le *Nouvel Observateur,* December 2, 1983, as excerpted by *Harpers,* March 1984, p. 22.

17. Manoff International Inc., "Bangladesh Family Planning Social Marketing Project"; "Nutrition Communications and Behavior Change Project: Indonesian Nutrition Improvement Program," 1983.

18. "Current Views on Nutrition Strategies," UNICEF, New York, 1983.

19. Flay, B.R., Tiessen, J.E., Edison, C.N., "Mass Media in Health Promotion," a bibliography, University of Southern California, Los Angeles, California, 1981, manuscript.

20. Gatherer, A., Parfit, J., Porter, E., et al., "Is Health Education Effective?" Health Education Council, London, 1979.

21. Berberian, R.M., *The Effectiveness of Drug Education Programs. A Critical Review,* Health Education Monographs 1976; 4: 377–398.

22. Berberian, R.M., et al., *The Relationship Between Drug Education Programs in the Greater New Haven Schools and Changes in Drug Use and Drug-Related Beliefs and Perceptions,* Health Education Monographs 1976; 4: 327–376.

23. Young, M., *Review of Research Studies Related to Health Education Practice (1961–1966); School Health Education,* Health Education Monographs 1968; 28: 1–97.

24. ORS/Therapy workshop, A meeting held at UNICEF, New York, January 10–11, 1983.

25. Schellstede, W.P., Ciszewski, R.L., op. cit.

26. Fraser, S., "Demographic Priority in China," *People,* Vol. 10/3, 1983.

27. Darlin, D., Abrams, B., "Procter & Gamble Co. Starts to Reformulate Tried-and-True Ways," the *Wall Street Journal,* March 30, 1983, p. 1.

28. Hollie, P.G., "Marketing Foods With Lower Salt," the New York *Times,* business section, April 9, 1983.

29. Hollie, P.G., "Straining to Be More Than Just Soup," the New York *Times,* business section, March 20, 1983.

30. Nunzio, J., "Third World Healthcard," *Advertising Age,* September 26, 1983, p. M29.

31. Ibid.

32. Ridker, R.G., "The No-Birth Bonus Scheme: The Use of Savings Accounts for Family Planning in South India," *Population and Development Review,* March 1980.

7

Executing the Social Marketing Plan: Lessons Learned

The development of the social marketing plan is a logical, orderly process. It is a gratifying experience to see the pieces fall into place as a pattern emerges from what had previously been an agglomeration of unrelated elements. But getting there is only half the job and may very well be all the fun. The real troubles surface once the implementation begins. Conditions presumed to exist during the planning stage are found in an altered state or not to exist at all. Like "the best laid schemes o' mice and men," social marketing plans, too, "gang aft agley" because they will vary from situation to situation and problem to problem. This is why the planning process and its disciplines are essential from project to project. In addition, there are lessons to learn and it may help social marketing planners to pan in the stream of past experience for the nuggets of wisdom we may find there.

Problems and People

It is essential to establish priorities. There is never enough time, energy, and money and these assets must be devoted to problems of first importance. It will help to avoid program clutter and diffuseness. When education attempts too much, learning suffers.

Before setting objectives, analyze the target audience for segmentation, and then assess the practicability of the behavioral tasks required. An *objective* is a goal and a *strategy* is the means of getting there. But getting there demands a series of critical decisions with respect to target audience identification. For a breast-feeding campaign it is not enough to target women who are either pregnant or lactating. Analysis of the barriers to breast-feeding should have revealed more profound distinctions. The concerns of women who work outside the home are different from those of women who don't. Special messages are needed to focus separately on these different concerns.

The national breast-feeding promotion campaign in Brazil[1] differentiated the salaried mother from the mother who worked at home and the one yet to have her baby. The objective for the latter was to motivate breast-feeding; for the at-home mother, to prolong it; and for the salaried mother, to arrange for the best accommodation to her job. Obviously, one message cannot satisfy all three circumstances. Secondary and tertiary target audiences must be defined to ensure harmony in the messages health professionals deliver and for policymakers to initiate new social action through legislation.

Setting objectives requires a demand assessment. What must a mother do to prepare a proposed weaning food? Are the ingredients easily available? Can she obtain the utensils, the fuel? Objectives must be framed by what is probable, not simply possible. Encouraging the enrichment of infant *lugaw* in the Philippines with dried fish was preceded by a market analysis to ascertain its year-round availability at an affordable price. One health educator with years of experience in India and Bangladesh, urged less comprehensive objectives so that

> setting the goal can become far more realistic . . . [Rather] than plunge in to improve the nutritional state of children in the slum as a whole, the project might might wait till a balwadi [preschool center] has been set up. . . . Instead of "all the children," the project should focus on those attending the balwadi. Rather than the vague ambition "to reduce the incidence of malnutrition," the objective could be more specific: "all the balwadi children will increase regularly their weight in the school year."[2]

The Special Roles of Research

A formative evaluation approach to market and consumer research of concepts, content, and message design is indispensable. This *formative* approach relies mainly on the *focus-group* interview or on variations of the technique. El-Bushra relates Sudan's experiences with mass media health education campaigns in which no formative inquiry was taken. The first such effort was tried at the time of a cholera outbreak in Khartoum in 1980 with short radio and TV announcements and daily newspaper insertions. Only after the launch was it realized that most of the target population had difficulty understanding the modern classical Arabic employed.[3]

In 1975, health authorities in Nicaragua included bicarbonate of soda in the recommended ORT formula. But research revealed how few of the villagers knew of bicarbonate of soda and how sparsely it was stocked among the local *tiendas*. The formula was accordingly revised. The Indonesia Nutrition Improvement Program employed formative research to involve mothers in the development of a homemade weaning food. Parameters were set for the types of food but the choice was left to the mothers and then assessed later according to preestablished nutritional values. Thus, mothers participated in product development the same way manufacturers engage them in product testing—uncovering consumer likes and dislikes in deciding the final formulation.

Field investigators for a weaning food program in the Dominican Republic uncovered the reasons for the problems mothers were having in the preparation and the feeding of the food. The original formulation had been decided without adequate inquiry:

1. There had not been enough observations in homes with young children.
2. The method of interviewing had not encouraged the pursuit of provocative statements by mothers.
3. Repeated trial with the same or similar families had not been provided for, thus making modification of the recipe impossible.
4. Mothers of malnourished children had not been well represented in the sample.
5. Health workers had not been intimately involved in the process.[4]

Many attempts to market fortified foods for the disadvantaged—Incaparina, CSM, Cerealina, Sekmama, and others—failed because objectives and target audiences were imprecisely established. These products turned out to be overpriced for their market. For those who could afford them, the need they were designed to fulfill was already being satisfied by existing items.

Community-based participation in the formulation of concepts and message designs is indispensable. Intuition and even expert opinion are unreliable for decision making. Qualitative research and message pretesting guard the social marketer against projecting personal values and perceptions onto the target audience. They shield the venture from the vanities of the planners, ensuring that the values and concerns of the target prevail.

Sometimes, community participation is reduced to a mere condescension. In rural Nigeria, malaria, schistosomiasis, onchocerciasis, and dracontiasis are severe public health problems. A team of 22 members from ten disciplines joined in a workshop to decide objectives. According to some participants the "team work was not without problems."[5] A subsequent "social and behavioral study" to identify community-felt needs and priorities still left unanswered such questions as: "How do you obtain community involvement in problems which are not seen as a priority by the people, yet have been identified as such by an external agency?" The premises of this inquiry—that the necessary actions might be "found to lie in sectors outside health delivery services" and that the community should be involved in determining its own priorities—are unassailable but the overload both in terms of personnel, time, and research strategy may have been unnecessary considering the results obtained. Fewer people, less time, and a simpler formative approach could have determined villagers' priorities and preserved resources for the action interventions.

Community participation implies involvement in subsequent activity. An American health worker, Maria de Zuniga, who worked in Nicaragua both before and after the revolution, describes that nation's effort to strengthen peoples' stewardship of their own health.[6] "In Cuba," she said, "it took 12 years to eradicate polio. Nicaragua took only three. . . . Nicaragua stresses preventive medicine with the primary service provided at the neighborhood level by people with no formal medical training but an awareness of basic good health practices." Nicaragua's immunization, breast-feeding, and oral rehydration campaigns are run by neighborhood health committees involving more than 83,000 *brigadestas.*

In the United States, an interesting experiment is being carried out through Communities Organized for Public Service (COPS). Due largely to the efforts of Ernesto Cortes, Jr., of San Antonio, COPS "rejects the top-down approach as paternalistic and insists that meaningful change can only come by building self-supporting community organizations."[7] Cortes's early experience was with community organizations originally cultivated by the fabled Saul Alinsky, a grass-roots activist who for many years before he died in 1972 was the inspiration for several successful community organizing efforts. Cortes spent months interviewing among the poor Mexican-American parishes unaware that he was pursuing a formative approach. It enabled him finally to determine that street drainage was the paramount issue among the people. The outcome of his labors over the past decade included improved streets and drainage, the demolition of substandard housing, the construction of new single-family homes, and protective zoning changes—ample evidence of how effective community participation can be on policy issues.

The difficulties involved in the planning and execution of baseline studies limit their usefulness for formative purposes. Baseline studies are expensive, subject to research overkill and often hurriedly implemented because of onrushing deadlines. The result is that many are defective, either in questions asked or unasked and subject matter covered. A Canadian journalist and TV producer, Warner Troya, has been involved in many mass media public education projects and describes much of research as feedback, a means for gaining insights "after the event rather than before." But he emphasized that the real need is for research that will uncover insights in advance and reduce to a minimum the need for eventual program revisions.[8] What he pleaded for was feed-*forward* capability to avoid pitfalls.

A proper baseline cannot be executed until all program elements—the target audience, messages, educational channels and media, and other program interventions—are verified; otherwise, the questionnaire and interviewer training cannot be correlated to the program. Baseline norms will either be incomplete or missing and, therefore, inadequate for subsequent tracking studies. Compensation in the tracking studies for these deficiencies cannot provide norms, however, against which to compare the new data. It may be advisable to consider less costly, more flexible approaches. These may include

1. Periodic tracking with formative evaluation (sacrificing exacting quantification for prudent trend measurements
2. A baseline delay for perhaps two to three months after the program start (sacrificing the possibility of an exact preprogram situation assessment for a more exacting measure of the program's long-term impact)
3. A control sample for comparison (not ordinarily possible when a program is national in scope)

Prudence as a Management Style

Researchers in Norway reported finding that heavy coffee drinkers have 14 percent more cholesterol in their systems than people who drink one cup or fewer. These findings would appear to correlate with other scientific findings more than a decade ago—that drinking coffee doubles the risk of heart attack. But on the other hand, critics of those studies found them flawed because there were other variables involved that failed to be measured; for example, coffee drinkers are likely to be heavy cigarette smokers. On the other hand, the Framingham Heart Study among residents of Framingham, Massachusetts, since 1949 has found no evidence that coffee contributes to arteriosclerosis. Norwegians responded that an analysis of their data showed that coffee drinkers still had more cholesterol in their blood even when factors like smoking, exercise, and alcohol were taken into account. "The relation seemed to withstand all adjustments," they declared in the June 16, 1983 issue of the *New England Journal of Medicine*. The National Coffee Association took all of this with a steadying cup of coffee.[9] The study, it declared, was designed to observe cholesterol levels, not heart disease, thus ignoring previous work that established a direct connection between the two.

What is the social marketer to make of this since the last word may not be known for some time to come, if ever? The scientific attitude of exactitude is not appropriate for public health educators who cannot wait until everything is known about a health problem. They have to settle for a prudent appraisal of whatever information is available. In general, prudence should dictate management style. In research, for example, it is prudent to decide how much is absolutely needed and to prevent research costs from consuming an excessive share of the program budget.

The conflict between prudence and exactitude presents a dilemma as to who should decide between the two. Traditionally, we have expected the scientists to tell us what we are permitted to say and when. But the scientific premises of the laboratory have questionable validity for determining what the public has a right to know. This is a social, not a scientific, decision involving probabilities, not certainties. Alan Lightman, the scintillating columnist of *Science* magazine, the Journal of the American Association for the Advancement of Science, suspects that "most people have a deep-seated reluctance to welcome probabilities into their private lives. . . . At least since the Greeks, mankind has harbored a passion for knowing some things with certainty. Probabilities by definition shimmer in a midst of uncertainty."[10] Lightman asked: "Who should not drive on Labor Day weekend if we are told that ten in each one million cars on the road will have fatal crashes?"

What should the public be advised about the dangers of high animal-fat consumption and its propensity for raising cholesterol and low-density lipid levels? Some scientists claimed that dietary patterns have not been proved to have a decisive effect on cholesterol and LDL levels associated with heart disease.[11] The historic findings reported by the U.S. government in 1983 on the connection between cholesterol and CHD were based on drug-induced not dietary control of cholesterol levels. This has encouraged some scientists to hold out for firmer evidence. Dr. Edward Ahrens represented this point of view when he earlier declared it "irresponsible to make the dietary recommendations that are being so widely proposed to the general public at this time. . . . It is anything but a service to the public to postulate *one* dietary solution for hyperlipidemia, no matter how well meaning one is in advocating it."[12] The American Cancer Society announced new dietary guidelines in 1983 to reflect findings that high-fat foods increase the risk of cancer while foods such as fruits and vegetables seem to offer a protection. High-fat diets, the society declared, were particularly linked to cancers of the colon, breast, and prostate.[13]

The National Heart, Lung and Blood Institute of the U.S. Department of Health and Human Services declared that while

> all the facts aren't in . . . a lot of scientific evidence points toward the heart-health benefits in eating foods low in saturated fats and cholesterol. Major scientific studies have shown that people with high blood cholesterol have more chance of developing coronary heart disease than people with lower levels of cholesterol.[14]

The nutrition committee of the American Heart Association urged a more prudent diet, one lower in fat, especially saturated fat, and lower in cholesterol. But its statement, published in the April 19, 1982 issue of *Circulation,* pointed out that "ironclad proof of its life-saving benefits is not yet available and because of high costs and other problems may never be obtained."[15]

One scientist at the University of California asked the fundamental question: "When a scientist offers data that bear on some question of public policy . . . should such data and their interpretation be called upon only when they achieve the level of certainty demanded within science itself? Or are lower levels of certainty significant when the issue is one of protecting health?"[16] He properly acknowledged that in fundamental science the demand is for

> incontrovertible evidence, else we would be building on shifting sands. . . . People do not ask for the level of certainty appropriate to pure science. . . . Given the level of public concern about cancer and the apparent delay between cause and effect, it would be just as unfortunate for the scientific community to be too late as too early in making people aware of trends that are developing in scientific data.

And so the debate is likely to last for many years to come while deaths from cancer and coronary heart disease continue as a major health concern. The dangers of not advocating a prudent diet have been highlighted. Yet those opposed to it have failed to make clear what the risks are even if subsequent findings reveal that it was not necessary. Our affluent diets are obviously too high in fat. It is not likely that the prudent diet will reduce fat consumption to dangerous levels.

Budgeting the Social Marketing Project

Cost estimates of social marketing projects must differentiate be-tween media materials and the media for their delivery. Film, slides, post-ers, radio scripts, pamphlets, and flip charts are materials. Media are needed to deliver them to their target audiences. Thus, TV and radio sta-tions, schools, and people—health agents (*promoters*)—are media. Cinemas and mobile film vans are media. Too many programs are hand-icapped from the start without a media strategy and plan or the necessary personnel and funds for them. They must be provided for in advance, and their costs and capabilities calculated. This is why so much educa-tional material never gets to its intended audience. On the other hand, print materials for mass circulation are often produced in amounts of 10,000, 30,000, 50,000—hardly enough to satisfy the need even if effective distribution exhausted their supply. The relationship of print runs to size of audience is rarely taken into account. Decisions are usually based on the amount of money available to pay for production and rarely on the frustrating chore of getting people to distribute them. The cost for dis-tributing such materials is almost never calculated. It is assumed that the organization will take care of it.

The distinction between media and media materials even escapes the most insightful of communications theorists. For example, Schramm compared results from using the "big media" with those obtained from the "little media." The former included TV, films, and computer-assisted instruction, while the latter comprised radio, tape recorders, film strips, and slides. Quite apart from the fact that the separations were purely judgmental and open to serious question, each was an apples-and-oranges collection of media materials that defied comparison.[17]

Social marketing programs must be supported at a sufficient level of effort with adequate time and money for materials, staff, and media. Mohan Singh, the well-known Asian health education philosopher, said that "health education, like the lotus, floats on still waters. Alas, while many admire their perfection, neither has visible means of support." This makes budgeting even more vital. It is better to know of budgetary limita-tions at the start and to plan accordingly than to have the program ham-pered when it is too late. Realistic goals and objectives must be projected. Resources have to be realistically calculated in terms of what will be avail-able to work with—the priority problems to be dealt with, the geographic area to be covered, the resources available to do the job. The tasks to be done must realistically reflect the constraints of limited money and per-sonnel and those for which no resources remain must be eliminated. The failure to do this during the planning process inevitably imposes cutbacks after the program has been launched. This cripples the project, leaving service gaps.

Social marketing is a trading of time and objectives for money and people. The less there is to work with, the less that can be attempted. A limited success is eminently to be preferred to a grandiose failure. Limited successes can always be expanded—rolled out—to enlarge on objectives or to embrace new ones. Food aid programs, for example, are intended to improve the condition of malnourished populations. But food aid alone is insufficient without health and nutrition education. Yet, how many food supplementation programs provide for education with budgetary allocations? Isn't there reason to consider such programs just as incomplete as if they supplied only half the food required?

Pilot projects—even the most successful—often neglect to take into account eventual costs of the regional or national extension—the roll out. Without these future costs the pilot project is fundamentally pointless. Leading international aid officials signaled this warning: "Care is needed in order to assure that design and development of local experiences do not create isolated artificial experiences with little or no chance of replication."[18] One of the guiding principles enunciated was the exercise of caution in setting the "rate of expansion and extension of new experiences . . . the speed of scaling." One health professional with years of experience in Third World countries asked the right question: "How are professionals dealing with the leap of faith, that where primary health care can be carried out on a small scale it can therefore succeed at the national and global level?"[19]

Often overlooked in budget planning is the indispensability of public sector subsidies for special projects. The social marketing of contraceptives and oral rehydration salts cannot be carried out on a nonsubsidized basis if the most vulnerable population segments are to be served, especially when commercial brands of these products are available but at price levels that place them outside the reach of those most in need.

Almost without exception, all health and nutrition interventions offer opportunities for educational components using the social marketing approach. The food supplementation program in Morocco reported better results with a nutrition education component than without it.[20] A similar report emerged from the Palawan Integrated Area Development Project in the Philippines, which provided for nutrition education by project design,[21] and the Nutrition Improvement Program in Indonesia,[22] where weighing and growth monitoring were combined with nutrition education. But only the latter employed the social marketing approach. Its results were acclaimed by the World Bank, the funding agency, in its cost-effectiveness evaluation: "Nutritionists have long held out the promise . . . that nutrition education . . . can make a difference in improving nutritional status. . . . The Indonesian experience is the first time it has been demonstrated in an operational setting."[23] International health experts, in calling for the integration of health education into all health programs, stressed the systematic approach for elaborating policy, strategy, formulation, planning, management, implementation and monitoring.[24] The vocabulary may be different but there is no mistaking the social marketing influence. The Indonesian example provided proof of its wisdom.

These experiences strengthen the holistic conception of the primary health care approach to public health. Each health intervention affects the whole health environment. Within this environment all problems are related. Even well-intentioned change can create ecological imbalances. Such possibilities must be assessed in advance to avoid counterproductive impacts. All in all, vertical programs from independent sectors are no longer deemed valid. They lead to lactation-inhibiting contraceptive pills, food supplements antithetical to the messages of nutrition education, and agricultural incentives that ignore priority nutrition needs. As Tarzie Vittachi of UNICEF declared

> The population problem is now seen more clearly . . . not as a single straight-line problem of people having too many children but as a complex of problems widely varied in nature, dimension and urgency interwoven with public health, education, jobs, sexual equity, fairer access for people to the material goods and opportunities which make life worth living.[25]

In addition, public health measures may depend on linkage to an enlarging role of women in development. Efforts to lower fertility have been aided when family planning programs were combined with schemes to ease women's work load and expand their education and income-producing opportunities.[26] "For some women a child-care center, a mill for grinding grain or a nearby woodlot" to ease their burden might make a significant difference. For others it could be provided by eliminating "school fees that drain household budgets or distant markets that prevent the easy sale of farm goods. . . . Each case suggests its own particular community incentive scheme."[27] For millions of working women around the world, lack of credit and access to marketing systems remain two major obstacles to their full participation in the economy. A strategy pursued independently of fiscal and legislative policies is likely to be less effective in leveling these obstacles. The evidence comes from projects tried in El Salvador, Bolivia, Bangladesh,[28] and other countries like Jamaica.[29] In 1983, Victor Soler-Sala, the UNICEF representative, foresaw that infant mortality in Indonesia could be reduced from 98 deaths per 1,000 to under 50 by 1990 by shifting UNICEF's efforts to reduce infant mortality into the country's family planning services network.[30] It will also piggyback nutrition programs onto existing family planning services and integrate the Extended Program Immunization (EPI) with this system. Implicit is the belief that the health sector alone is powerless to prevent malnutrition and disease, though it can ameliorate their effects or stimulate action by other sectors.[31] ORT cannot reduce the incidence of diarrhea, only its mortality rates. The provision of good water and sanitation needs the involvement of other sectors and governmental departments.

Use all the media that can be afforded and managed consistently with target audience strategy and the messages to be delivered. Health and nutrition education interventions complement and reinforce each other. Message duplication is a plus provided it is harmonious. Mass media cannot substitute for formal systems. If messages from both are in harmony, they reinforce each other.

Mass media extend the reach of health workers and educators. Since a vital fraction of the population does not avail itself of the local health centers, an effort is needed to bring the health center to these people. Those who do not come are usually the most vulnerable—either unmotivated or unaware. Because preventive health messages are mostly simple, direct, and nontechnical, they are ideally suited to mass media delivery. Mass media also helped to reduce message dissonance by standardizing the social marketing messages for all health and nutrition educators (as well as for the public), influencing them to harmonize their messages on the same subjects.

Selection of message delivery systems—the media—must be made carefully. Media need to be appreciated for their differences, not summarily lumped together without distinction. No two media are identical, either in their uses, their advantages and disadvantages, or their target audience efficiencies. The modern health educator needs to understand social marketing's appreciation for media diversity and the special advantages of each medium in terms of target audience and message (see Chapter 8). Sometimes the process of coordinating the media effort is complicated by the number of independent agencies involved. For example, the Films Division of the Information and Broadcasting Ministry in India handled distribution of cinema messages. The Directorate of Advertising and Visual Publicity controlled wall paintings, public service advertising in the print media, and poster production and distribution. Meanwhile, the Field Publicity Section was responsible for publicity in the field. All India Radio, of course, controlled the airwaves. The Song and Drama Unit was responsible for traveling theatrical groups. Unless all agencies and component sections are coordinated and all messages executed as designed, the consistency so essential to social marketing impact will be frustrated. In the United States, the Department of Health and Human Services in evaluating a national health promotion media campaign concluded that "multi-channeled communications are essential, as suggested by both the target audience survey and the case studies."[32]

Limitations to Social Marketing

There are limitations to social marketing because its strategies are not capable of solving every health problem, some of which are economic or structural. The provision of potable water to a Third World village requires an economic intervention, a structural change. This is also true of hospital practices. In Recife, Brazil, eight of nine maternity hospitals changed to rooming-in. Breast-feeding in the first 12 hours is now almost 100 percent versus 24 percent when infants were separated from their mothers. Diarrheal infections are nonexistent as compared to a 15- to 20-percent incidence before. The use of breast-milk substitutes is now only 20 percent of its previous volume. Baby abandonment, formerly a serious problem, has virtually ceased to exist.[33] Breast-feeding education would have been ineffectual without this change by hospital administration.

Goiter is an economic, not an educational or medical, problem. Education becomes practical only after salt is iodized and made available at an appropriate price. Then, education encompassed in a social marketing project becomes a timely and appropriate intervention. There are many other limitations imposed on social marketing by other cultural, environmental, and structural impediments (see Chapter 11).

Because social marketing cannot make up for deficiencies of social and economic systems, health professionals are obliged not to lend their skills to problems education cannot solve. Apparently, even primary health care is not beyond being exploited as a diversion by governments unwilling to make the necessary systemic changes. One who has spent most of her life working for Third World health education programs asked: "Is primary health care a revolution trying to counteract the political greed and insensitivity of nations and within nations . . . or is it, as some have claimed, an alibi, using health care to cover up the depth of the global crisis?"[34]

Poverty is the critical structural constraint. Typically, the most severely underserved population is the bottom 20 percent of the poor, the most in need and the most difficult to reach.[35] Long-term health incentives are less likely to appeal to these people than those that offer immediate economic benefit. A small farmer's project in Nepal provided easy credit through the International Fund for Program Development (IFAD). The resulting advance in income and standard of living reportedly improved the climate for health education efforts. Another program offered institutional credit to women to enhance their chances in the economic life of the country. In Brazil, a program for rural production credit for small holders (PRAMENSE) helped almost 7,000 families in about 400 production groups. Its effectiveness encouraged the Bank of Brazil to extend the program to wider areas of the northeast. One key benefit of the initial trial was the spur to collaboration between the health sector and the farm-extension service.

Obviously, antagonistic commercial marketing practices obstruct social marketing effectiveness. Sometimes even well-intentioned collaboration of the private sector can have an adverse effect, such as the creation of a market dependence in people accustomed to self-reliance. As farmers in Zaire became more dependent on new energy resources to improve food production and to ease access to markets for their produce, they abandoned previous means over which they had direct control. When energy costs soared after 1974 to 1975, the farmers' new dependence turned into a bane. By 1983, they found themselves "cut off. . . . from regular communication" with the effect that it "slowed down access to markets and further depressed food production."[36] However, in the Kisantu health zone of Zaire, health workers with an appreciation for the need of rural people to make judgments on the appropriateness of technological aid and to assume the authority for such decisions managed to minimize this dependency backlash. The villages of Kisantu "remained relatively unsold by dependence-creating efforts from the national level."[37]

Green Revolution farmers have suffered a similar setback in India and elsewhere from their dependence on high-yielding seeds and their high inputs of petrochemical-based pesticides and fertilizers. The sudden surge in energy prices created a cul-de-sac from which they could not easily extricate themselves. They had made no provision for storing seed strains used in the past. The latter afforded flexibility that was abandoned in the stampede to transfer to the new miracle grains. When in the past one strain failed, farmers could easily transfer to others. Not so with the new ones. The Green Revolution inadvertently persuaded the farmers to exchange self-reliance for a dependence on market factors beyond their control. Only the most perceptive could have foreseen the unhappy development.

The campaign to teach Filipino mothers to enrich weaning food at home was eventually converted into a commercial enterprise in which the formulation was packaged as Nutripak for sale to mothers. This market dependence created economic problems for the disadvantaged no matter how generously the government subsidized them. Fluctuations of supply in the cost of raw materials inevitably reflected in hardship prices to consumers. Growing dependence on the market can be justified when there is steady income improvement; without it, the economic woes of the disadvantaged must worsen.

To appreciate the limitations of social marketing reduces the danger of overburdening the target audience and protects the social marketer from unwitting service as a surrogate for official inaction. In the state of Santa Catarina, Brazil, new legislation in 1979 enabled inspection of business establishments to compel compliance with a previous law requiring crèches. In one year, 85 percent of them established nursing facilities. Controlled marketing of feeding bottles in Papua, New Guinea, reduced second- and third-degree malnutrition, an achievement that would have been well nigh impossible had the unbridled promotion of bottled feeding been permitted to continue.

The Message: The Vital Element

Design of messages is the major task of social marketing. When improperly executed, it can constitute social marketing's critical weakness. There's a widespread misconception of what constitutes appropriate messages for social marketing endeavors. This applies to all messages, however delivered. A slogan is not a message; neither is a restatement of the words of the objective, nor a repetition of the theme, the problem, the desired behavior, or the benefits to be derived. None of these, singly or together, constitutes a complete message no matter how well it is put together.

A well-designed message goes beyond the problem, the desired action, and its benefits to deal with the *resistance points*—behavioral constraints that act as barriers to desired behavior change. The complete message will focus on the resolution of these resistances. Messages that acclaim the superiority of "mama's milk" do not deal with the heart of the breast-feeding problem. Though everyone agrees that "breast is best," a wide chasm separates belief from behavior. Formative research has produced rich insights into *resistance points* of new mothers. These range from self-doubt and insecurity, born of the loneliness of a nuclear family or the practical problems of a working woman. Messages that deal with these in an effective mode enable the new mother to comprehend that she is not alone in her uncertainty and give her renewed assurance and a relief from anxiety. Put succinctly, it is the problem within the problem that is the thrust of the social marketing message to overcome the *resistance points* that create the gap between belief and behavior.

Traditional evaluations of health and nutrition education mistakenly assume that their quality is a constant in all situations. But these cannot have a monolithic value. Their worth is as variable as the people involved and the inputs they make. Consequently, their results will differ. Yet, evaluations invariably focus only on measuring the impact of these efforts instead of also attempting to assess their quality.

1. What was the content of the education?
2. What was its relevance to local problems, to the target audience?
3. How well designed were its messages and how rigorously were they tested?
4. Do they deal with priorities or with a diffusion of problems?
5. How relevant were its motivational elements to identifiable *resistance points*?

The mass media are similarly stereotyped. The value of radio in these efforts is automatically presumed to be a constant. Evaluations characteristically proceed to ascertain media impact rather than to analyze how effectively the media were used.

1. Was the radio format appropriate?
2. Did the time periods deliver audience goals?
3. Were the messages relevant to priority problems and effective in resolving *resistance points*?
4. Was the duration of media exposure as planned? (Was the campaign a short-burst effort?)

The biomedical orientation still dominates the public health field with the consequence that social and behavioral factors are neglected in research. One WHO expert committee in 1983 declared that "research on mass communications systems should be considered as a part of the research on health education."[38] Evaluations will accept pretesting as proof of message efficacy without assessing the efficacy of the pretesting procedure.

The Inside Communications Task

Health education is an inside/outside responsibility with health educators requiring continuing education along with the public. In Brazil, few members of the National Working Group responsible for the National Breast-Feeding Program were aware of the successful experience with rooming-in in Recife. Several were unaware of the Santa Catarina experience in setting up work place crèches. No more than 10 percent of the health professionals in five different cities knew about the WHO/UNICEF International Code for the Marketing of Breast-Milk Substitutes, even though Brazil had voted for it at the 1981 World Health Assembly. Others could benefit from inside communications as well. A WHO Expert Committee on New Approaches to Health Education in Primary Health Care[39] issued a declaration that

> In addition to teachers one group of professionals that can make important contributions to health education are media personnel . . . who . . . have come to recognize their social responsibilities in the development process and, in particular, the power of the mass media in creating a political will in favor of health, raising the health consciousness of the people, setting norms, delivering technical messages, popularizing health knowledge and fostering community development.

A recommendation of another WHO group was that national policy should "recognize that health is not strictly a medical issue but environmental, cultural, biological, social and economic as well and provide for the . . . intersectoral cooperation necessary." They should also assure a "central unit . . . staffed by specialists in health education and placed on the same administrative level as other essential health services" and that "health education responsibilities are incorporated into the functions and training of *all* health workers, teachers and media personnel."[40]

In general, the inside job is devoted to sharing experiences with professional personnel and reporting on program development and modifications. The communications devices to be employed are workshops, seminars, newsletters, and bulletins. These devices can be designed for participating agencies to issue under their own names. "Educated governments, administrators and planners can alter mortality patterns and rates," declared Paul Hindson, president of the International Union of Health Education.[41] "We can educate our decision makers by keeping them better informed . . . in the health aspects of the community they serve . . . about the real needs of our population."

Until recently, none of the pharmacists in Nepal was legally qualified though they were selling more than 4,000 drugs and freely dispensing advice about use and dosage. Recognizing this potential health hazard, the government launched a massive program in 1983 to train more than 2,000 of these retailers by 1986. The 40-hour course was heavily marketed by radio and newspaper. Enrollees were taught the appropriate advice to give in the use of drugs and how to handle and store them. A handbook summarized this information as well as the diagnosis and treatment of malaria, tuberculosis, diarrhea, and other widespread diseases covered by the course. Thus, this inside training provided an informed pharmacomedical corps to compensate for the severe shortage of health professionals outside Khatmandu. Since drug retailers were customarily solicited for health and medical advice, officials wisely decided not to fight the system but to absorb it inside the health care infrastructure by qualifying it through training.

In Sudan, problems hampering health education programs have been identified by one authority as

> (a) lack of understanding of basic techiques; (b) lack of coordination which results in conflict and duplication of effort; (c) lack of clear understanding of the division of responsibilities leading to institutional frictions; (d) lack of policies with respect to basic needs and health priorities; (e) lack of integration with other government services required by the program, e.g., water, agriculture, etc.; (f) lack of adequate research facilities.[42]

In Turkey, where infant mortality is more than 120 per 1,000 births, the more than 5,000 pharmacies are influential sources of health information. Yet on a recent trip I made to that country, an informal survey of a dozen establishments in Ankara produced not one pharmacist who knew the proper treatment for the infection. The typical advice was to administer an antibiotic, give water, and suspend milk feeds.

Notes

1. Manoff, R.K., "The Brazilian National Breast-Feeding Program," a report of Consultant's Visit, March 21–31, 1982, consultant to INAN (National Institute of Nutrition of Brazil) and INCS (International Nutrition Communication Service).

2. Griffith, M.H., "Urban Health Workers in Search of a Role," *Future*, IPPF London, first quarter, 1983.

3. El-Bushra, J., "Health Education by Television and Radio in the Sudan: A Brief Review" in *Health Education by Television and Radio*, (Ed. M. Meyer), K.G. Saur, Munich, 1981, pp. 395–398.

4. Manoff International Inc., "Report of Technical Assistance Provided USAID/Santo Domingo, Dominican Republic," September 29–October 10, 1975.

5. Adeniyi, J.D., Brieger, W.R., Ramakrishna, J., "Involving Communities in Tropical Disease Control," *Education for Health, WHO Newsletter*, Geneva, Switzerland, 1984, inaugural issue, pp. 39–47.

6. Steele, J., "Grass Roots Democracy That Sets Nicaragua Apart," the Manchester *Guardian Weekly*, September 4, 1983, p. 8.

7. Skerry, P., "Neighborhood COPS," *The New Republic*, February 6, 1983, p. 21.

8. Troya, W., "Consultative Task Force on Social Marketing and the Child Survival and Development Revolution," a meeting held at UNICEF, New York, April 4, 1984.

9. "Coffee Drinkers Said to Run Risks," an AP dispatch to the New York *Times,* June 16, 1983.

10. Lightman, A., "Weighing the Odds," *Science* 1983, Vol. 4, No. 10, p. 21, American Association for the Advancement of Science, Washington, D.C.

11. "The Lipid Research Clinics Coronary Primary Prevention Trial Results," *Journal of the American Medical Association,* January 20, 1984, 251/3, pp. 351–364.

12. Ahrens, E.H., "Dietary Fats and Coronary Heart Disease: Unfinished Business," *The Lancet,* December 1979, 22/29, pp. 1345–1348.

13. "Cancer Society Prepares Diet Suggested for Reduced Risks," the New York *Times,* September 30, 1983.

14. "Everything You Wanted to Know on Cholesterol," National Heart, Lung and Blood Institute, *Nutrition Week,* Vol. 14/15, April 12, 1984, p. 4, Community Nutrition Institute, Washington, D.C.

15. Brody, J.E., "Heart Panel Urges That Everyone Cut Fat and Cholesterol," personal health column, the New York *Times,* April 14, 1982.

16. Gropstein, C., "Should Imperfect Data Be Used to Guide Public Policy?" *Science* 1983, Vol. 4/10, p. 18, American Association for the Advancement of Science, Washington, D.C.

17. Schramm, W., "Big Media, Little Media," Information Center on Instructional Technology, USAID, Washington, D.C., 1973.

18. "Current Views on Nutrition Strategies," UNICEF, New York, 1983.

19. de Sweemer, C., "Reaching the Village: Alibi or Revolution?" *People,* IPPF, London, Vol. 10/3, 1983.

20. Gilmore, J.W., Adelman, C.C., Meyer, A.J., Thorne, M.C., "Morocco: Food Aid and Nutrition Education," A.I.D. Project, Impact Evaluation Report No. 8, August 1980, Washington, D.C.

21. Levinson, J.F., "Toward Success in Combating Malnutrition: An Assessment of What Works," presented to the Eighth Session of the UN/ACC Sub-Committee on Nutrition, Bangkok, Thailand, Document No. SCN 82/20, February 15–19, 1982.

22. Manoff, R.K., Griffiths, M., Cooke, T.M., Zeitlin, M., "Mothers Speak and Nutrition Educators Listen: Formative Evaluation for a Nutrition Communications Project," in Special Territory of Yogyakarta, Central Java, South Sumatra, *Volume I: First Stage: Concept Testing Before Developing Education Materials,* submitted to Indonesian Nutrition Development Project, Nutrition Communication and Behavior Change Component, July 23, 1980.

23. *Nutrition Review,* Population Health Nutrition, the World Bank, Washington, D.C., April 19, 1984, p. 51.

24. *WHO Newsletter,* WHO, Geneva, Switzerland, inaugural issue, 1984.

25. Vittachi, T., "World Population—Back From the Brink," the Manchester *Guardian Weekly,* September 9, 1979.

26. Rihani, M., "Development As If Women Mattered," Overseas Development Council, Washington, D.C., 1978.

27. Jacobsen, J., "Promoting Population Stabilization: Incentives for Small Families," Overseas Development Council, Washington, D.C., 1983.

28. "Recognizing the 'Indivisible Woman' in Development: The World Bank's Experience," Washington, D.C., 1979.

29. Lewis, M., "Developing Income Generating Opportunity for Rural Women," *Horizons,* January 1983.

30. Smith, D., "Indonesia Sets New Targets," *People,* Vol. 10, No. 4, 1983, p. 32.

31. "Current Views on Nutrition Strategies," UNICEF, New York, 1983.

32. "Evaluation of the National Health Promotion Media Campaign," Office of Disease Prevention and Health Promotion (HHS), U.S. Department of Health and Human Services, Washington, D.C., 1982.

33. Manoff, R.K., "The Brazilian National Breast-Feeding Program," op. cit.

34. de Sweemer, C., op. cit.

35. "Current Views on Nutrition Strategies," op. cit.

36. de Sweemer, op. cit.

37. Ibid.

38. "New Approaches to Health Education in Primary Health Care," a report of the WHO Expert Committee, WHO, Geneva, Switzerland, 1983.

39. "Two Major Events," a report of the WHO Expert Committee Meeting, 1982, in Education for Health, *WHO Newsletter,* Geneva, Switzerland, inaugural issue, 1984.

40. "Technical Discussions," a special session of the thirty-sixth World Health Assembly for 300 representatives from all six WHO regions, as reported in *WHO Newsletter,* WHO, Geneva, Switzerland, inaugural issue, 1984.

41. Hindson, P., "Intergalactic Health Education," in Hygie, *International Journal of Health Education* (IUHE), Geneva, Switzerland, October 1983, Vol. 2/3, p. 18.

42. El-Bushra, J., op. cit.

8

Using the Mass Media for Social Marketing

Travelers to India who see for the first time the exquisite erotic temple sculptures of Khujarao and Bubaneshwar are stunned by their uninhibited and diverse depictions of the sex act. Some historians suggested that they were the inspiration of ambitious rulers who, in need of bigger armies and work forces, saw in these sculptures an ingenious device for promoting fertility. If so, then they were among the earliest of social marketers and extraordinarily ingenious. Using the temple as a mass medium ensured maximum target audience in those days. It also lent authority to the message and sanction to its instruction: make love freely. And the messages, each with a beautifully graphic demonstration of the joys of sex, not only employed the most motivating appeal, but also executed it brilliantly. Engraving them on temple walls ensured continuity of exposure—all in all, a good example of social marketing; so good, in fact, as to be more than slightly responsible, perhaps, for India's population plight today.

Preempting temple walls then was the equivalent of using radio and TV today. No place in those ancient communities was more heavily trafficked, proof our ancestors had a fair grip on the task of getting the message out. True, they did not have anywhere near the mass communications capacity we have today but they made the most of what they had to an extent that we have yet to attain. And they instinctively knew how to go about setting a sound media strategy though they would have been dumbfounded to be told so.

Setting the Media Strategy

Message and media strategies are inextricably linked. One should not be decided independently of the other. Inexperienced practitioners who make media decisions a priori ("Let's use radio") and then design the message to fit ("O.K., how about a jingle?") deserve the inevitable denouement. (Evaluation: "The results are not conclusive that radio can effectively be employed to attain behavior change objectives in public health education.") The only problem is that the record of such inept experience clutters the literature and weakens the case for social marketing. The disciplined approach to media strategy development involves seven key factors

1. The target audience
2. The media value requirements of the message
3. Reach
4. Frequency
5. Media weight
6. Continuity
7. Cost efficiency

The Target Audience

Once target population determinations have been made, media possibilities must be examined to identify those with the maximum potential for audience delivery. This does not necessarily mean the most popular, because the aim is not to reach all the people but only selected segments, which might include secondary audiences of material importance to the objectives. Thus, Ward et al., in a study of a mass media campaign for hypertension control for "the general public and . . . persons aware that they have high blood pressure,"[1] reported that it also served as a conduit to health professionals. Yet, their conclusion that "communication practitioners should further examine use of general mass media [TV, radio, magazines, and newspapers] in professional education efforts" seems unwarranted for cost-efficiency reasons. Most of the reach of these media would be squandered for so small a target. Other media possibilities (professional journals, direct mail) would seem more appropriate to that aim.

In the United States and other countries with highly developed communications data-gathering infrastructures, information on audience composition is readily available. The A.C. Nielsen Company with its

Nielsen TV and Nielsen Station Indexes (NTI and NSI) provide both national and local program and time-period audience data. Arbitron (ARB) TV Local Market Services is primarily a source for such information about local stations in more than 200 TV areas. Radio audience data is obtainable from the Arbitron Local Market Radio Service for over 250 radio markets. The primary source for radio network audience information is Radio's All Dimension Audience Research (RADAR). These services provide information on audience size and composition by sex and age for all time periods. In addition to this demographic information, special services like the Simmons Market Research Bureau (SMRB)—the result of the merger of Target Group Index (TGI) and W.R. Simmons and Associates Research—provide market information, media usage patterns, and such life-style insights as consumer usage of more than 500 brands of products. The latter is available on a program-by-program basis so that advertisers can pinpoint their best prospects. The Magazine Research Inc. (MRI) also provides complete demographic and readership information for all magazines. Newspaper data are available from individual market studies conducted by the papers themselves or from such services as Scarborough and Three Sigma. Comparable information is available in almost all industrialized countries and, to a lesser degree, in the Third World.

Commercial marketers make ingenious use of such information in designing their media strategies against the competition. Social marketers can do with less. But there is a basic need to know the stations and time slots—or newspapers and magazines—that deliver the highest percentage of desired audiences.

This information is sold by the services and is for the privileged use of subscribers. It is expensive. Almost all advertising agencies have access to such information. Many large marketing organizations subscribe directly. The information is not usually sold on a one-time basis. Social marketers will find some advertising agencies willing to offer *pro bono publico* cooperation and, thus, can gain access to this information.

In countries where such media information is not available, it can be developed on an ad hoc basis by including appropriate communigraphic questions in both the qualitative formative or the quantitative baseline studies to uncover answers to such questions as: What is the penetration of the mass media? How many radio/TV sets are in operation in homes or in communal settings? How many are not working? How many cinemas? How many newspaper and magazine readers? Which ones and which parts? How often do they use these media? What are the most popular radio/TV stations? The most popular programs? In general, what are their reading, listening, and viewing habits? It is surprising how conveniently this information can be elicited in the course of research.

In many of these countries, either local advertising agencies make such surveys on behalf of clients or the clients do so themselves. Among the latter are branch operations of major multinational marketers to whom basic media and audience information are indispensable.

In Pakistan, a survey for the Population Planning Council established valuable data on radio penetration, listenership patterns of men and women, frequency of listening, and urban versus rural listening patterns that proved critical for media strategy decisions.[2] Similar data were obtained on newspaper and magazine readership by the Research Division of Adcom, an advertising agency in Karachi. More recently Manoff International, serving as consultants to Population Services International in Bangladesh, developed similar data in the course of the baseline study for the motivational component in PSI's contraceptive social marketing program (SMP). It produced critical intelligence, namely that rural Bangladeshi women cannot be reached by radio when the men are at home because they are virtually prohibited by the men from access to it.

According to Atkin, failure to identify audience characteristics can mislead us to those inclined to ignore our message, to misconstrue it, and to reject it as inapplicable.[3] There is ample documentation for this observation in innumerable marketing experiences. But as cited by Atkin, it has also been confirmed by communications researchers like Klapper,[4] Bauer,[5] Roberts and Maccoby,[6] and Wright.[7]

The Media Value Requirements of the Message

Media differ in their communications values and these differences are critical for social marketing programs. TV, with sight, sound, and motion, is supreme for messages that include demonstration. A message for Oral Rehydration Therapy would be handicapped without a demonstration of a mother preparing the ORT formula—the liter of water, the measuring of the ingredients, the feeding to the infant. But if TV is not available and radio is the ideal alternative, then ingenious message design must make up for the loss of sight and motion with a graphic use of words and sounds to build a lucid, memorable word picture. Obviously, the print media with the opportunity for illustration and detailed instructions may be the best of all, considering, too, that the message can be saved by the reader. But what if the targeted audience is largely illiterate?

These media-value considerations pertain to all means of communications. A face-to-face live demonstration has both the advantages and the drawbacks of TV. Once it is done it may be forgotten though TV offers an easier opportunity for repetition. A leaflet left by the demonstrator is no more effective than a newspaper or magazine message if the audience is incapable of deciphering it. One obvious advantage of face-to-face live communication is its two-way capability and the opportunity for discussion.

Media-value comparisons should not suggest the absolute superiority of one medium over another but merely identify relative strengths and weaknesses for given tasks. Obviously, a combination of media—the media mix—is the most desirable strategy whenever affordable. The use of more than one medium increases reach and should be limited only by budgetary considerations. This media mix is an essential component of media strategy formulation. The addition of special interest magazines with well-defined readerships augments a TV schedule unable to reach the whole of the desired population. A media mix is also useful to increase frequency through media that appeal to the same audiences. This is known as audience duplication—to be sought after or avoided depending on need. There is little to fear that a use of media combinations may reach a point of diminishing return even with the gargantuan budgets of the commercial world. In marketing, whether social or commercial, the media policy of the more, the better is almost always valid.

The availability of color (e.g., magazines, billboards, TV) is a value of some importance to the presentation of foods. But though it may be right for the message, it must also be right for the audience. Billboards or hoardings have the limitations of audience distance and fleeting impression. This obliges messages to be brief, but inexperienced message designers sometimes find it a discipline most difficult to observe, resulting in a wordy roadside sign or poster embellished with disparate design elements and an undersized typeface impossible to read at a distance in the brief exposure time. The billboard is essentially a reminder or auxiliary medium with potentially good reach but effective only for reinforcing a key concept of a message—its slogan and/or symbol. For some social marketing messages the medium can be ideal: "Immunization Week July 15–21!—The Shot That Can Save Your Child's Life"; "Have You Checked Your Blood Pressure Lately? It's High Time You Did." These are topical campaigns. Detailed information and motivational elements need media that afford longer messages and more time for their delivery.

Direct mail offers an opportunity for sharply targeted communications now that computerized mailing lists are available in demographic and life-style breakouts. The Direct Mail Advertising Association maintains a U.S. roster of agencies for this service. Similar firms operate in countries throughout the world. Costs for direct mail run high on a per capita basis but the waste circulation is minimal, thus reducing the real cost. Telemarketing, a similar service by telephone, has become popular among commercial marketers, but the high cost of this service and its limited applicability to ordinary public health education activity makes it a questionable medium.

Reach

The ability of a medium to cover an audience is its reach. In the United States, where TV penetration is almost total (98 percent of all homes), TV has a theoretical reach of almost 100 percent. This means that all America can be got to with TV. The same is true of radio with a 98-percent penetration plus 60- to 70-percent out-of-home listening as well. But these are theoretical possibilities. While TV reaches almost everyone in the country, not everyone in the country sees everything on TV. This is why effective reach—the percent of the target, not the total, audience—is a more useful measure.

With print media, effective reach is just as elusive. The total circulation is never exposed to every printed item. The effective reach of a newspaper or magazine is the percent of circulation likely to be exposed to a printed message. Messages precisely designed to attract the attention of target readers (e.g., "Attention, Mothers of Infants") and repeated—increasing the frequency—are the surest means of expanding their effective reach. To begin with, only newspaper sections or magazines identified for their high readership by the target group should be selected. The print media, with their special sections (newspapers) and special interest focus (magazines) are particularly advantageous for reach (e.g., professional journals for nutritionists, doctors, lawyers, businessmen).

Radio has this advantage over TV because its broader spectrum, allowing a proliferation of stations, has forced audience specialization upon its operators. Thus, stations in the United States are known for their music—classical, top-forty, hard-rock—or for weather and news. Audience demographics are thus more sharply defined station by station, a valuable equity for those who may find in one station precisely the audience profile they need.

U.S. family planning social marketers who want to target their message to the teenage population have found radio an ideal medium.[8,9] For targeting children, there is no better access than Saturday and Sunday morning and some late afternoon hours on TV. TV sports programs offer a heavy male audience although this may not guarantee a particular male segment. That is why the accumulated audience data are useful for target segmentation purposes. In the absence of such data, one either is forced to collect them as practically as possible or, like a keen-eyed Columbus, to strike out in a likely direction and happen on a great discovery.

Frequency

While reach measures the percentage of homes (or listeners, viewers, or readers) exposed to a given message, frequency tells how often it was received. A frequency of six, for example, is an average for all the homes reached but not all homes received the message six times because not all were tuned in during the same hours. By analyzing the average frequency—and Nielsen data make this possible—we can ascertain the frequency distribution. A quintile breakdown of the audience on this basis may look like this: the top 20 percent will have a frequency of 22; perhaps the next, 5; the next, 3; the next, 2; and, finally, the bottom, 1. (Incidentally, this is a typical usage configuration for many consumption categories in the American marketplace: domination by a heavy-user segment). In our hypothetical case, the top 20 percent (heavy users) is responsible for almost 80 percent of the total exposures; the bottom 20 percent (the light-users), for only 3 percent.

This frequency distribution is a function of two circumstances: the difference in media usage habits—some homes are heavier consumers of TV time than others ("20 percent of the TV viewers do 80 percent of the watching" is an old media rule of thumb) and the placement of the messages. The first is outside the control of the media strategist but not the second. Ideally, both circumstances will be advantageous if the target audience is also an aggregate of heavy TV viewers. This is not often the case because groups targeted for one circumstance (cigarette smoking) do not necessarily correlate for another (heavy TV viewing).

What can the media strategist do when, as in almost all developing countries, there are few data sources for making frequency distribution analyses? Some attempt should be made to generate the information from local universities, research organizations, media, or advertising agencies that may already have done research. One need but make inquiries in the right places to uncover it. Rudimentary facts about media habits can be elicited in the course of other scheduled research. In the end, judgment will have to play a big part in the ultimate decisions and this will depend on the social marketer's growing familiarity with the media environment and the messages from other sources that have a bearing on the venture. This is referred to among commercial marketers as monitoring the competition.

Advertising is looked upon as the automation of selling—substituting advertising for the salesperson. Therefore, it is important to know how many advertising sales calls the competition is making—how many potential customers (reach) and how often (frequency). Other conditions being equal, the more sales calls, the more sales. In social marketing the competition depends on the nature of the venture. For a campaign to promote breast-feeding, it is the advertising and promotion activity of the breast milk-substitute marketers readily apparent in the local media. The record of radio and TV advertising is recorded in station logs generally required by law in most countries. In the United States, logs are available for public inspection on request.

But the competition for other social marketing ventures is not so easily identified. For an immunization campaign, for example, competition is simply a matter of determining the share of voice needed to be seen and heard above the crowd and the clamor of messages competing for public attention. Some sense of this activity is necessary to determine the media share of voice needed for a reasonable impact on the target audience. Where the level of such activity is moderate, the public should be easier to reach with less frequency to achieve message goals.

Subsequent tracking studies of the campaign will reveal whether media schedules are working out. Creative message design has a vital role to play in all this. Given the same reach and frequency, one message design can outdo another's impact on the same subject. The media offer an opportunity to be seen and heard but only message design—its clarity, appeal, motivation, and capacity to engage the imagination and interest of the audience—can determine the extent to which that opportunity is realized.

Cinema is clearly not a primary medium for reach or frequency. Both the number of cinemas and the frequency of attendance give cinema only an auxiliary role to that of the more intrusive mass media. The majority of cinemas in the world are concentrated in urban areas and are a pastime of higher socioeconomic groups, especially in the Third World. In 1972, there were an estimated 326 cinemas in all of Pakistan with a total of 204,000 seats for a population of 65 million.[10]

The value of folk media in social marketing has yet to be evaluated formally although enthusiastic claims appear with undiminished frequency but unimpressive evidence. Folk media comprise the traveling theater, dance, and other performing groups like the puppet and shadow theaters of Sri Lanka and Indonesia. The repertoire consists of a rich cultural product whose roots are to be found in national and local religion, history, and tradition. In more recent years these groups have found their way onto radio and TV. But their particular appeal as folk media is their outreach to villages with limited access to other communications and their presumed influence on the beliefs and attitudes of the people.

Family planning educators and others have sought to use folk media to convey family planning messages. Quite apart from the question as to whether these precious cultural treasures should be tampered with for more temporal matters, the possibilities for effective message design and delivery seem limited at best. One way has been to work family planning references into the dramas. Because of the constraints of the story lines, messages cannot possibly be designed to deal with deep-seated *resis-*

tance points or other essential message elements. One description of a folk media experience in Orissa, India, was typical both in the ecstatic response of the reporter and the paucity of substantive information on its impact: "Today word has gone out that the PHC [Primary Health Care program] has visitors who want to see how the folk media are used . . . and the villagers respond with enthusiasm. Magicians, dancers, minstrels and puppeteers throw out ideas (sic) in ways which make the cleverest mass media seem sallow."[11] To throw out ideas is not precisely what social marketing messages are meant to achieve.

In other situations, folk media have been preempted for specially created family planning and health education dramas. It would appear that they then seek to fulfil the same purpose as contemporary dramas created especially for radio and TV. This suggests that the value of folk media ought to be measured by the same tests proposed for all media— that is, cost efficiency, reach, frequency, and continuity. But these criteria play little part in the judgment of ardent folk media proponents. When asked whether puppets can be used as health message communicators, the UNICEF consultant to a puppet theater experiment in the slums of Colombo, Sri Lanka, replied positively, saying, "Drama helps to put across any kind of message . . . in a far more tangible and meaningful way than any discussion or film show . . . [Folk] drama belongs to the kind of people messages are directed to and can be understood and appreciated by them. . . . Using puppets . . . was just an experiment."[12] These are reasonable remarks, but social marketing will require some more objective basis for deciding whether the folk media represent a viable alternative given the budgetary constraints that always make alternative choices obligatory.

Media Weight

This is the factor that determines the reach and frequency of a mass media campaign, irrespective of the form of the message—whether delivered as a program or a spot on radio and TV or as a message in the print media. How many times should the message be delivered, where, and, if on radio or TV, at what times? The answer is in the rating, the measuring device for audience size. In the print media the readership score tells the percentage of total readers that saw the message, read it ("read most") and associated it correctly ("seen and associated"). Ratings are developed through various media research techniques. For radio and TV, the A.C. Nielsen Company has for years attached electronic recording devices to TV sets in a carefully selected sample of homes whose identity, for obvious reasons, is the best kept secret of the industry. From these recordings collected on a regular basis, Nielsen is able to ascertain the audience size for all TV time periods for local stations and the networks. These data are used for arriving at media weight, reach, and frequency calculations. Other services offer similar information based on different methods of data collection—home diaries, telephone surveys.

The basic unit for measuring media weight is the TV (or radio) rating, a percentage of the homes with TV (or radio) sets that were tuned in at a given time period. This measure of a past viewing (or listening) experience is presumed to be a reliable measure for the future audience. In effect, a 15-rating time period means that the message at that time ought to reach 15 percent of the TV homes within the ADI (area of dominant influence) of the station. Were the message also to be telecast at four other times in a week with respective ratings of 18, 14, 12, and 16, it would be said to have a weekly schedule of 75 gross rating points (GRPs). On the surface, this suggests that 75 percent of the TV homes in the area will have been reached. But we have already learned that in the real TV world there is audience duplication. Some homes will have received the message more than once (frequency). Thus, the percentage of homes actually reached will be considerably less than 75 percent.

For example, in Pennsylvania there are only 32 commercial television stations with a TV penetration of 4,261,500 homes out of a total of 4,338,200 homes, or virtually every home (98 percent). Further, an analysis of television advertising for a selected week (in this case June 6, 1983) indicated the proportion of advertising time devoted to various food products. For that week there were a total of 15,690 commercials beamed into that area—10,248 on local television and 5,441 from the networks. One-fourth were for food products of which almost a third were for soft drinks, cereals, candy and gum, cookies and crackers, coffee, tea, and cocoa. When a commercial advertiser makes such an announcement just once during the day and then repeats it just once in the prime evening hours—with average ratings for both day parts—seven days a week, those two announcements a day will have reached 52 percent of the homes in the television area an average of two times that week. At the end of four weeks, the advertiser will have reached more than 80 percent of the homes more than five times. At the end of 13 weeks the message will have penetrated 91 percent of the homes more than 17 times. These conclusions are based on data from NTI and NSI.

This little exercise is intended to demonstrate the importance of media research and analysis to the targeted use of the mass media. "Feeling Good," an ambitious public health campaign planned and developed by the Children's TV Workshop in New York, was a grave disappointment despite its elaborate production values. The series never attracted a sufficient audience to warrant its continuance on the air. Only 1 percent of the population was reported to have watched it.[13] How to explain the audience failure?: (1) the program format may have attracted only those who were already motivated; (2) the time period may have been wrong for the program; (3) the program may have been wrong for its target audience; or (4) vice versa. One thing is certain: without an audience, there can be no success. In the case of "Feeling Good," greater reach and frequency might have been achieved with a strategy of short messages. Not only would the cumulative audience ("cume") have been greater but the memorability of the messages enhanced, as suggested by Miller et al. in a study of short radio messages confined to simple salient ideas. Their conclusion was that such messages, delivered with a frequency strategy, appeared to have greater likelihood of being sorted out and retained from the clutter of other messages in the radio environment.[14]

John Maynard Keynes once declared that "if you owe a bank $100, it's your problem but if you owe the bank $1 million, it's theirs." Students of the German philosophers, Kant and Hegel, will recognize this witticism as a latter-day postulation of the transformation of quantity into quality: if the quantity of a force is increased steadily, at some point its effect undergoes a sudden and violent qualitative change. There is no more dramatic demonstration of this principle than the media experience; increase both reach and frequency and extend continuity and, at some point, a qualitative change in audience knowledge, attitude, and behavior may take a leap. What that point may be is the continuing challenge to the social marketing professional. There is no fixed point toward which he or she can set a venture. Each one is a new experience, a new empirical exercise; each one instructive, conveying the promise that it will improve the next.

Continuity

Reach, frequency, and media weight are short-term concerns but social marketing efforts burdened with intricate goals and deep-seated *resistance points* in its target audience need the long-term strategy of continuity. Reviewing the disappointing results from antidrug campaigns aimed at U.S. youth, Atkin singled out as a reason that all of them "tended to be of short duration."[15] There is no assurance that continuity makes the qualitative difference, but given the complicated nature of the teenage drug problem, short-burst media strategies are a design for failure. A brief campaign may be effective for announcing a new service but not for achieving modifications in behavior. Few evaluations of health campaigns have taken note of this deficiency.

The short-burst media strategy is a common failing of most involved social marketing efforts and it is not always because of budgetary constraints. More often it is a planning deficiency of professionals with limited media experience. Some efforts do not need more than limited media exposure; a drive for immunization within a given period of time suggests a strategy of a short high-reach-and-frequency cycle for maximum coverage of the target audience as often as possible in the shortest period of time. But a sodium-avoidance educational campaign suggests an investment in year-round continuity at lowered levels of reach and frequency—to emphasize continuous message delivery at the cost of more gradual audience accumulation and message repetition. The nature of the problem dictates the strategy. High sodium consumption in the United States is an ongoing problem. New additions to the vulnerable population arrive every year. The long-term need for continuity takes precedence over the short-term expediencies of reach and frequency.

The health problem of cigarette smoking, like drug addiction, presents the same long-term imperative. Ouellet and Melia report on a Canadian antismoking campaign initiated by the government that was one of the few to take cognizance of this strategic need and plan for "a minimum 20-year effort."[16] The campaign recognized that the "decision to smoke was ultimately a product of a lifelong (birth to age of smoking onset) socialization process." The campaign will, therefore, address each of the key stages in the lifelong cycle. The mass media program, launched in spring 1982, will be continuous, probably in pulsed cycles within each year and will be coordinated with educational efforts in the school system and with other governmental and nongovernmental agencies "essential to the success of the program." In deciding on a continuity strategy over a 20-year period, the planners acknowledged the fact that "smoking programmes to date have typically been short term (less than two years)" and, presumably, had proved inadequate.

Continuity does not require an uninterrupted media plan. Pulsing is a pattern of interspersing hiatus periods among exposure periods, for example, two weeks in, two weeks out. This media tactic obviously reduces reach and frequency goals in favor of continuity. One question often asked of social marketers is: "How long a period of time is needed to achieve communications objectives?" Regrettably, there is no ready answer. Variables from situation to situation are never the same, even given the same problem and successful past experience in dealing with it. Differences in target audiences, environmental influences, media systems, and message design, make each new situation, or even the same situation at another time, unpredictable. Experience enlightens each successive effort but it cannot predict precisely what will happen and when. Only periodic tracking studies can provide the answer.

Cost Efficiency

The measure of how well time or space units compare in terms of audience delivery is their cost efficiency and the basic calculation is the cost per thousand (CPM), the cost for reaching a thousand homes or, in more effective terms, a thousand members of the target audience. If a schedule of announcements (spots) on TV, for example, is priced at $2,000 weekly and the aggregate GRPs promise to deliver 200,000 members of the target audience weekly, then CPM is $10.00. Comparing this to other available schedules and to past buys provides a basis for decision. CPM calculations can be made for all media.

Comparative Cost Efficiencies
Target Audience: Adult Females 18–49

Time			CPM
Day network TV	(:30)	(10–3:00 P.M.)	$ 5.95
Prime network TV	(:30)	(8–11:00 P.M.)	14.20
Day spot TV	(:30)*	(10–3:00 P.M.)	6.60
Prime spot TV	(:30)*	(8–11:00 P.M.)	17.85
Radio AM drive time	(:60)	(6–10:00 A.M.)	3.50
Radio housewife time	(:60)	(10–3:00 P.M.)	3.20
Radio PM drive time	(:60)	(3–7:00 P.M.)	3.70
Daily newspapers	(1000-li. b/w)		19.65
Magazines (4-color page)			13.25
(selected men's and women's magazines)			

*Top 100 ADIs (above information based on Nielsen NTI, early 1984)

Message length or size of space in print media obviously makes a difference. A one-minute announcement is more expensive than one for 30 seconds during the same time period. CPM calculations must take this into account. Lengthier messages (but not necessarily larger space units) can mean lowered *reach, frequency,* or *continuity* for the same budget. The shorter the message, the more that can be purchased and the greater the potential reach, frequency, and continuity. However, small space units usually deliver less impact. By the same token, the more expensive the time period (prime time) or the print medium (higher circulation), the greater the reach but the lower the frequency and continuity for a given budget. Obviously, the same budget in less expensive time periods (non-prime, fringe prime) or print media (lower circulation) produces lower immediate reach but greater frequency and continuity. These may offer a more cost-efficient access to the target audience (e.g., daytime TV for women) but if reach is a prime objective, one consideration must be balanced against the other. The addition of another medium, like women's magazines, to the daytime TV schedule may adequately compensate for the limited reach of the latter at an overall lower cost and with less waste circulation than prime-time TV.

Production costs for materials should enter into total cost-efficiency calculations. These obviously differ from medium to medium. In calculating TV/radio production costs, a fairly reliable rule of thumb for most Third World countries is a 10-to-1 TV/radio ratio. In developed countries the spread is even greater because TV (live, film, or video) costs fluctuate wildly depending on number of scenes and shooting days, on-location shooting, size of cast, and optical effects. Radio production costs, by contrast, fluctuate within a much narrower range. Print production costs, engravings, and photography are fairly standardized. The usual procedure for estimating cost is to submit all materials for preproduction bids to more than one supplier. The lowest bid is not necessarily the choicest. Considerations of quality and reliability must be weighed against price.

The Satellite Revolution

Satellite communications development has outpaced even the bold prophecies of the English scientist and science fiction visionary, Arthur C. Clarke, who in 1945 conceived a fantastic scheme for orbiting satellites to convey messages from one part of the earth to another. Today, satellite technology has created a global communications network providing developing countries with worldwide links for the first time. This has opened up communications possibilities that would have taken decades to develop and at prohibitive costs with presatellite technologies. With only 7 percent of the world's telephones, Third World countries by 1980 already accounted for 38 percent of total satellite communications traffic.[17] These countries are able to bypass traditional long-distance telephone line installations and the costly cable and relay facilities previously necessary for radio and TV transmissions. The falling price of earth receiving stations has accelerated the rate at which they are being erected so as to redistribute transmissions to homes in surrounding areas. It appears to be the cheapest method for mass information delivery ever and, possibly, the most effective.

SITE, a joint project of the United States and India in 1976, was designed to employ a NASA synchronous-orbiting satellite for direct telecasting to a population of more than five million in 2,400 villages of six areas of India. The linkup from earth receiving stations to TV monitors in the villages brought educational programs in family planning, health, nutrition, agriculture, and professional instruction for teachers and students. The one-year program was evaluated as a notable achievement. The launch of an Indian-built system became a top priority, finally realized in the summer of 1983 when the most important piece of cargo on the space shuttle Challenger was Insat B, India's own unique satellite, combining telecommunications, weather forecasting, and telecasting capabilities all in one. When Professor U.R. Rao, director of India's space research agency, was asked, "Why, with all its problems of poverty, overpopulation, malnutrition, poor health and illiteracy, should India go into space?", his answer was "to help solve those very human problems." He added that SITE had proved "satellite TV coverage could change the face of rural India if it is properly used by raising education levels, improving health, family planning and child-raising practices."[18]

In the United States, however, satellite telecasting has done little more than expand the variety of TV entertainment. Programming currently coming to U.S. homes by satellite is more abundant than the feed from the networks and, with a few less than notable exceptions, just about as uplifting. It consists of popular movies, sports and entertainment programs, business teleconferencing, religious programming, business reports, and stock market quotations, all in all a threatening deluge of the same old fare. Without a policy of reserving satellite telecasting capacity for health and related education purposes, this extraordinary breakthrough may ironically contribute to the clutter that worthwhile material already finds hard to penetrate.

The future of satellites is not without its problematic aspect. Some countries are fearful of the prospects. Jerry Grey, author of *Beachheads in Space*, said that because "television is too powerful a medium, they're afraid of . . . broadcasts [from other nations] going from a satellite to their citizens." Nandasiri Jasentuiiyana of Sri Lanka, executive secretary of the United Nations Conference on Outer Space, asked, "Who am I to say that ideas on family planning and birth control should be broadcast to people of a different region?"[19]

Materials Versus Mass Media, Media, and Channels

We have no desire to add more bafflement to ongoing mass media references. The problem goes beyond the customary difficulties with definitions or semantic arrangements. New definitions will not necessarily do any better than old ones. Definitions, like archery targets, are destined to be shot at. It is safer not to stand behind either. Better to take up the bow and be the one who lets the arrows fly. I have a few in my quiver.

To begin, a USAID reference to the importance of using the mass media for ORT in antidiarrheal programs declared, "mass media campaigns, radio, newspapers, billboards and *special materials* [author's emphasis] are effective tools which should be used."[20] I heartily endorse the sentiment of this statement but am sorely troubled by the indiscriminate lumping together of "special materials" with true mass media and "mass media campaigns." Similarly, Kline and Pavlik[21] propagated a comparable confusion when they reported that others had "found that some media such as *film, pamphlets, books* [author's emphasis] and magazines were characterized by a high level of 'informativeness.' . . . On the other hand, some media such as radio and billboards were characterized by a relatively low level."[22]

This confusion of media materials with the mass media themselves is not uncommon. It is pervasive even among professionals and results in much wasteful effort producing materials whose delivery is inadequately provided for. Confusion also exists about the distinction between a *medium* and a *mass* medium. This is more than a matter of semantics, although the literature sometimes reduces it to this absurdity. Kline and Pavlik, in a sincere attempt to let in light on the subject, might have increased the haze by declaring

> A channel is the vehicle that transmits a message from a source to a receiver. Frequently, a channel and a source can be one, as in the case of a peer, a parent or a teacher. At other times, however, the channel and source are separate. Such is generally the case with the mass media. While in some situations a mass medium can be both source and channel, they more often are a voice box for some other spokesperson.[23]

This reasonable definition of a *channel* offers no relief from the confusion surrounding the *distinctions* among channels or, if you will, media. "A voice box for some other spokesperson" may also be a telephone and, though the telephone would not be construed by them as a mass medium, that misperception is far from uncommon.

The telephone can have singularly effective uses for social marketing. Public health organizations are making good use of the telephone for hot line purposes. USDA's Food Safety and Inspection Service offers consumer advice for those who call the Meat and Poultry Hotline, initiated in 1980 as a pilot program called the Consumer Response System. But the premise of the operation recognizes the limitations of the telephone as a medium for transmitting information on a mass basis. To build traffic for the service, the hot line uses the mass media to promote itself.

Tel-Med, a nationally franchised U.S. health information service by telephone operating since 1973, is free to callers in over 100 communities in the United States. Recognizing that its success depends on public awareness of its existence, Tel-Med depends on media—individual as well as mass—to get the word out. The most effective media, according to one study of the system, are newspapers, TV, radio, and friends and relatives (the people medium). Doctors' offices and others locations were also effectively used as media for the distribution of a brochure (the media material).[24]

An even more revealing example of this misclassification of media materials as media is the video cassette recorder (VCR). Examples of its effective use in health, nutrition, and food activities have won it wide-scale respect. But the video cassette is nothing more than electronic film, with some admitted advantages over the latter; it affords instantaneous production and replay, requires no elaborate production and developing facilities, is battery operable, and can be viewed in the open light. But like film, video is not a medium because it still requires a means of delivery to its target audience: human beings with means of transport and roads to travel by. Like film, it is a more sophisticated version of the old talk-and-chalk presentations of field educators.

In fact, the opposition both to VCR and film by traditionalists stems from fear that they represent too slick a transformation of the material for most unsophisticated audiences and create dependence on expensive technology. In many situations and for some subjects the charge is probably valid. The baited trap of technology ensnares the unsuspecting when simpler and less costly materials would be more appropriate. But what escapes critical notice in all of this is that neither film nor video is a medium, although they are erroneously perceived as such. They are materials in need of a medium for their transmission. This has crippling cost implications and people-power investments that severely limit their effectiveness when it is already too late to do much about the situation. One Latin American project dependent on the use of VCR equipment was beset with "problems of international financing . . . salaries for the national staff . . . [and the fact that] many trained and capable national staff have left the project for better prospects elsewhere. . . . It has been a tooth-and-nail fight every inch of the way."[25]

It is unlikely that the VCR can provide its predicted educational impact. India was reported to have more than 300,000 VCRs in 1984 with more than 15,000 being added monthly.[26] Other estimates ran as high as one million. Like TV, it is proving to be an entertainment medium offering the selectivity of book buying in the film and video market. But this consists almost entirely of popular entertainment and pornography, creating very little incentive for dealers to stock educational items. Even though sales of VCRs are burgeoning, it would be overoptimistic to view it as a new important learning tool in the hands of the public, though it does have distinctive presentation and training advantages for audiences of governmental officials and health professionals, among others.

The failure to take into account this difference between materials (film, video, pamphlets, posters) and media (walls, hoardings, radio, TV, cinemas, magazines, newspapers, and people) leads to serious budgetary and logistical problems. Lumping them with media overlooks the need to budget for time, money, and means for their dissemination. This is why many film and video productions rarely achieve the exposure we intend for them, especially in rural areas of Third World countries. There are not enough trained people for the task, the cost is too high, and the mobile vans too few and break down too frequently in places where repairs are not readily available. In 1975, the Pakistan Population Planning Council maintained the biggest fleet of mobile audiovisual vans. In an interview, Joint Secretary M. Alludin expressed much discouragement with that means of reaching the public because of the difficulties in maintaining the vehicles, generators, and projectors in repair and the turnover of educational personnel in the field.[27]

To prevent such misjudgments, social marketers learn to differentiate between media and materials, show reverence for existing media, and accord them priority. They seek first to design materials appropriate for these media and eschew the high risk of those that require new media systems, unless circumstances allow no choice. The difference can be crucial. Radio and TV are established systems operating daily for hours on end. Messages designed for broadcast, therefore, do not demand the enormous start-up costs in people and monies. Even the expense of purchasing air time is a fraction of that required to set up a new communications infrastructure. When it falters under this tremendous financial and human overhead, its highly speculative nature becomes only too apparent, too late. This argues for the clear-cut distinction in advance between the costs of materials and the additional costs (in money, equipment, and/or people) of the media. We automatically do this with radio and TV. With other media, however, we have still to learn because we erroneously endow some materials with a magical capability for self-delivery. The undistributed stacks of literature and posters in the supply rooms of health agencies and the intermittent screenings of expensively produced films and video are silent testimony to this voodoo faith.

Formats: The Many Faces of the Mass Media

There are many different ways in which a medium delivers its offerings to the public. On TV there is comedy, news, serious drama, variety shows, musical extravaganzas, panel discussions, talk shows, interviews, sports, women's-interest programs, children's programs, soap operas, and more. Radio is mainly music, news, weather, and call-in or talk-show programs. The print media are variegated through news columns; features; and special sections like food, sports, theater, music, op-ed, editorials, and letters. These format variations are obviously intended to broaden the public appeal of the medium. *The mass media, marketing's primary tools, are not exempt from the need to market themselves.*

For social marketers, these varied formats reflect major target audience differences within the same medium—radio/TV station, newspaper, or magazine. It can make a significant difference in message delivery if a special news item on the dangers of alcohol consumption were to appear in the general news, the sports, or the food section of a newspaper. Readership varies with each (data are usually available). Of course, the decision is ultimately up to the editors—and this is one of the weaknesses of publicity as a social marketing tool, although that decision can sometimes be influenced by the way the item is prepared.

The unpredictability of publicity, hence its unreliability for educational purposes, has been noted by journalists themselves. Goody L. Solomon, a nationally syndicated columnist in the United States, in a speech to the National Food Processors Association, decried the sporadic attention given by the news media for food and nutrition affairs:

> During the 1970s, the food beat began to attract newspaper people. . . . Food sections started to go beyond the mere publication of recipes and delved into inflation, ersatz foods, the healthfulness of the diet of Americans and the activities of consumer groups. [They] tackled tough political questions and probed into alleged cancer risks of . . . suspect additives . . . even food stamps and the WIC [a national Women's Children and Infant Nutrition] program, received attention on food pages.

But in the 1980s, Solomon added,

> The pickings are slim when you look around for gutsy reporting about food issues. . . . there has been a sharp decline in reporting on national nutrition policies and the many questions that affect the quality and healthfulness of the American food supply. . . . The void leaves consumers ignorant of important nutrition aspects of the food they buy.

Though crediting food editors with "a healthy appetite for certain kinds of nutrition information"—the newsy, low-salt, low-sugar, low-fat issues— Solomon deplored much of it as "little or poor advice."[28]

For the broadcast media, the question of format has taken on special importance. For one thing, these are the most powerful of the mass media tools. For another, the significant distinctions among the available broadcast/telecast formats for social marketing messages remain badly blurred. In general, the problem reduces itself to the question—How does the health and nutrition educator decide which format to employ—a discussion (panel, interview, talk show), drama or soap opera, lecture, or the well-known advertising technique? At one time or another all have been tried and each undoubtedly has its value depending on the circumstances. The answer to our question can be provided only in terms of the target audience; the message; and the reach, frequency, and continuity objectives of the media strategy.

Given the preventive nature of public health education strategies and the need for simple, lucid instruction and motivation on a single diet or life-style practice, elaborate, highly delineated messages are usually contraindicated. This argues for the short message technique of advertising—social advertising, if you will—as a fundamental strategy for social marketing. Of course, a 15- or 30-minute program covers more ground and can provide more detail some subjects may require. But so much of what must be disseminated is one-idea-at-a-time material, not requiring a program format for its presentation. The usual strategic objective is to present a single idea with enough reach, frequency, and continuity to give the message insistence and impact. Put plainly, 30 one-minute or 60 thirty-second announcements in the course of one TV or radio week have a reach and frequency (and one-week continuity) far in excess of the half-hour program that appears one time, one day. Even when subject matter is more complicated, the experienced social marketer analyzes it for its component individual messages so that these may be transmitted in individual short message units. Because of the placement flexibility afforded by the technique, these messages, rotated frequently through the broadcast schedule, accumulate a sizeable total exposure.

There are several disadvantages of the longer-length program formats

1. They must compete with other programs of greater popular interest.
2. They, therefore, tend to attract and hold motivated audiences, while others tune away.
3. They are far more expensive to produce.
4. Even when the program is a regular feature (once or more a week), the demand for new material each time becomes insatiable, threatening deterioration in production quality.

The result is that such programs tend to have small audiences despite the flowing claims so often made for them. An actual example from the Dominican Republic illustrates the point. In that country, there had been for some years a radio program called "Hacia una Nueva Familia" ("Toward a New Family") that was funded by the International Planned Parenthood Federation. Its subject matter was family planning but in the broadest definition of that term so that while its major purpose was to en-

courage birth control practice, it also dealt with other aspects of family responsibility. It was broadcast from some eight locations in the country so
as to cover virtually the whole population. In Santo Domingo, the capital,
it was broadcast over Voz de Tropico, one of the top 15 or 16 stations in the
city, from 8:00 P.M. to 9:00 P.M., Monday to Friday. The radio program
was claimed to attract 28 percent of the women's audience—an unusually
successful venture, if true.

In 1976, Manoff International consultants, in the country for a nutrition education project, were extremely doubtful that any one program on
only one of many stations could attract such an audience. Inquiries of
local advertising agencies unearthed a report of a one-week survey of
radio listening made in October 1975 by the Association of Advertisers.[29]
It revealed that the 8:00-to-9:00 P.M. hour was one of the poorest in audience size. For all the stations combined, it represented only 8 percent of
the total daily woman's audience. In turn, Voz de Tropico had only a
minor share of that 8 percent. The average daily audience for the program
was only four women (within the fertile years) out of a total sample of
17,230 women interviewed!

But even were the results more encouraging, certain conclusions are
inescapable:

1. In a typical radio market in almost all countries a campaign needs more
   than one station for reach because audiences are too fragmented.
2. The message needs more than one time period because people listen at
   different times and no one time period can deliver more than a small
   share of the target audience.
3. By contrast, a program format usually occupies one time period daily on
   one station and is confined to a narrow audience.
4. Therefore, only by scattering the messages over several stations and in
   many time periods is it possible to fulfill the audience reach objectives and
   the frequency requirements of the task.

Peter Riding, a TV health program producer, relates a discouraging
experience in reviewing previous health programs. After studying some
four examples from the United States and England that, with one exception were all unsuccessful, he concluded that three main reasons for their
failures were: "(a) the series did not have a good transmission time [i.e.,
media strategy]; (b) there was only one program [i.e., frequency] on each
subject; (c) the programmes were only concerned with facts [i.e., message
design]."[30] The one exception was Canada's "Participaction," a series of
"very *short* films" [author's italics] offered to TV stations as a public service. "Their approach was to keep plugging away at the same theme for as
long as possible" because the "organizers believe that to change peoples'
life-styles is a long, slow process."

The result of this study led him to produce a series that would seek to avoid the pitfalls of the past. His program, "Feeling Great," was aired on BBC-1 as a ten-minute series in a fixed 6:30-P.M. Sunday time slot. The average audience proved to be only half that of the preceding program. It was still a respectable three million but three million others tuned away. Riding did not inform us which half he lost, those who needed it or those already converted. The question here is not whether such a series is beneficial. No sensible social marketer would argue it. The issue is whether a more effective use could have been made of TV for the same purpose and the same time, effort, and money.

Some purposes are well served by the program format—even on a one-time basis. Greenberg and Gantz assessed that the successful impact of "VD Blues," a U.S. TV special, came from its wide audience and the increased perception of the seriousness of the problem. The day after the telecast thousands streamed into VD clinics.[31] A similar experience is reported by Mendelsohn for the "National Driver Test," which attracted 30 million viewers, a mail response of more than a million letters, and motivated thousands to sign up for driving improvement courses.[32] The obvious appeal of this special was the unusual subject, the presentation of difficult driving situations, and the challenge to the viewer's ability to deal with them—another version of the ever popular quiz show. Such programs are unusual both for the topicality of their subjects and their relatively limited objectives. But the examples illustrate again the particularity of formats vis-à-vis objectives.

There is a popular notion that messages can be worked into the scripts of popular programs like soap operas, but it is largely illusory. For one thing, writers and producers are constitutionally opposed to having dramatic story lines tampered with for what they pejoratively describe as propaganda. When they are receptive to the idea, the constraints of the story line reduce the message to such subtlety—not to speak of content or message design—as almost to pass without notice. Even the eminently successful family planning soap opera, "*Acompañeme*" in Mexico ultimately needed to have a special three-minute advertising message on family planning inserted as an epilogue "to provide the information required to put the new behavior into practice."[33] This does not negate the program's value but illustrates the difficulties of accommodating the soap opera format—or any program, in fact—to the needs of an explicit social marketing message. Either the story line or the message is compromised. This is not to suggest that these formats are worthless for social marketing. But only with realistic assessments can social marketers use them to best advantage.

Every generalization has its exceptions. The "Radio Farm Forum" has been a successful format worldwide and the experiences in Canada and in India are perhaps its most notable examples. In India it is an early morning program, broadcast before farm families take off for the fields. The format permits presentations of new agricultural or community development ideas in the form of brief lectures, discussion by forum participants, interviews with experts and farmers, and question-and-answer sessions based on inquiries sent in by the farmer audience. In each village the farm forum is made up of about 20 members who listen regularly as a group to the half-hour, twice-weekly broadcast. Following the broadcast, the village forum considers whether the ideas received from the program are applicable to the local situation. The discussion is led by the forum leader, who is the liaison with the program producers for feedback, comments, or questions.

Originally tried in Poona in 1956, the "Radio Farm Forum" was expanded in 1959 and made part of the Five-Year Plan after that. Much credit for the Green Revolution has been given to the program by farmers and officials, both.[34] The "Farm Forum" format is popular and effective throughout the world and is believed to have originated in Canada where it is still broadcast. It is not difficult to assess the reasons for the appropriateness of this format for the social marketing task: the target audience was precisely defined; the subject material, expansive and diverse and related to the economic interests of the audience; the audience, strongly motivated toward it; and the time period, right. Given such a set of circumstances, the program format proves indispensable.

There is no one right format for every problem and its messages. The right decision is forthcoming from the answers to these questions: How do we reach our target audience? What format will enable us to reach the greatest number of them? What format will enable us to reach them with maximum frequency—and with a consistent message to enhance memorability? What message format will make sure that the message is simple, clear, complete, and memorable?

Notes

1. Ward, G.W., Morrison, W., Schreiber, G., "Pilot Study of Health Professionals: Awareness and Opinions of the Hypertension Information in the Mass Media They Use," *Public Health Reports,* National Heart, Lung and Blood Institute, Bethesda, Maryland, March–April 1982, Vol. 97, No. 2.

2. Akhloq and Owais Research, an unpublished report for the Population Planning Council in 1975, Lahore, Pakistan.

3. Atkin, C.K., "Mass Communication Research Principles for Health Education," in *Health Education by Radio and Television* (Ed. M. Meyer), K.G. Saur, Munich, Germany, 1981, pp. 41–55.

4. Klapper, J., *Effects of Mass Communication*, Free Press, Glencoe, Illinois, 1960.

5. Bauer, R., "The Obstinate Audience," *American Psychologist*, 19/1964, pp. 319–328.

6. Roberts, D., Maccoby, N., "Information Processing Persuasion," in *New Models for Communication Research*, (ed. P. Clarke) Sage, Beverly Hills, California, 1973, pp. 269–302.

7. Wright, P., "Factors Affecting Cognitive Resistance to Advertising," *Journal of Consumer Research*, February 1975, pp. 1–9.

8. Kline, F.G., "Adolescents and Family Planning Information," in *The Uses and Gratifications Approach to Mass Communication Research* (eds. J.G. Blumler, E. Katz) Sage, Beverly Hills, California, 1974, pp. 113–136.

9. Manoff, R.K., "The Mass Media Family Planning Campaign for the United States," in *Readings in Public and Non-Profit Marketing* (Eds. H. Lovelock, C.B. Weinberg) Scientific Press, Palo Alto, California, 1978, pp. 93–97.

10. Research Division of Adcom Advertising, Karachi, Pakistan, December 1972.

11. Chabra, R., "Building on Success in Orissa," *People*, IPPF, London, 1983, Vol. 10, No. 3, p. 8.

12. Aloysius, C., "Can Puppets Be Effective Communicators?" *PSC Newsletter*, UNICEF, December 1983, New York.

13. Atkin, C.K. Op. Cit., p. 47.

14. Miller, P.V., Morrison, A.J., Kline, F.G., "Approaches to Characterising Information Environments," International Communications Association, New Orleans, Louisiana, April 1974.

15. Atkin, C., Op. Cit., p. 43.

16. Ouellet, B.L., Melia, P., "Toward a Generation of Non-Smoking Canadians," Hygie, *International Journal of Health Education*, IUHE, July 1983, II/83/2, pp. 34–38.

17. Hudson, H.E., et al., "The Role of Telecommunications in Socioeconomic Development," International Telecommunications Union, Geneva, Switzerland, 1979.

18. Stevens, W.K., "India to Pursue Down-to-Earth Goals from 22,300-Mile Orbit," the New York *Times*, August 29, 1983, p. B6.

19. As quoted in "Crosscurrents," *Science* 84, American Association for the Advancement of Science, December 1984, p. 99.

20. "AID Bulletin," *Horizons*, USAID, September 1983, Vol. 2, No. 8.

21. Kline, G.F., Pavlik, J.V., "Adolescent Health Information Acquisition from the Broadcast Media," *Health Education by Radio and Television*, (Ed. M. Meyer), K.G. Saur, Munich, 1981, pp. 92–117.

22. Miller, P.V., Morrison, A.J., Kline, F.G., op. cit.

23. Kline, G.F., Pavlik, J.V., op. cit., pp. 100–101.

24. Diseker, R.A., Michielutte, R., Morrison, V., "Use and Reported Effectiveness of Tel-Med," *American Journal of Public Health*, March 1980, Vol. 70, No. 3, pp. 229–234.

25. Fraser, C., "Adapting Communication Technology for Rural Development," *Ceres*, FAO, Rome, Italy, September 10, 1983, No. 95, p. 23.

26. Stevens, W.K., "Bazaars of India Are Now a Toyland of High Tech," the New York *Times,* February 2, 1984, p. 2.

27. Manoff International Inc., "Mass Media and Nutrition Education," report of an assessment visit to Pakistan for USAID, Manoff International, New York, March 5, 1975, p. 26.

28. Solomon, G.L., "Food Editors Slip on Nutrition News," *Nutrition Week,* Community Nutrition Institute, Washington, D.C., November 24, 1983, p. 4.

29. *Association Dominicana De Anunciantes,* audience measurement study of radio stations in the Dominican Republic, Santo Domingo, Dominican Republic, October 1975.

30. Riding, P., "Producing for Health Education: How to Reach the Target Audience," *Health Education by Television and Radio,* (Ed. M. Meyer), K.G. Saur, Munich, 1981, pp. 343–351.

31. Greenberg, B., Gantz, W., "Public Television and Taboo Topics, The Impact of 'VD Blues,'" *Public Telecommunications Review,* April 1976, pp. 59–64.

32. Mendelsohn, H., "Some Reasons Why Information Campaigns Can Succeed," *Public Opinion Quarterly,* 37/1973, pp. 50–61.

33. Paniagua, L., "Selling Values through Social Soap Opera," *People,* IPPF, London, Vol. 10, No. 3, 1983.

34. *New Educational Media in Action: Case Studies for Planners,* Vol. 1, reprinted offset, Aubin, Poitiers, 1969.

9

Designing the Social Marketing Message

The scene is a little village about 20 miles from Managua, the capital of Nicaragua. Maria Rodriguez had noticed that Pablito was sick. It was diarrhea again. "Make him Super-Limonada," her older daughter said. "Like they say on the radio."

For weeks she too had been hearing it on the radio from Managua. "Super-Limonada fights diarrhea," the voice said. "Make it when your baby gets diarrhea. A liter of clean water, lemon, sugar—like lemonade—and a 'pinch' of salt to make it 'super'—Super-Limonada."

It had been a one-minute drama between a mother of a baby sick with diarrhea and a wise village woman, Donna Carmen. It came on like Coca-Cola or the jingle for cigarettes. "Super-Limonada," Donna Carmen had said, "puts back water the baby lost from diarrhea." The salt kept it in. Sugar and lemon were for flavor and other reasons she couldn't remember.

"I'll ask Carmelita Robles," she answered her daughter.

"She will tell you 'yes,'" Lena replied. "Yesterday I saw her give it to her Juan. 'Super-Limonada,' she said, 'to fight diarrhea.' Just like on the radio, mama."[1]

Maria related this incident to me. Such are the uses to which marketing techniques were being put as early as a decade ago.[2] Today social marketing is a major instrument in Indonesia's Nutrition Education Improvement Pilot Project,[3] Brazil's breast-feeding campaign,[4] and several others.

The advertising technique is an adaptation of a wisdom as old as Man, the Teacher, evident in the Ten Commandments, the Rock Edicts of Ashoka, the five tenets of Hinduism, the strictures of Islam, of Buddhism, and of every philosophy that has ever sought suzerainty over the human mind. The essence of the advertising technique is the short message delivered frequently to a defined target audience. If it is perceived as a commercial eccentricity, it is because commercial marketers have adroitly monopolized it.

This does not suggest that social advertising should mimic the commercial food marketer who is competing with other brands of the same product—a soft drink, a snack food, a coffee or tea. Because of superficial differentiation between brands, there is little meaningful content to their advertising. It becomes a contest of moods and emotions; content is derationalized. The seduction of the audience is attempted by an ingeniously contrived product image. This explains the dominance of jingles, humor, and sex in commercial advertising. None of these is relevant either to the product or to the consumer's purchase decision.

The needs of health educators are a sharp contrast. Meaningful content and rational presentation are indispensable. In Indonesia, the Nutrition Education Improvement Pilot Project used radio to educate rural mothers about nutrition for pregnant and lactating women and their infants, the treatment of diarrhea, and the benefits of monthly weighings. The approach taken was to use social advertising, the commercial technique given a new educational dimension.

Because health education is a prevention strategy, its messages are instructive and simple and the advertising technique can be highly effective. The key lies in the message. Not only must it convey meaningful content and motivation but also overcome audience resistance to change. This overcoming of *resistance points* may be its crucial function. In the Philippines, resistance to enriching the *lugaw* was traced to rigid adherence to tradition. Also, green vegetables were opposed because they cause gas and diarrhea in infants. In the United States, a national family planning campaign had to deal with ethnic antagonism to the idea of birth control. Segments of the black community perceived it as being aimed at them by a hostile white community. The advertising was designed so that its intent for all population groups was clearly evident.[5] In a vasectomy promotion campaign for Planned Parenthood in Houston, concern among males for their masculinity was relieved by having the radio messages delivered by men who had undergone the operation and who offered to consult with interested listeners.[6] In Ecuador, indifference to iodized salt was rooted in ignorance of goiter (*coto*) as a serious disease.[7]

In Indonesia, the use of only the left breast in feeding was commonplace presumably because of the Muslim injunction that the right hand is for food and the left for toilet. Therefore, a busy mother breastfeeding on demand was compelled to keep her right hand free (and her right breast unused) for her cooking chores. This led her eventually to conclude that the right breast was for water (no suckling, little milk) and the left for food.

These *resistance points* are obstacles social advertising has to overcome. Otherwise, they may achieve high awareness—for example, that "breast is best" or, in family planning, that "a small family is a happy family"—but be unable to convert that awareness to practice. Only messages designed to deal decisively with *resistance points* stand a chance of narrowing the gap between awareness and practice. The Resistance Resolution Model in message design can be helpful. While our example deals with the short messages of social advertising for radio, the model is applicable to all mass communications situations.

The Resistance Resolution Model

Searching out *resistance points* has been referred to as a major purpose of qualitative research (i.e., the focus-group interview or the individual in-depth interview) in advance of strategy and message development. The theory is that no communication, whether interpersonal, intergroup, or mass media, can be effective without overcoming hurdles of custom, religion, or psychology. It is based on the experience that messages which fail to resolve such *resistance points* risk the possibility of rejection. This is consistent with the widely observed phenomenon that awareness and understanding of an instruction do not necessarily guarantee its acceptance (e.g., cognitive dissonance) even where it includes a strong incentive for doing so.

In the Philippines, investigators for a nutrition education campaign to persuade mothers of a new way to enrich *lugaw*, the local weaning food, were repeatedly confronted with the objection that "it is not the custom."[8] It became necessary to demonstrate the adaptability of custom to changing circumstance in order to obtain cultural permission for urging a revision in the traditional *lugaw* recipe. In the Andes of Ecuador, the natives of Imbabura believed that endemic *coto*, the Quechua word for goiter, was a normal condition. The communication to persuade adoption of iodized salt had first to convince Imbaburans that *coto* was a disease.[9]

Conventional attempts to create paradigms or models of this process do not usually embrace this interaction hypothesis in their linear analysis of the sending-receiving process. When they attempt to do so, they become increasingly complex and cumbersome. According to Howell,*

---

*I am indebted to Dr. Howell for his fascinating interactive dyadic model of interpersonal communications that first suggested the theoretical approach I have taken. Some years ago I gave the name *resistance points* to those impediments to communication that lurk in the mind of every audience. When in the course of searching for a suitable theoretical framework I came upon Dr. Howell's construct and its concept of the internal dialogue, I saw immediately their compatibility with my thoughts on social marketing communications.

Extended analysis identified more variables and since the parts are presumed to add up to the whole, none can be left out of a diagrammatic representation. Thus, modern models of the communication process are not quickly and easily memorized and used.

A holistic approach to model design authorizes the designer to cluster groups of unspecified variables in ways that dramatize the point he wishes to make. This makes it possible to create simple models that say a great deal, because the mode is metaphor rather than realistic or literal symbolization. Instead of supplying all the details, the metaphoric model guides the reader into a sequence of his own thoughts, opinions and experiences. Non-Western cultures are, incidentally, much more comfortable with the metaphoric model than with detailed analytic representations. Their scholars expect to have directions suggested to them rather than to be instructed literally and exhaustively.[10]

To epitomize mass media communication, we may employ a modified version of Howell's interactive dyadic model of interpersonal communication: the Resistance Resolution Model. Though both consist of communication between two sources, mass media communication is reactive; interpersonal is interactive. The absence of interaction leaves no immediate opportunity for adjusting the mass media message to unexpected resistances. Thus, the mass media message designer must identify these in advance to overcome them in the messages and, through pretesting, to confirm the effect.

Let us examine the point by reference to the situation of a Filipino mother listening to her radio in Iloilo province on the island of Panay, an actual case from Manoff International's experience.[11] She was tuned into a music program from the commercial station in Iloilo City. Instead of the ubiquitous jingle for Coca-Cola, she heard for the first time a new one-minute minidrama. It caught her ear because it was about a child of five months, the same age as her Gregorio.

The minidrama was one of the radio messages designed for a nutrition education campaign launched by the Institute of Nutrition.[12] The key elements of the message were:

Element A: Enrich *lugaw,* the traditional rice-porridge weaning food, through a new recipe. Add:
1.   A drop of oil.
2.   Green vegetables.
3.   Fish.

Element B: Reasons why and benefits to be derived:
1.   A baby of 5 months needs *lugaw* in addition to breast milk.
2.   But the rice and water are not enough.

   3.   A five-month old needs:
        (a)   Fish for protein and growth.
        (b)   Green vegetables for vitamins.
        (c)   Oil for more calories.

Element C: Proper preparation of enriched *lugaw:*
   1.   Wash salt from fish.
   2.   Chop and cook vegetables well.
   3.   Add oil.
   4.   Mash altogether with *lugaw.*

Element D: Call on the local support system:
   1.   More help and details are available from Community Health Worker
        (CHW), Home Management Technician (HMT), or doctor (MD).

   The ideal situation occurred when all four elements were heard, remembered, integrated with one another in her mind, and accepted so that
the knowledge conveyed by the minidrama message was agreeably received and her attitude positively affected. Consequently, she was persuaded to use the recommended recipe and adopted the desired behavior
change. Obviously, in real life such an outcome is the product of a more
elaborate process involving far more frequent exposure to the message
over time, reinforced by its socialization through word of mouth from
other mothers who have been exposed to it and by its institutionalization
through the health care system (the CHW, HMT, and MD).

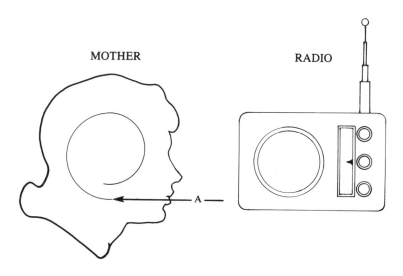

Figure 9.1.   Message element A is received/accepted.

In our theoretical construction let us assume the combined influence of these factors and focus exclusively on the message design to examine the ways in which apperceptions of existing behaviors and perceptions of new ones affect reaction. It will help to illuminate the need for anticipating *resistance points* and dealing with them in the message design. The failure either to identify the source of the *resistance point* or to resolve it inadequately in the message creates a dissonance in the mind that Howell aptly calls the internal dialogue.

We can attempt to depict the process through a model in which the mother is listening to the message on her radio. In our ideal situation, Element A is received and accepted by the mother and she is in harmony with what it says, its language, its tonality, and its people. This is depicted in Figure 9.1 as the first ring of an uninterrupted spiral.

In Figure 9.2 we see how Element B advances the spiral through its second ring of acceptance.

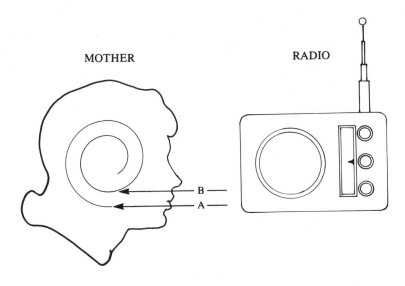

Figure 9.2.   Element B is received/accepted and integrated with A.

Figures 9.3 and 9.4 support the process of acceptance through the third and fourth rings to complete the convergence that is intended to symbolize the reaching of our target—hitting the bull's eye, as it were, of persuasion with the arrow of a perfect message.

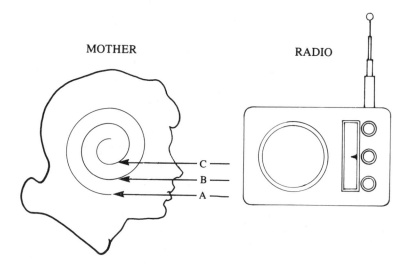

Figure 9.3. Element C is received/accepted and integrated with A and B.

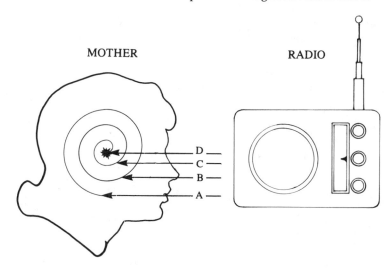

Figure 9.4. Element D is received/accepted and integrated with A, B, and C.

In real life, the perfect message is an ideal, forever thwarted by circumstances either beyond our knowledge or ability to control. But the message designer is engaged in a continuing struggle to know and control. Figures 9.5 to 9.8 pictorialize a more realistic situation with our Filipino mother and illustrate why this struggle is important. In Figure 9.5 message Element A is delivered and received but almost immediately it encounters a *resistance point* and what should have been the first spiral ring now turns into a closed circle of internal dialogue.

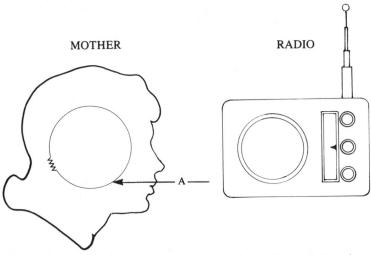

Figure 9.5. Element A encounters a *resistance point,* and turns into a closed ring of internal dialogue.
ww = resistance point

Our mother cannot accept the suggestion of a recipe to enrich the *lugaw*. It triggers a conflict with custom and, because it offers no resolution of the conflict, distracts the mother from the matter at hand.

A second internal dialogue is provoked as we see in Figure 9.6 by Ele-

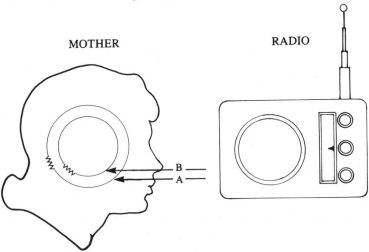

Figure 9.6. Element B encounters another *resistance point* and becomes the subject of a second internal dialogue.

ment B despite its reasons why and benefits to be derived. She resists once more because of the belief she shares with many others that such foods are inappropriate for infants, causing gas and diarrhea. For the second time this leads to a closed circle of internal dialogue and a disconnection from the preceding message element.

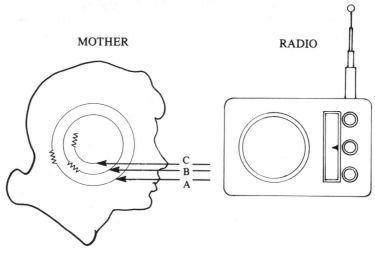

Figure 9.7. Element C encounters a third *resistance point.* The incomplete ring suggests all communications has broken off.

In Figure 9.7 the process of disconnection worsens. Element C,

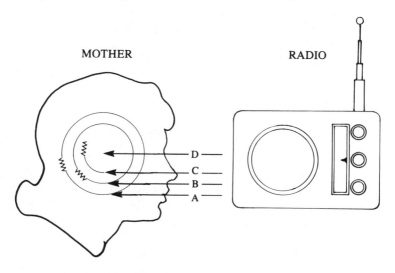

Figure 9.8. Element D in this example fails to register at all.

which discussed preparation of the *lugaw,* is rejected out of hand as ir- relevant because of the resistance to the recipe to begin with. The internal dialogue is scarcely begun before the whole matter is summarily termi- nated. Her patience seems to have been exhausted.

In Figure 9.8, Element D stands no chance at all. Either the mother is preoccupied with the internal dialogues provoked by A and B or, in reject- ing the whole idea, ceases to listen at all.

Far from being perfect, our message is a failure. The model illustrates several key insights about message design. It makes clear once again that cognitive treatment of messages is not enough, that usually facts do not speak for themselves. Conative and emotive factors are invariably pro- voked into *resistance points,* cognitive material is sidetracked, and an in- ternal dialogue preempts its place. This is similar to the "powerful ex- traneous element [that] takes over the thinking mechanism of each par- ticipant" in interpersonal communications, according to Howell.

> Trying to account for apparent absurdity crowds out the business to be transacted. Such an irrelevant train of thought preventing the normal use of resources to solve problems and do other works we term an "inter- nal dialogue." . . . The cause of dissonance must be identified, con- fronted and resolved. Only then, when internal dialogue is controlled can the interaction proceed to combine resources of participants in ac- complishing their common objective.[13]

Interpersonal communicators are privileged to deal with the dissonance in the course of the interaction. The social marketer, making use of the mass media, must rely on preparatory research into audience knowledge, attitude, custom, and behavior to elicit target audience reaction to pro- posed behavioral concepts and objectives before their translation into message elements. This is perhaps the most important of the disciplines of message design and at this point it would be useful to discuss them all.

The Disciplines of Message Design Strategy

Designing a social marketing message is like playing with a *ma- trushka* doll, the ancient Russian nesting of identical hollow wooden dolls, each one small enough to fit inside the other. Lift off the first and, presto, there is one more slightly smaller, an apple-cheeked, buxom peas- ant woman in the leaping colors of her traditional garb. Lift her off and there is yet another and another. Experienced social marketers know how an apparently simple problem turns out, on probing, to be a *matrushka*— a nesting of problems.

Is it possible, for example, when designing a message for breast-feed-ing mothers not to peek inside her and discover that she is more than one? She works at home. She is a salaried worker. She is rich. She is poor. And for each of her there are distinct concerns to cope with and psychological barriers to lower before she can be helped to breast-feed.

Peer deeply into the breast-feeding *matrushka* again and there is more than a nesting of mothers. There are doctors who discourage breast-feeding, hospitals that separate a mother from her newborn, milk com-panies that woo her with bottle feeds, legislators who are numb to need-ful laws, businesspeople who violate them when they pass, and officials who are blind to the violations.

Even the message is a *matrushka*. For example, improving infant nutrition means exclusive breast-feeding for the first four months of age; after four months, the introduction of a proper weaning food in addition to breast-feeding; and at eight or nine months, the transition to food the family eats. Each stage calls for a special message to the mother. Nor is that all in many poor countries. What about diarrhea management at every age? And the importance of weighing? More messages. What of the mother? Improving her infant's nutrition demands a better diet for her. What about the expectant mother? Again, more messages.

How shall the social marketer and the message designer deal with all this? First, obviously, is the principle of priority. At any given time, one audience and its problems take precedence and the rest can be ranked in importance. Second, is the principle of zero-sum knowledge, which counsels never to accept anything on faith, to start with a presumption of total ignorance. This means challenging every opinion, every conclusion. It may slow matters and offend the vanity of some authorities at the start but it will advance the cause more rapidly and with greater assurance once it is engaged.

Chapter 6 set forth the process for making planning decisions. Though the tasks involved may be the responsibility of others, the mes-sage designer should be familiar with them. They are the source for all the material from which messages will be fashioned. Once priorities have been set, strategies agreed to, target audiences described, objectives iden-tified, and necessary messages chosen, the task of message design will benefit from a strategy of tested disciplines born of social marketing ex-periences in Ecuador, India, Pakistan, Bangladesh, the Philippines, In-donesia, Brazil, several East African countries, as well as the United States.

Message design strategy is guided by disciplines affecting factors of

1. Content
2. Design

3. Persuasion
4. Memorability

Each of these has an important part to play in overall message impact. Not every message will make either the same use or any use at all of these factors but they should be considered seriously every time. They serve the designer as a checklist so he or she will be less apt to overlook the decisive contribution some factor could make.

Content Factors (1.0)

Content factors include

1.1. The problem
1.2. Target audience
1.3. *Resistance points*
1.4. Solution
1.5. Required action
1.6. Authoritative source

(1.1) *The problem* has to be dealt with so everyone comprehends it clearly. It is not satisfactory to identify the problem as the decline of breast-feeding. This is the overall problem of the program. But for an individual message directed at the mother with a job outside the home, for example, the specific problem is how to manage a breast-feeding regimen around her job.

Thus, focused identification of the (1.2) *target audience* is a significant factor. We have already noted that mothers are a segmented group. A message designed to build maternal confidence must somehow invoke her presence so as to create an empathetic environment for winning her attention. Typically, she is riddled with self-doubts and other (1.3) *resistance points*. The research should have detected them. They must be countered and neutralized so she is freed to respond to the message.

The objective is for her to be receptive to the (1.4) *solution*. The solution depends on her carrying out (1.5) *required actions*. Presumably these were concept-tested earlier with a sampling of the target group and the determination made that the actions are reasonable, practical, and acceptable.

The message may benefit from an *authoritative source* to lend credence to its claims. This may be a doctor or another respected member of the community, the community health worker, the midwife, or the lady home visitor. Sometimes it can be a famous personality or government official. The Population Crisis Committee quoted a Tunisian peasant woman: "If President Bourguiba says I can take the pill, who is my husband to say no?"[14] Choosing an appropriate authority depends on the message, the authority, and popular perceptions of the relevance between the two.

Design Factors (2.0)

Design factors include

2.1. The single idea
2.2. Language and cultural relevance
2.3. Situation and character identification
2.4. Distinctive message style
2.5. Low fatigue index

Each message—a radio spot, poster, film, or booklet—is more effective when it is confined to a (2.1) *single idea* directed at a special problem of a specific target audience. Such messages are more likely to be absorbed, concentrated on, and reacted to. Furthermore, a single idea message enables the designer to say more in less time and to weave into it the elements necessary to enhance its effectiveness. Too many ideas, thrown haphazardly together, produce a clutter in which no single idea can be vigorously advocated. The heart of the idea—a recipe, for example, or a new health practice—should be demonstrated if possible. One advantage of TV is its capacity for demonstration with sight, sound, and motion. But even radio offers the opportunity to picture the instruction with the spoken word; print, with pictures or drawings and the written word. Whatever the medium, demonstration enhances impact and comprehension. Even in booklets and other printed materials, ideals should be sorted out and developed individually for easier reference and greater impact.

(2.2) *Language and cultural relevance* is the guiding rule of presentation. The style and expression employed must be suitable. The designer is aware that the purpose is to advocate change. But the proposal must be set in a compatible cultural context. The discipline calls for relevance but not rigidity, and warns us not to be enslaved by idiom. Every language has its cliches; every culture, its deeply etched patterns. Social marketing's objective is to revise, to overturn a preconceived idea or notion and to persuade people to view it from a new perspective and, thus, to be receptive to a new accommodation. This rearranging of people's views may be aided by fresh arrangements of words and ideas, not necessarily by the familiar ones to which old practices are anchored.

So in social marketing programs, the retreat to idiom in language and ideas may rob us of persuasive impact. An intrusive, mind-jarring effect is the social marketer's obligatory style for messages to change old ideas. Communications began the day the human animal discovered he or she was not alone. From that moment on new ideas either added to or replaced received wisdom. Thus, change is unremitting and the primary tool for its control is the message. If there are personalities involved, the (2.3) *situation and character identification* must be thoughtfully established. Slavish mirroring of target types is often inadvisable. People may more readily identify with aspirations than with their realities. A well-known sports personality or a famous woman may offer more potent identification value to target audiences than people like themselves. The testing of alternatives can help the designer decide.

In Iran, Robert W. Gillespie of the Population Council reported in 1970 the test results of six versions of a family planning poster in which the mother was pictured in traditional garb. A seventh version had been included at the last moment showing her in the fashionable dress of a middle-class Teheran woman, which provoked a heated debate about whether village women could identify with it. This last-minute entry won the test hands down, evidence that for social marketing purposes identification with aspiration may be more advisable than with status quo.

Since the campaign is likely to employ more than one message and in different media, it will benefit from a (2.4) *distinctive message style.* The sounds, look, tonality, and key language should be consistent, message to message, medium to medium. Such treatment has a cumulative effect on public awareness. Music can be a helpful device so long as it supports rather than dominates the message.

Messages accumulate impact with repetition so long as they maintain their consistency. No message lasts forever. Eventually it wears out, loses its effect, and must be replaced with a new version that retains the old content in a new guise. Sometimes it is replaced prematurely because those close to the campaign are usually the first to tire of it. The message designer must fend off such assaults. The surest weapon is a message with a (2.5) *low fatigue index*—that remains interesting and captivating as well as instructive and persuasive for as long as possible. The finest creative instincts of the designer are called for. But message familiarity is sometimes mistaken for message fatigue. Familiarity is what we aspire to and is not to be abandoned once achieved. It is precisely at that point that our message performs its most valuable function—reinforcing awareness and winning acceptance. It is the social marketer's responsibility to assure a media strategy that provides for continuity of exposure.

Persuasion Factors (3.0)

Persuasion factors include

    3.1. Reason why
    3.2. Empathy
    3.3. Concern arousal
    3.4. Action capability
    3.5. Believability
    3.6. Creativity
    3.7. Benefits

A message is obliged to offer the (3.1) *reason* for its proposal and *why* it is desirable. This *reason why* may help dispel doubt before it arises and throws up a barrier to the rest of the message.

Because emotion always affects decision, (3.2) *empathy* with the audience is essential. The audience must sense an emotional assurance that someone cares and understands the problem. Advice is rarely taken from an unsympathetic or indifferent source. But what is called for is the affinity, the harmony of empathy—not the compassion of sympathy, which runs the danger of patronizing the audience. Empathy is the response to the other person's perception of his or her own feelings. The question of true feeling does not enter here because it is not answerable. In fact, it is not even a useful question.

But the audience must also be made to feel concern with the problem, otherwise, why bother? (3.3) *Concern arousal,* not guilt or paralyzing fear, is a valuable message equity. It is the incentive to give attention and to adopt the idea. To a mother, growth is meaningful but even more meaningful may be lack of growth. It is no accident that pellagra, beriberi, rickets, scurvy, and goiter have been more memorable concepts than the positive statements of good health, strong bones, or a balanced diet. It is an ancient wisdom that the negative statement can sometimes be the most positive instruction. Eight of the Ten Commandments are negative.

(3.4) *Action capability* is the compatibility between what the message asks of the audience and what it is capable to perform despite limitations of income, time, transportation, food availability, water supply, and fuel. Even the slightest conflict between the two fatally impairs the message.

(3.5) *Believability* of the statement of the problem, solution, message environment, and promised benefits depends on the belief systems of the audience. These vary among audiences. Messages must contain themselves within the audience's permissible limits. The temptation to go beyond—to oversell—can be overwhelming. The results are almost always damaging; the audience becomes disillusioned and is lost to the effort.

There is no formula for (3.6) *creativity.* Talented message designers, like talented writers and artists, bring to the task an imagination and a feel for reaching people's minds and hearts. They add the extra dimension that turns an educational message into a creative experience. But this creative flair is subject to rigid disciplines. No matter how brilliantly conceived messages may be, they must first respond to the approved strategies. Seduction by a clever idea or an enchanting jingle that are off-strategy is not uncommon but it must be resisted. My favorite response to such message designs is, "This is a brilliant idea. Now find me the problem."

But the promise of (3.7) *benefits* from the new behavior is something the audience expects to hear. Otherwise, there is little incentive. The benefits must be realistic, neither overblown nor indifferently offered. Too often, family planning campaigns make their promise in empty, meaningless slogans. In India, Bangladesh, and other countries, "the small family is a happy family" has been the thematic cornerstone. Such a message may promote awareness (which is, incidentally, rarely a problem in most countries today) but accomplish very little in dealing with the deeper level blocks—the *resistance points*—that limit the conversion of awareness into practice. For one thing, the claim is not believable. There are many large happy families in these countries and unhappy small ones. In fact, one cause of unhappiness is the inability to have the desirable number of children. Family planning message strategy must be based on other incentives to which the target population can respond. The challenge to the creative social marketer is to prospect for them through ingenious inquiry among the people.

Memorability Factors (4.0)

Memorability factors include

4.1. Idea reinforcement
4.2. Minimizing distractions
4.3. Reprise (repetition)

To seat the new idea and persuade its adoption calls for (4.1) *idea reinforcement.* The aim is for maximum awareness in the well-founded belief that it will make a qualitative difference in attitude and behavior. Repeated references to key phrases maximizes awareness. Here again, themed music (but rarely entire jingle messages, despite their popularity) can be a potent reinforcement device. They are usually remembered for the wrong reasons—not for the serious idea we aim to transmit. Commercial jingles are effective because their objective is simple awareness of a brand name and a slogan. Health messages have much more meaning to convey.

Keeping out clutter means (4.2) *minimizing distractions,* like offering more detail than the audience needs to know. "What will happen if they do not know this?" is a good test of the information. Every element must be essential to the message or be eliminated. Time and attention of the audience must not be trifled with. (4.3) *Reprise* is the repetition of key elements to enhance memorability.

The Anatomy of an Actual Message

In all human endeavor perfection is a goal to strive for despite the unlikelihood of its attainment. "A man's reach," the English poet, Robert Browning, wrote, "should exceed his grasp, or what's a heaven for?" The legendary American advertising man, Leo Burnett, once said, "Reach for the stars. You may never get one but at least you won't come up with a fistful of mud."

Message designers for social marketing must also reach for the stars. The message design disciplines as well as the insights of our communications theory are intended to provide this grasp for perfection despite its ever-elusive nature. Only the upward striving can produce the improvements in message design on which the impact of social marketing ventures ultimately depend.

An analysis of an actual message used in the Philippines project referred to earlier will illustrate their application. In the Philippines, the research and concept testing revealed sources of potential *resistance points* as well as of action incentives. These findings were critical inputs in the design of the six messages for radio, each 60 seconds in length, with the same content but with variations in situation and emphasis. Here in English translation from Illongo, the local tongue, is one of them, a mini-drama between a young mother, Lita, and her mother.

LITA: Mama, what are you putting in my baby's *lugaw*?
MOTHER: A drop of oil, some chopped green vegetables and fish.

LITA: Where did you get this strange idea?
MOTHER: From the doctor on the radio. Listen!
DOCTOR: *(filter)* After six months a baby needs *lugaw* as well as breast
             milk, but *lugaw* must be mixed with fish that gives protein
             for muscles and brain. Green vegetables for vitamins. Oil
             for more weight on his body.
LITA: But, mama, six-month old baby can't digest such foods.
MOTHER: Sh-h. Listen to the doctor on the radio.
DOCTOR: *(filter)* A six-month old baby can digest these foods. Just
             wash the salt from the dried fish, chop the vegetables and
             cook them well, add a little oil, and mash with the *lugaw.*
LITA: But, mama, you didn't feed me like that.
MOTHER: How could I know? I didn't even own a radio. Times
             change. You live and learn.
LITA: Mama, you must be sad that all the old ways are changing.
MOTHER: Not all the old ways are changing. But only a fool remains
             with an old way when there is a new, better way.
DOCTOR: *(filter)* For help with your baby see the home management
             technicians or community worker or the local doctor.

A line-by-line analysis of this message reveals the determined attempts to prevent internal dialogue by utilizing the insights gained from the formative research. We also note, where appropriate, the effort made to observe the disciplines of message design with commentary about their usefulness to the message. We do this by noting the number of a specific factor from our outline discussion of disciplines—for example, (1.6) *authoritative source*—to indicate how it relates to each message element. Table 9.1 is a reproduction in outline of these disciplines together with a scoring chart for the message. The reader may want to refer to it while reading what follows.

First, there was the selection of the doctor as authority (1.6). In many parts of the developing world, the doctor is not the practical resource in either health care or illness unless death threatens. For one thing, doctors end up as city creatures even when in rare instances they originate in the countryside. They are the health ministers of the middle class. We all know about this problem of doctor distribution in every country. While he or she may be resorted to only when serious illness strikes or death threatens, the doctor is regarded as the ultimate authority. Even in countries in which folk medicine and the shaman are still formidable institutions, the authority, if not the practice, of the formally trained and licensed medical establishment has penetrated the countryside.

Furthermore, the doctor is a dialectic authority, representing a tradition in which knowledge accumulates, is changed by its accumulation, and to which human behavior is in continuous adaptation. This philosophy of the admissibility of change and of human adaptability to its

Table 9.1. Outline of The Disciplines of Message Design

Discipline Factors	Number of Reflections in "Lita and Her Mother"
1. Content	
1.1 The problem	x
1.2 Target audience	x
1.3 *Resistance points*	xxxx
1.4 Solution	xx
1.5 Required action	xx
1.6 Authoritative source	x
2. Design	
2.1 The single idea	x
2.2 Language and cultural relevance	xxx
2.3 Situation and character identification	xxx
2.4 Distinctive message style	x
2.5 Low fatigue index	xx
3. Persuasion	
3.1 Reason why	x
3.2 Empathy	xxx
3.3 Concern arousal	xxxx
3.4 Action capability	x
3.5 Believability	xxxx
3.6 Creativity	xxx
3.7 Benefits	x
4. Memorability	
4.1 Idea reinforcement	xx
4.2 Minimizing distractions	xx
4.3 Reprise (repetition)	x

implications is not in historic opposition to ancient custom. Change has always been a custom—its rate varying from one period to another. Thus, the notion that modernity encourages change and custom opposes it is mythical.

Human culture in all its aspects—physical, social, and economic—has always been the product either of human adaptation to the environment or of environmental adaptation to human need. The pace of cultural response to environmental change is a reliable measure of the health of a society and its survival capability. Today, the rapid rate of environmental change demands equally swift cultural responses as a matter of cultural health and survival. It is not debatable. What is debatable is whether the rate of environmental change is in society's best interest and, if not, what measures can be taken to arrest it. Once taken, these measures dramatically ease the pressure for social behavioral change. The message designer's responsibility is to provide proper balance between the two, never to be laggard when change is clearly indicated, never to rush rashly to change when it is not.

The choice of the doctor figure in our message for Iloilo is a deliberate cultural decision based on the strategic objective to change a weaning food practice. The doctor is an ultimate authority. He or she is also a symbol of the change that is taking place in the countryside—the availability of local health clinics and MCH centers and the new education and care they dispense (2.2). This is why the doctor was selected instead of some other established village health figure who may be the custodian of local custom but is not necessarily perceived to have as much authority. Moreover, they may be linked to practices whose validity is under question.

Now, why was the minidrama chosen as the format (2.3, 2.4)? For one thing, the *novella* or soap opera is an extremely popular form of entertainment. For another, it provides an excellent format for the presentation and resolution of the conflict that is always provoked by a new idea. The interplay between the characters affords a chance to have the idea offered by one and challenged by the other. This replicates reality. It gives us a chance to air the arguments against the idea revealed by our research and to refute them.

The confrontation of the *novella* also gives us a chance to hear certain psychological truths: mother's concern for her child, mother's unwillingness to accept the new idea, her emotional retreat before the inevitable, her chagrin for not knowing what was right, and the reassurance that it can be assuaged by willingness to learn (1.2, 2.3). The aim was to bend the rigidity of custom, to eliminate it as a *resistance point:* to help our target mother to loosen the grip of custom her mother had clamped on her and her mother's mother before her (1.3).

The obvious way, which was rejected, was a typical confrontation between a modern daughter and a traditional mother in which the daughter argues for making the *lugaw* the new way. This was not culturally acceptable (2.2). It would have aroused feelings of hostility toward the daughter for opposing her mother. Sympathy for the new way would have been destroyed. Two struggles would have been required to win one. Sympathy for an idea requires empathy with the sponsor (3.2). So the conflict was turned around. The grandmother was made the sponsor of the idea and her daughter, the opponent (3.6).

Remember?

LITA: Mama, what are you putting in my baby's *lugaw*? (3.3)
MOTHER: A drop of oil, some chopped green vegetables and fish.
LITA: Where did you get this strange idea? (3.3)

Lita's concern is aroused by her mother's behavior. The health of her child is involved. This technique of role reversal releases the audience from preestablished positions of partisanship. Everybody becomes a free agent. The job, however, is to bring credibility to the situation (3.5). Something unusual must happen to make the reversal of roles plausible. That something is the doctor on the radio within this radio message. The grandmother confesses where she heard this new idea:

MOTHER: From the doctor on the radio. Listen!

And she invites her daughter to hear it for herself, which means for the radio audience to hear it as well.

Thus, the conflict has been turned around and the stage set for the presentation of the idea. After all, the grandmother is the proponent; the guardian of tradition has become the sponsor of change. The daughter is incredulous and here she is really speaking for the radio audience, which, we anticipate, must be taken aback by this unexpected twist of circumstance (3.6).

At this point our audience presumably sympathizes with the modern daughter in wondering, as she does, where the old woman got this strange idea. This is to be preferred to the alternative dramatic situation in which hostility toward the mother would have been aroused for opposing the grandmother so disrespectfully (and in a 60-second minidrama mere brevity alone would have incurred a curt, brusque disrespect) and for coming up with an outlandish modern idea that is not the custom (1.3, 3.6).

But in our situation there is no hostility toward either the daughter or the old woman. If anything, the old woman might be considered off her rocker but she is quickly seen to be perfectly sane (2.3, 3.5). She is redeemed in our estimation by the doctor on the radio. This element in the message also provides additional benefits. First, it associates the old woman with modernity—age is not synonymous with cultural antiquity. Old people can learn new ideas. Second, it helps to lend authority to our medium—particularly our use of it. Third, it reinforces the authority of the doctor and the health centers in which he can be found. All the elements in our little minidrama are relevant components (4.2). We need them for our purposes, but we also use them to make their purposes even more important.

This is a form of symbiosis in communications that rejects irrelevant elements and distracting devices in order to permit our audience to become emotionally and intellectually involved in the central issue of our message and finally to accept the overriding wisdom of its idea (4.2).

We are now ready to hear the doctor give the essence of our message. Notice that the message is designed to make this the high point. Often messages contain all the essential elements but lack deliberate design to emphasize the central point. The result is a message that may lack impact though heard or, if heard, not listened to for what it says (2.1).

Lita's mother focuses the audience's attention on the doctor because he holds the key to the conflict between mother and daughter. So the drama is used to serve the purpose of our message, not merely for interest or convenience, but for underscoring our point.

DOCTOR: (*filter*) After six months a baby needs *lugaw* as well as breast milk, but *lugaw* must be mixed with fish that gives protein for muscles and brain. Green vegetables for vitamins. Oil for more weight on his body. (1.1, 1.4, 1.5, 3.1, 3.3, 3.7)

Here is the nub of our message, presented crisply, simply, and in ways that build on a mother's understanding as well as her concern for the health and growth of her child (2.2, 3.3). Observe how many of our discipline factors are acknowledged here. With it all, however, we are also mindful of a major *resistance point* identified by the research to be such a radical change in infant feeding behavior. It demands Lita's immediate objection.

LITA: But, mama, a six-month old baby can't digest such foods. (1.3)

Lita's objection is a replay from the research. The widely held belief is that infants cannot digest such foods—that they result in diarrhea. The belief was easily challenged when mothers were told that proper preparation of these foods prevented such ill effects. This was a crucial *resistance point* that had to be dealt with in the message and it was given to the doctor for the authority he represents. Thus, Lita's mother is quick to reply:

MOTHER: Sh-h. Listen to the doctor on the radio.
DOCTOR: (*filter*) A six-month old baby can digest these foods. Just wash the salt from the dried fish, chop the vegetables and

cook them well, add a little oil, and mash with the *lugaw*.
(1.4, 1.5, 4.1, 4.3)

This is not only a reprise of the recipe but also a simple statement of a routine that research revealed was within every woman's capability (3.4). The next task is to resolve the conflict in favor of Lita's mother because she is the sponsor of the idea. The only believable thing a daughter can say to her mother under these circumstances is:

LITA: But, mama, you didn't feed me like that. (1.3)

This is tantamount to saying, "Okay, I believe this doctor but why didn't you know enough to feed me this way when I was a baby?" Lita still resists; she is finding it hard to abandon custom to a new idea. It also affords the opportunity to reinforce the subordinate notion that learning is a dynamic process—that education is continuous (4.1).

So Lita's mother says it in the most believable way using the circumstance of the doctor on the radio:

MOTHER: How could I know? I didn't even own a radio. Times change. You live and learn.

Now, the audience response to this should be affirming. From the research, we learned that they accept the radio as a new instrument for delivering modern ideas. Thus, Lita's mother's explanation is plausible and understandable (3.5).

Before the message is done there remains one other emotional task: sanction the change by eliminating any taint of blame that might attach to Lita or her mother or the doctor (3.2). The audience must also be relieved of any such imputation lest it end up rejecting the good advice because of an emotional resistance to abandoning tradition. So it is Lita who says to her mother:

LITA: Mama, you must be sad that the old ways are changing.

With this statement Lita concedes that the new way is inevitable. She has now shifted from the struggle against her mother to a concern for the emotional price the older woman may have to pay for winning the argument. Good communications design never overlooks the need to balance the emotional budget (3.2).

Lita is the agent for arousing audience sympathy for Lita's mother. After all, changing custom is a burden we all bear and resist. Who cannot feel sorry for her? At the same time the audience is subtly encouraged to feel kindly toward Lita for expressing compassion for her mother. Thus, in this one simple, honest question, the message strives for three important things: to resolve the issue with Lita accepting her mother's (the doctor's) new idea; to have Lita articulate the anxiety her mother could be experiencing despite her seeming assurance and, in so doing, to give expression to the same concern that many in the audience may be feeling; and to bring the audience into sympathy with Lita's mother and with Lita and create an inviting emotional environment for the audience also to accept this new idea.

But now that the question has been asked, lurking in the minds of the audience is a curiosity as to what Lita's mother's response will be? After all, some will be wondering: "How can such a traditional mother be so easily accepting of change? It just isn't believable." This also enhances the drama in the situation—a bit of suspense (2.5).

So Lita's mother's answer must be painstakingly thought out. She isn't really so eager to see change take place. She says:

MOTHER: Not all the old ways are changing.

which is to say: "Hold on there. Who says all the old ways are changing?" And, of course, they are not. The audience should be reassured by this. "Aha! So you see Lita's mother is no empty head—accepting any silly idea that comes her way. No. Not at all. She is obviously a sensible person."

And Lita's mother continues:

MOTHER: But only a fool remains with an old way when there is a new, better way.

And who can deny that? Because even the most tradition-bound individual knows change is inevitable but also welcomes it when its value is clear. This bit of suspenseful stage business also may turn out to be the dramatic climax for which the audience will come to look forward each time the message plays (2.5). So Lita's mother is a credible soul. She has done what any sound, sensible person would do under such circumstances (3.5).

Now here is a summary of what the message was designed to cover:

1. A formula for a new way to prepare the baby's porridge
2. The reasons that it is necessary and the benefits to be derived
3. The authority of the doctor
4. The confrontation with custom
5. Dealing with the delicacy of the relationship between the generations in a traditional society
6. The need to articulate the anxiety that change in custom is bound to arouse and then to alleviate that anxiety
7. Establishing the credibility of the protagonists to give the audience a willingness to accept what is being said
8. Reassurance to the audience that such change does not mean the end of the world as they know it, but merely one of those occasional improvements they have the capability to accommodate

All of this has been composed in a message only 60 seconds long, including a standard opening and closing to identify the campaign with a theme used in all six versions.

All messages were tested from the very first draft. This was done by recording them on cassettes and having them played back for a sampling of target mothers in the villages. Interviewers' guidelines were prepared and on the basis of mothers' reactions they elicited, changes were made, and the messages rerecorded. These, in turn, were tested again, then revised in accordance with the findings. The script analyzed here appears in its final version and much of the analysis presented is, in fact, a restatement of the observations and insights gathered from the test experience. In the beginning, there was no certain way to know the eventual impact of the messages except that their vital elements were now positively received, *resistance points* were effectively reduced, even if not entirely eliminated, and the characters in the minidrama were accepted both for who they were and what they had to say (see Chapter 10 for a case history of this Philippines project).

Perhaps the reprise element could have been strengthened. Though the idea of the recipe is repeated three times in the body of the message, it would be more forceful if one of those could have been managed at the close. Instead, the ending was reserved for reference to other local authorities from whom more assistance could be obtained—a necessary element in a message of this kind to integrate the effort with ongoing service agencies in the community (1.6). Music might have been employed to aid the audience in remembering the recipe—putting it into lyric form against a musical phrase. This is a matter of creative judgment that is always open to question.

The Role of Research in Message Design

In our many references to predesign research (Chapter 6 deals with the subject in greater detail), the emphasis on qualitative methods has meant to serve our primary interest in uncovering new material—problems, concepts, *resistance points,* and perceptions—of the target audience than in quantitative measurement of preconceived notions. Either through focus group or in-depth individual interviews, these inquiries are anthropological in nature. The dynamics of the interviews are organic, dependent on the interaction between the parties, and not constrained by rigidly structured, closed-ended questionnaires. This is the first essential contribution of research to message design.

After messages have been drafted, research plays its important role in testing them with samples of the target population. Message drafts are exposed under circumstances approximating real-life situations. Various testing techniques are available, depending on the nature of the message and the media for which it is intended (see Chapter 6). Thus, radio messages are produced on cassettes and played back for small groups or individuals who are then probed for reactions to ascertain level of comprehension, motivation, and presence of language or cultural blocks. Once again the interview follows a guideline rather than a rigidly constructed quantitative questionnaire.

These formative inquiries are as important, if not more so, as the evaluative studies to measure results, because their purpose is to make messages more effective. In that sense, formative research is an important determinant of the outcome of the summative evaluation, which is a routine audit of the program. Past programs in health and nutrition education have tended to give greater research emphasis to the latter. Social marketing seeks to restore the balance.

Message Design for Print Media

In general, the message design disciplines apply to all media, though our illustrations intentionally favor broadcast, which generally promise far more impact for social marketing purposes (see Chapter 8). Print media's dependence on literacy is a source both of its strength and weakness. In Third World countries, the most vulnerable populations cannot be reached through newspapers, magazines, or other print communications. Even in a country like the United States, millions of people are functionally illiterate—and almost all are among the most disadvantaged—unable to understand or carry out simple printed instructions. Millions more who can read have undoubtedly been weaned away from the reading habit by the more convenient, entertaining appeal of radio, TV, and the cinema. The singular strength of print media is their usefulness for reaching opinion makers—government officials, public figures—and in providing the opportunity for greater detail.

The notion that illiterate populations can be communicated to entirely through the use of nonverbal communications techniques may be mostly myth. While valuable use can be made of ingeniously conceived graphic devices, they are almost never capable of capturing whole ideas except, perhaps, those that have already been established through interpersonal communication or other nonliterary means. Then, the graphic representation is, in fact, nothing more than a reminder. Words, in the end, are the sine qua non of communication. Pictures also require their own form of literacy—graphics literacy, if you will—the ability to translate the picture into the reality it is meant to symbolize.

For people unaccustomed to such symbolic representations, the communication is not always clear or meaningful. A poster showing a thin woman with a heavy basket on her head and another fat perspiring woman sitting alongside was meant to illustrate that keeping body weight normal produces vigor and better health. But local people gave it another interpretation: the sitting lady was lucky to be so rich that she could eat well, grow fat, and afford a servant to carry her burdens. When a poster on the danger of flies pictured them in the foreground enlarged by the perspective, villagers expressed gratitude that the flies in their village were "not as huge as these."[15]

Several studies[16] demonstrated the limitations and pitfalls, and the precautions necessary to avoid them. For example, the presentation of a single idea at a time is found to be as valid for print as it is for broadcast. In an instructional booklet, each page is more effective when it avoids having more than one message and contains the minimum of detail necessary to convey its meaning. Abstract symbols are best avoided unless already well established in the graphics literacy of the culture. Otherwise, the more realistic the illustration, the better. Regional cultural differences may require multiple versions of the material—an essential, although costly, procedure. Colors may not be casually selected and their choice should be decided by testing in advance. Colors have different meanings for different people. In general, because intellectual conventions of one culture may not exist in another, the logical flow of instructional steps, for example, especially when represented through pictures, may have totally different meanings for those without such a learning tradition.

In the end, there is no substitute for predesign research—the formative inquiry. Uncovering target populations' perceptions, their view of their problems, their willingness and capability to accept the solution, the *resistance points* that thwart motivation, their response to proposed message elements, and then testing and retesting as necessary—all these are indispensable to the success of the print message outcome.

Of all the elements of social marketing, perhaps the most important (except when a social product is involved) is the message. It is the reason for the program, and all other components—the research, materials, and media—are meant to serve the message.

The late Marshall McLuhan's famous dictum is specious. The medium is not the message because only the message can be the message. One medium may be better than another for a message because of its particular environmental values but all media without a message to deliver are empty vessels. TV offers a more dramatic message environment than radio (see Chapter 8) and radio can be more dramatic than print. None of these media, however, has meaning by itself. McLuhan's characterization has validity when the media, abandoned to entertainment, have little to say; when psychostimulation, not thought, is their preeminent employment. In such a time the medium does, in fact, become the message because there is no message. When the message is meaningful, the messenger is barely noticed. When the messenger arrives empty handed, what else is there for us to see?

Are Global Messages Possible?

The universality of certain health problems has provoked interest in the possibility of global messages appropriate for all countries. No doubt such prototypical messages are possible given a special problem and solution that surmount cultural differences. They are possible but not very likely. Awareness of the possibility comes from a growing realization of the universality of a city culture on the one hand and a village culture on the other throughout the world. One observer declared

> The West . . . now includes small enclaves in most of the Third World's great cities, part of the same jet-and-electronics network we belong to. Beyond are the two million villages where a very sudden closing of the 5000 B.C.-1980's A.D. technology gap should now be possible. . . . On a

> 1980 visit to the North China Plains, I found that once you stepped inside a village family's household walls, property, marriage and the family mattered just as much as in any other village culture. . . . A universal village culture does exist."[17]

This may very well be as Aristotle told us more than 2,300 years ago that the three elemental values of village life were property, marriage, and family. Every creature's mode, he concluded, is determined by how he obtains his food—"If you change agriculture, you change culture." Anyone who has traveled among Third World countries will bear testimony to their commonality. But for social marketing purposes, these resemblances may be too gross to rely on for sensitive message designs.

One might generalize that the opportunity for a global message would bear an inverse relationship to the complexity of the required behavior change. The more it depends on specific local human and environmental resources, the less the likelihood that the message can be prototyped. A nutritional message on the preparation of a weaning food would defy prototying because the circumstances from culture to culture are so varied in terms of food availabilities, preparation patterns, and food coding systems (e.g., hot and cold foods). On the other hand, a health message promoting an immunization drive would appear to be a possible candidate for prototyping, although how can we really decide without knowing whether indigenous differences in *resistance points* exist?

TransTel, a nonprofit organization jointly operated by ARD and ZDF, the West German TV networks, provided programming for stations in overseas markets. Increasingly, it has been providing TV fare for Third World countries. "*TransTel—Ratgeber Gesundheit,* (Health Adviser)," a series of short, five-minute spots, has been an ongoing production of the organization for stations in Africa, Asia, and Latin America. The productions were originally done in Germany but were criticized overseas as being inappropriate for local audiences. In designing a subsequent series on tropical diseases, TransTel responded by attempting to localize the scripts and production values. For reasons of cost, it decided it could make no more than three regional versions, one for each continent. However, it selected a single location for the three versions on the assumption that it could pass muster in all the regions and in all the countries they include. They chose Surinam in the Caribbean to which they transported actors and technical advisers from Africa, Asia, and other parts of Latin America. In all, 13 spots were produced and in each there are two central characters, Brother Careful, who always does the right thing, and Brother Careless, who never does.

No evaluation information is available on this effort and though it might have been successful, the approach it typifies is highly risky. If assistance is to be given, then it ought to be help in planning, designing, and executing such projects with local resources and a disciplined approach to the task to ensure its relevance to people, custom, and the special circumstances of the local situation. Anything short of that obviously threatens to impose alien ideas and inappropriate solutions. Its messages are certain to be insensitive to target audience *resistance points,* which cannot be identified in Surinam for a community high in the Andean region of Ecuador, not even with an army of experts especially imported from that area.

Given its central importance, the message cannot be a casual construction. Nor can it be simply a matter of letting the facts speak for themselves. If it is to persuade and move an audience to action, then it will require the services of skillful message designers who know how to determine where emphasis will be placed, the proper message environment for the target audience, appropriate language and idiom, and the reasonable action to expect. Finally, they will know how to blend these together so the message (facts included) will have a maximum chance to attain its objective. This will require strict adherence to the disciplines of message design. They are the distillation of much experience both from commercial enterprise and from social marketing projects around the world. Though they focus primarily on messages to be designed for delivery through the mass media, they have validity for other channels as well. In the final analysis, effective message design follows certain fundamentals regardless of media.

Notes

1. Manoff International Inc., "Radio Nutrition Education—Using The Advertising Technique To Reach Rural Families: Philippines and Nicaragua," final report, December 1977.

2. Ibid.

3. Manoff International Inc., "Mothers Speak and Nutrition Educators Listen: Formative Evaluation For A Nutrition Communications Project," in special territory of Yogyakarta, Central Java, South Sumatra, July 23, 1980.

4. Matthai, J., *The Brazilian National Breast-Feeding Programme,* Document 8201, UNICEF/Brasilia, Brazil, January 1982.

5. Richard K. Manoff Inc., pretest of family planning advertisements conducted for Planned Parenthood/World Population, 1972.

6. The Carolina Population Center, University of North Carolina at Chapel Hill, "A Test of Advertising Vasectomy on Radio," a research report by Winfield Best, William A. Flexner, Richard K. Manoff, and Stephen D. Mumford, June 1977.

7. Manoff International Inc., "Using Modern Marketing Techniques for Nutrition Education: Ecuador," final report, December 31, 1975, prepared for USAID.

8. Manoff International Inc., "Radio Nutrition Education—Using The Advertising Technique To Reach Rural Families: Philippines and Nicaragua," final report, December 1977.

9. Manoff International Inc., "Mass Media and Nutrition Education: Ecuador," 1975.

10. Howell, W.S., "Theoretical Directions for Intercultural Communication," in *Handbook of Intercultural Communication,* (Eds. M.K. Asante, E. Newmark, and A. Blake) Sage, Beverly Hills, California, 1979.

11. Manoff International Inc., "Radio Nutrition Education—Using The Advertising Technique To Reach Rural Families: Philippines and Nicaragua," final report, December 1977.

12. Ibid.

13. Howell, W.S., op. cit., pp. 30–31.

14. Population Crisis Committee, "Accelerating Fertility Declines," as cited in *Worldwatch Paper* 54, p. 34, Worldwatch Institute, Washington, D.C.

15. Ritchie, J.A.S., *Learning Better Nutrition,* p. 105. Food and Agriculture Organization, Rome, Italy, 1967.

16. Fusell, D., Haaland, A., "Communicating With Pictures," a study for the National Development Service of Nepal and UNICEF, 1976. Available from UNICEF, 866 U.N. Plaza, New York 10017. Other reports are also obtainable from PIACT (Program for Introduction and Adaptation of Contraceptive Technology), 2030 M St., N.W., Suite 700, Washington, D.C. 20036; WHO (World Health Organization), 1211 Geneva, Switzerland; AED (Academy for Educational Development), 1414 22nd St., N.W., Washington, D.C. 20037; USAID (U.S. Agency for International Development), 21st and Virginia Ave., N.W., Washington, D.C. 20523.

17. Critchfield, R., "Science and the Villager," *Foreign Affairs,* fall 1982, Vol. 61, No. 1, p. 14.

Part III

Social Marketing: Cases and Caveats

10

Case Histories

No social marketing project I know of would rate better than a 12/75 or a 9/60 PRISM. (see Chapter 6). Reasons vary but two recur frequently: mediocre message design and substandard media planning and execution. The data base for media planning is sparse in most Third World countries and little ingenuity has been employed to make up for it. In the United States, where there is a plethora of information, media expertise in using it is rare among health professionals. Only recently have they begun to call on the services of advertising agencies and their media specialists. But even this has not sufficed. These new clients are not knowledgeable or demanding, and agencies are less than exacting in behalf of *pro bono publico* campaigns. These difficulties are further aggravated by the access problem. The public media are exorbitantly expensive and social marketing programs have yet to attain a budgetary status commensurate with the education tasks involved.

After almost two decades of social marketing experience, I have gained some familiarity with several hundred mass communication projects around the world. Most have been token mass media campaigns with a minimum of planning. All but a handful have paid obeisance to the social marketing approach and these have been almost entirely for the distribution and sale of family planning devices. None of these would merit a maximum 12/100 PRISM. The demands imposed by product marketing brought them closer to the model but without much of its substance. Research has been marked by a poverty of discovery—message design by marginal vision. Disciplined development and execution of social marketing plans, inventive media analysis, and critical process evaluation have been minimal.

The four case histories that follow were selected because they represent diverse experiences and highlight some aspect of social marketing ingenuity. Two are from developed countries; two from the Third World. The Indonesian Nutrition Education and Behavior Change Project was an innovative integration of major program elements—a sizable corps of specially trained volunteers, growth monitoring with monthly weighings and growth chart record-keeping, the use of new communications materials, and the mass media—in substantial observance of social marketing principles. The Social Marketing Program of Population Services International in Bangladesh (SMP) is a good demonstration of the social marketing of contraceptives. It was extraordinarily successful in its stated objective: to expand the market and usage of nonclinical contraceptives by marketing through the commercial system. The performance has not been faultless but given the political and religious obstacles unceremoniously tossed in its path, SMP has been a commendable effort.

The Karelia Project from Finland illustrates ingenious use of the mass media—this time an unusual TV program format for addressing high health-risk behaviors. The Stanford Three-City Project demonstrates how an integration of diverse components can be made to work for the same objective and how yet another use of the mass media can have a significant "multiplier" effect.

Other commendable efforts deserve more than mere citation here but their details would require several volumes.

1. Costa Rica, Dialogo, the population campaign ongoing since 1970
2. The Honduras and Gambia ORT Projects, USAID funded, technical consultants, Academy for Educational Development
3. Nicaragua, the Super Limonada ORT, funded by USAID, Manoff International Inc., technical consultants
4. Philippines, Masagana 99, an international program to increase rice production
5. Tanzania, "Man is Health," a radio campaign on disease control and priority health problems
6. Tanzania, "Food is Life," a nutrition campaign
7. Philippines, a weaning food campaign to teach Filipino mothers how to enrich the traditional weaning food (USAID), Manoff International, technical consultants
8. Trinidad and Tobago, a breast-feeding campaign by the Housewives Association with the assistance of the local Association of Advertising Agencies
9. The Brazilian National Breast-Feeding Program, ongoing since 1981 by the National Institute of Nutrition of Brazil with UNICEF assistance
10. Ecuador, Rural and Urban Nutrition Education Campaign on priority dietary practices (USAID), Manoff International, technical consultants
11. New Mexico, United States, a nutrition education campaign on nutrient education, the promotion of food stamps, and the school lunch program by the University of New Mexico, the Office of Economic Opportunity, and Manoff International, technical consultants

12. Norway, an antismoking campaign, 1974
13. South Korea, Mass Media and Nutrition Education Campaign by CARE, 1970
14. India, Mass Media and Nutrition Education Campaign for proper weaning food practices by CARE, 1972

They represent serious efforts to advance the state of the art. The list is by no means complete and apologies are offered for unavoidable omissions.

Indonesian Nutrition Education and Behavior Change Project

Primary Health Care (PHC) strategy emphasizes community participation, cultural relevance, and the use of paramedical personnel to provide services using simple but appropriate technologies. It also underlines the importance of integrating health promotion with education, water, sanitation, agriculture, and economic development. Social marketing is its natural tool.

The progress of PHC since Alma-Ata has not been even. Community participation, for example, has become a byword. Hardly a program exists that does not pay its respects to the principle. Yet differing interpretations of community participation assign contrasting roles to village people. Some delegate responsibility merely for implementation of programs designed at national, state, or provincial levels. Others go to the opposite extreme, letting communities decide programs entirely on their own.

The National Nutrition Education and Behavior Change Project of the Indonesian Nutrition Development Program set out in 1977 to employ a better balance between official responsibility and local initiative because it promised a higher level of effectiveness for nutrition education.[1] It called on Manoff International for assistance in the belief that the social marketing approach offered the most appropriate address to the situation. The principle of intersectoral integration ensured message harmony from all sources. The principle of appropriate technology was pursued through a village weighing program as the core device for nutrition education as well as for growth monitoring and was the responsibility of trained volunteer nutrition workers. These *kaders gizi,* not the equivalent of PHC paramedical workers, were specially recruited to work among the villages in which they lived. The messages delivered by the mass media— in this case, radio—were designed to reflect inputs from the villagers.

This project sought to go beyond the limitations of previous approaches to analyzing target audience perceptions by penetrating beneath the skin of the problem, as it were, to its inner realities, or to soliciting the villagers' assessment of the practicability of one solution versus another. The effectiveness of health education is circumscribed when resistances inherent in local custom elude the formative evaluation process. The subsequent communications strategy development and message design are critically impoverished.

This project sought to remedy defects of the standardized formative evaluation process.

1. An innovative qualitative research scheme was prescribed as most likely to encourage rural mothers to reveal crucial attitudinal issues.
2. Mothers were afforded the opportunity to determine the ingredients for the proposed enrichment of the traditional weaning food.
3. A behavioral trial was provided for assessing its practicality and nutritional value.
4. The target audience participated in the formulation of messages.
5. The insights gathered from the villagers were instrumental in designing strategies and messages.

This project is one component of the Indonesian Nutrition Development Program funded by the World Bank. Its Director is Dr. I.B. Mantra, the head of the Health Education Directorate in the Ministry of Health. It was begun in five subdistricts of three provinces in Central Java and South Sumatra. The total population involved was 225,000 in 40,500 households. In its first two stages, from 1977 to 1979, the project retrained and equipped about 2,000 *kaders* and initiated a weighing program in each village. In the third, from 1979 to 1981, focus was on research for the development of communications strategies and the design, production, and dissemination of the materials. The fourth, in 1982, was devoted to implementation and evaluation.

The major nutrition problems had already been identified:

1. Undernutrition of pregnant women
2. Undernutrition of lactating women
3. Protein-calorie malnutrition in children from birth to four-months old (lactation practices)
4. Protein-calorie malnutrition in children five- to eight-months old (time of introduction of solid foods)
5. Protein-calorie malnutrition in children 9- to 24-months old (quantity of food consumed)

6. Infant diarrhea
7. Vitamin A deficiency in young children
8. Goiter

The communications infrastructure offered potential for both interpersonal and mass media. But the corps of *kaders* was poorly trained and suffered a high dropout rate. Radio coverage, except for some few areas, was generally good.

The work began in planning sessions with project managers in Jakarta with the commitment to the special formative evaluation framework. First, a concept investigation was intended to yield qualitative information rather than extensive quantitative data. It was to be program oriented, quick and inexpensive, and designed to reflect local reality, reveal the perceptions of mothers of malnourished children, solicit mothers' opinions for improving infants' diets, and uncovering the *resistance points* to the behavior change goals.

Individuals selected for the investigation team converged on the villages designated for the training and from which they would disperse to conduct their work. Since this phase was to compel a field reexamination of the validity of preconceived ideas, it called for detailed observation of the methods of food preparation with particular reference to infants' first solid foods (the traditional weaning food is rice porridge), the age of introduction, and the method of preparation. It meant inquiring into responsibility for infant care for its target audience implications.

In every community, the first step was to introduce the investigators to the village mothers, to allow village leaders to endorse the investigation, and to receive suggestions from both groups. The investigative staff then met to develop a question guide based on these inputs. The guide was organized by topic to explore the suitability of local foods to nutrition demands, whether they were within the means of the families, and mothers' reactions to preparation suggestions from the community meeting. Investigators were trained to use the guides with simple interview techniques.

Equipped with village maps, investigators pinpointed low income neighborhoods. A total of 330 households participated in some aspect of the investigation, which also included midwives, shopkeepers, health workers, and officials. Village volunteers, either a *bidan*—a midwife—or a *kader* were recruited to help locate families with either a pregnant woman, a lactating woman, a malnourished child, or a child with diarrhea, preferably under the age of two. To help identify the malnourished, children were weighed and checked against weight charts. Interviews were tape recorded and included a 24-hour recall of the baby's diet.

Using an innovative 24-hour dietary recall sheet, investigators were instantly able to calculate deficiencies in protein, calories, or vitamin A and to determine the recommendations to be made to mothers. Investigators then followed the guide to observe such matters as the arrangement and use of the kitchen, the condition of the home and backyard garden (if one existed), or evidence of the availability of fresh greens.

At this point the interview departed significantly from the conventional household survey. Based on the age of the child and the outcome of the dietary recall, the investigator pursued the appropriate behavioral change. The mother of a six-month old was probed for her ideas on what to add to the porridge. Together, the investigator and the mother developed a recipe for an enriched weaning food. Since they did not follow a rigid format, they were able to use the ingredients the mother had on hand, her methods for preparing foods, and her recipes. In the investigator's presence the mother fed the new food to her child and both observed the child's reaction. The investigator promised to return in three or four days after the mother's pledge to serve this food the prescribed number of times a day. Invariably, the mother would modify the recipe to suit her needs. Her reasons were invaluable. This technique for product development—for trial, adaptation, and retrial—by the mother is an important element in the methodology and was adapted from product-testing procedures of commercial food marketing that ensure a consumer role in product formulation.

The information from 330 household interviews provided the basis for the communications strategies and the content of the messages. There were many new insights. The well-known prejudice against colostrum (the initial breast-milk fluid) was not firmly held for reasons important to the message designers. It was also discovered that women in Central Java primarily used the left breast to feed. Many hypotheses abounded (the Moslem injunction that the right hand is for food and the left is for toilet was one) but not until focus group interviews were conducted with health workers was it discovered that the left breast was commonly perceived to contain food and the right breast water. Women offered the food first and if the child seemed content, the water was never proffered. This observation led to an important breast-feeding message element: use both the right and the left breasts equally.

The weaning food trials revealed a preference for virtually the same ingredients but for different methods of preparation. The inclusion of a fat source to improve caloric density was essential and to make it universally acceptable the recipe was modified by area custom: frying the *tahu* or *tempe* before mashing in the porridge, or adding drops of coconut oil to cooked rice, or cooking all ingredients in coconut milk.

A major insight was the realization that there were seven, not two, target audiences to deal with—not merely the pregnant woman and all other mothers with children from birth to five years of age. Past experience instructed that target populations are not monoliths, that even a seemingly homogeneous group is differentiated at any moment by heterogeneous concerns and motivations. This target audience segmentation is vital to identify. It enables delivery of the precise message needed by a specific target audience segment at the right time.

The seven identified target audience segments were:

1. The pregnant woman
2. The lactating woman
3. Mothers of infants from birth to four months
4. Mothers of infants from five to eight months
5. Mothers of infants from 9 to 24 months
6. Mothers of children with diarrhea
7. All mothers of children under 5 years (weighing)

Each target segment represented a distinct nutrition or growth problem. For each one, distinct behavioral objectives were established, for example, mothers of infants from five to eight months:

1. Breast-feed, using both breasts.
2. Feed *bubur campur* (enriched rice porridge) four times a day.
3. Introduce the supplementary food patiently.

This is the message developed for radio:

Tune: In, up.
Slogan: Good Nutrition—Healthy Child
Mother 1: Hah! What are you making?
Mother 2: I'm making *burbur campur* for my child, Atik. *She is five months now.* [identifying the child's age]
Mother 1: That is a strange combination. And a bother.
Mother 2: No, it's easy and cheap. Rice, green vegetables, *tahu* or *tempe,* and coconut milk.
Mother 1: But why?
Mother 2: To help my baby grow faster, be healthier and stronger.
Mother 1: A five-month-old baby can digest these foods? [Now the idea of feeding such foods to a five-month-old baby is a revealed *resistance point.* It had to be dealt with in the message.]
Mother 2: Yes, ask Bu Kader. If the ingredients are *mashed* well. And

the vegetables, fish, *tahu,* or *tempe* are fried and also mashed, then mixed into the *bubur campur.*

Mother 1: That's a lot together with breast-feeding.

Mother 2: Oh, no. A five- to eight-month child needs this much food. And the breast-feeding should be from both breasts, not only one. Breast milk as before and *bubur campur,* four times a day. Otherwise, our children do not grow enough. But you are not listening.

Mother 1: I am thinking. Breast-feeding from both breasts and *bubur campur*—rice with well-cooked green vegetables, mashed *tahu* or *tempe,* cooked with coconut milk. You are sure of this?

Mother 2: Ask Bu Kader. You should weigh your child every month at the weighing post. If you need more information, you can ask the *kader,* the *bidan,* or the Health Center staff.

Mother 1: Always new ideas these days.

Mother 2: Not always good ones like *bubur campur*!

Slogan: Good Nutrition—Healthy Child

Tune: Up, out.

Implementation began in August 1980 and ran for over a year before it was evaluated. The first steps of implementation involved acquainting officials in each area with the messages and materials. Then the *kaders* were trained in the specifics of the desired behavior changes and in the use of materials. They were encouraged to make as many home visits as possible. The radio spots were distributed to stations that broadcast to the five subdistricts. Air time was not paid for, since the messages were to be played as a public service. However, even on the government-owned radio stations, the messages did not receive the targets set for reach and frequency. (The access problem reared its ugly head.)

Figure 10.1 shows an innovative poster version of this message conceived initially for areas of low radio penetration but eventually employed in all. It is called an Action Poster because it was an effort to overcome poster passivity, an inherent communication weakness of the traditional poster. It conveyed the same message for radio with a vital difference. It showed a mother's worksheet requiring her to keep a record of her performance. It was given out mainly at weighing sessions although *kaders* also distributed them during home visits. Thus, a mother received only those messages designed for her circumstances at a given time. Whenever she breast-fed or served *bumbur campur,* she was instructed to mark or pierce one of the little boxes under the appropriate illustration. Each horizontal line of boxes represents one day, four boxes for the four daily feeds of *bubur campur,* and as many as ten for demand breast-feeding. Thirty lines cover the monthly period between weighings. The effectiveness of the Action Poster was not to be measured by the number of marks or holes. Religious compliance with this obligation was not expected. But the awareness of the obligation was a stronger reminder than a passive poster and helped to fix the message more firmly in the mind.

All media materials, including the Action Poster, were pretested. Artists and writers participated in the field investigations. Revised materials were taken back for retesting.

In November 1981, an extensive evaluation investigation was begun under Dr. Marian Zeitlin of Tufts University among a total of 1,000 households—600 in the project areas and 400 in the comparison areas. The latter were selected for comparable demographics. They also had an ongoing nutrition program involving *kaders* but without the special nutrition education component. The results suggested that the project had considerable effect on knowledge, attitude, and the dietary intake of mothers and infants and significantly affected the growth of the children.

Children in the nutrition education areas grew significantly better after five months of age than children whose families participated in other nutrition programs. The chart (Figure 10.2) shows the mean weights for each age group of children in the nutrition education program and in the comparison group. Notice that at 22 months program infants' mean weight is almost one kilo more than for the comparison group. The growth curve flattens at seven months for the program infants and at five months for the comparison group. Mean values for the program infants never fall below the normal zone, whereas the mean values for the comparison group drop below at 13 months and do not reenter. Differences between the groups are significant ($p \leq .05$) at 2 and 3 months, 7 and 8 months, and 14 months onward.

Parents in the nutrition education villages knew more specific information about nutrition problems and what to do about them. Nutritional knowledge was measured two ways. The first was a total knowledge scale, composed of all message elements used in the nutrition education messages. The second scale was a personalized knowledge scale based on the age of the mother's child and the specific messages she should have received for herself and her child. The nutrition education program participants averaged 49 percent in correct recall of the messages on the total knowledge scale and 38 percent on the personalized knowledge scale, while the mothers in the comparison areas scored 28 and 22 percent, respectively.

Parents in the nutrition education villages offered their children the foods stressed in the messages. (These foods included greens and coconut milk.)

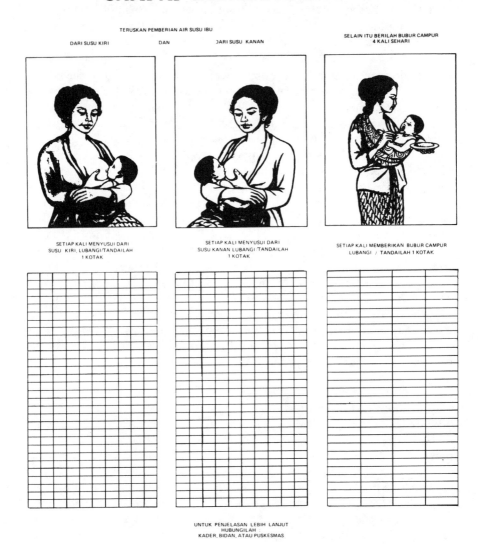

Figure 10.1. This "Action Poster" instructs the mother of an infant 5 to 8 months of age to breast-feed and supplement with an enriched weaning food at least four times a day. Note the emphasis on using both breasts. The underlying boxes provide a record-keeping reminder of balanced feeding with both breasts on demand and a four-times-daily frequency of supplementation.

Percentages of Infants in Each Age Group Who Received Greens and Coconut Milk in a 24-hour Recall Period

Food	Age of Child	NE Program	Comparison
Greens	5–8 months	54.3*	27.9
	9–16 months	71.2*	35.6
	17–24 months	85.3*	58.2
Coconut milk	5–8 months	35.0*	13.2
	9–16 months	27.0 (ns)	20.0
	17–24 months	43.0 (ns]	34.2

*Significant at $p \leq 001$.

Children of the families in the nutrition education villages had higher protein and calorie intakes. With the focus of the messages on increased consumption, the changes in dietary practices translated into improved nutrient intakes.

Percentages of Children Consuming Less Than 50 and 67 Percent of Recommended* Calories and Protein

	NE Program	Comparison
Calories $\leq$ 50%	13	38
Calories $\leq$ 67%	37	64
Protein $\leq$ 50%	18	40
Protein $\leq$ 67%	32	61

*Twenty-four hour recall data for infants were translated into calorie and protein intake using values from Indonesian food tables. Breast milk intake was assumed to be constant for infants within the age groups zero to 6 months (650 grams), 6 to 12 months (450 grams), and 13 to 24 months (200 grams). Calorie adequacy was calculated as a ratio of intake to requirement, where requirement was based on Food and Agriculture Organization (FAO) (1973) standards and median National Center for Health Statistics (NCHS) reference body weight for sex and age. Protein adequacy was calculated similarly, using protein levels 50 percent higher than the current FAO standards for 6 to 24 month old infants and 30 percent higher for those under 6 months to compensate for infection.

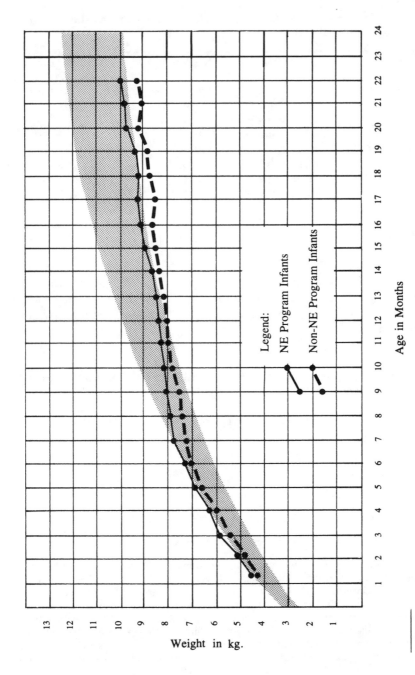

Figure 10.2. Growth Comparison, NE versus Non-NE Program Infants; Indonesia Nutrition Education and Behavior Change Pilot Project.

The World Bank, in making a cost-effectiveness analysis of its nutrition projects, declared that *"if projects are compared in terms of annual cost per beneficiary the least expensive by far is the Indonesian Nutrition Education [Improvement] Program at $2.00"* (author's emphasis) (Table 10.1).

It concluded its analysis by declaring

> The low-cost nutrition education as practiced in Indonesia looks particularly attractive. That it was cheaper than programs requiring food commodities comes as no surprise; the question is whether it is effective. The evidence has shown that nutrition education alone *can* make a difference in improving nutritional status. *Nutritionists have long held out the promise of this possibility; the Indonesian experience is the first time that it has been demonstrated in an operational setting.* (author's italics)[2]

The Stanford University Heart Disease Prevention Program

This is the one domestic program that comes closest to satisfying the standards and disciplines of social marketing. Started in 1972, it was an experiment to explore alternatives to conventional health education in dealing with the mounting morbidity and mortality from coronary heart disease, specifically with the dietary and behavioral factors implicated.

The study was designed to measure results from a combination of mass media and face-to-face instructional groups. Three California towns with well-matched characteristics as to size and demographic composition were selected. One served as the control without either intervention. Another received the combined mass media campaign and personal instruction for high-risk individuals. A third was given the mass media campaign only.

The goal was positive behavior change with respect to high-risk factors associated with cardiovascular diseases. The ultimate measure of disease reduction was presumably deemed beyond what available personnel and funds would allow. Moreover, much clinical and epidemiological evidence already supported the assumption that significant changes in behaviors associated with the high-risk factors must inevitably reduce cardiovascular morbidity. The specific factors that enter into the probability that a person will suffer a cardiovascular incident in a 12-year period include age, sex, history of heart disease, systolic blood pressure, weight, smoking, and serum cholesterol levels. The behavior change aims were obesity reduction, smoking cessation, increased physical exercise, and reduced consumption of sugar, salt, cholesterol, saturated fats, and alcohol.

Table 10.1. Financial Costs of Some Components in Bank-Supported Nutrition Projects[a]

Project, Component, and Date	Annual Component Cost (thousands of dollars)				Population in Area Served	Number of Beneficiaries	Annual Cost per Beneficiary (dollars)	Total Project Cost to Deliver 1,000 Calories (dollars)	Annual Component Cost per 100,000 Population (thousands of dollars)			
	Nonrecurrent[b]	Recurrent							Nonrecurrent	Food	Other	Total
		Food	Other	Total								
Brazil												
Food Subsidy (PINS), 1980	0.04	722.93	151.59	874.56	219,000[c]	41,026	21.32	0.30[d]	0.02	330.11	69.22	399.34
Preschool feeding and education (PROAPE), 1980	6.86	435.45	594.06	1036.37	not available	22,298	46.48	0.53[e]	—	—	—	—
Colombia												
Food subsidy, 1981	—[f]	2652.84	1551.38[f]	4204.22[f]	960,000	120,000	35.04	0.79[g]	—[f]	276.34	161.60[f]	437.93[f]
Indonesia												
Weighing and feeding program (NIPP, Bojonegoro area), 1982					194,000							
—Weighing and screening	387.73	76.71	74.22	189.66		14,886	12.74		19.96	39.54	38.26	97.76
—Feeding						2,307	56.01					
Nutrition education, 1977–81								not applicable				
Initiation phase[h]	83.38	0.00	63.26	146.64	225,000	37,272	3.94		37.06	0.00	28.12	65.18
Expansion phase[i]	36.18	0.00	40.30	76.48	225,000	37,272	2.05		16.08	0.00	17.91	33.99

234

Tamil Nadu
Weighing and
feeding program
(Nutrition delivery services,
block level, Madurai

district) 1982	3.68	43.09	28.29	75.06	100,000[j]		20.76		
—weighing and screening						6,084	20.76	3.68	43.09	28.29	75.06
—feeding						2,307	12.34			
1985 (projected, at 1982 prices)	3.68	17.24	28.29	49.21	100,000[j]		37.82		
—weighing and screening						6,084	37.82	0.72[k]	3.68	17.24	28.29	49.21
—feeding						1,301	8.04			

[a]For detailed component cost, see T.J. Ho, "Economic Issues: Costs Affordability and Cost Effectiveness." Department of Population, Health and Nutrition, World Bank, 1983.

[b]Annualized over the respective project component periods which vary from 3 to 5 years. See individual cost tables for details.

[c]Estimate derived by tripling the 10,000 families of two minimum salaries or less targeted for the subsidy program since around 1/3 of families in the project area fall in that category, then multiplying by 7.3, the average family size the lowest group in the urban northeast Brazil.

[d]Based on 600 calories per person per day at 50 percent subsidy for 27,000 recipients for the full year (i.e., some of the 41,026 beneficiaries participated for less than full year).

[e]Based on 500 calories per person per day at 100 percent subsidy for 14,055 children for 217 days, 4,270 for 131 days and 3,973 for 60 days.

[f]Costs are estimated. Costs included under other recurrent costs may include some training costs, which should fall under nonrecurrent costs. There is no information on this breakdown, however, nor on any other nonrecurrent costs from previous years; hence no estimate of nonrecurrent costs is made.

[g]Based on 5,227 tons of food, the value of coupons redeemed.

[h]Includes fixed costs.

[i]Excludes fixed costs.

[j]Average block size is 100,000.

[k]Number only of children fed.

Source: World Bank Data.

In autumn 1972, a baseline survey was undertaken with 550 subjects in each of the three towns. The mass media campaign was started immediately after the survey and ran for nine months through to August 1973, when a second survey of the sample was made. This pattern was repeated in 1974 and 1975, covering the full three-year period of the experiment. The nine-month media campaign was repeated in 1973 and 1974 but was reduced for 1974 and 1975.

In the town selected for the combined intervention, high-risk individuals were selected for a ten-week period of intensive instruction either individually at home or in group sessions. Another high-risk group, half the size, but not given instruction was observed as a subgroup during the study. Similar high-risk subgroups were formed in the other two communities. Communication objectives included: agenda setting (directing attention to issues and problems); informing (presenting the propositions that set the stage for individual action); motivation (incentives to behavior change); training (learning to overcome barriers and accepting the personal cost); and self-maintenance (resisting pressures to revert). Having defined these key elements, the project directors, however, did not foreswear the possibility they might have to be modified in practice. One of the reports made this clear.

> These five campaign elements are by no means definitive nor mutually exclusive. No doubt messages may serve different functions for different receivers, e.g. a message which provides information to one person may perform an agenda-setting function for another. Messages may serve different functions for the same receiver, e.g. a message may simultaneously persuade, inform and motivate a single receiver.[3]

Although it is not clear from public reports of the study precisely how messages were tested, it appears that the same procedure may not have been utilized in every case. But formative evaluation appears to have played a central role in pretesting as well as in overall planning and media decisions.

TV, radio, newspapers, billboards, transportation (buses), direct mail, and the school system were used as media. A special kit of materials was prepared for schools. It is not clear to what degree mass media usage was calculated on the basis of audience-targeted radio and TV programs and reach-and-frequency goals or whether a postanalysis was made of these media values. Reference to the number of spots produced for radio and TV leaves unclear whether this is the total of actual messages produced or of on-air exposure. Perhaps even more crucial, however, is the missing information regarding cumulative reach-and-frequency ("cumes"). Were the media schedules in the two communities comparable? This is essential to meaningful interpretation of the results. The unfortunate categorization of some media materials as media rendered the media impact analysis even more difficult. Except for these apparent shortcomings, overall evaluation of the process was ongoing throughout the campaign.

The results of the three-community study were clearly positive. The program in both the full-intervention community and the media-only town produced considerable improvement in the targeted behaviors compared to the control town. While the full-intervention town had the most marked improvement, behavioral change in the media-only community was significant.

The conclusion of the evaluation is that "certain kinds of behavior associated with risk reduction can be learned through exposure to the mass media alone."[4] This has been restated many times since by the directors as a group and individually, Farquhar,[5] Maccoby,[6] and Maccoby et al.[7] But results are better with a broad-based education effort including the mass media. This confirms the social marketing principle: more impact impacts more.

This success prompted a five-city study in 1978 to run for five to eight years in larger communities and to embrace a broader age base. This time actual changes in cardiovascular morbidity and mortality rates not undertaken in the earlier study will be audited. It will also aim to establish a model in terms of cost effectiveness and adaptability to other communities. The training and coordination of health professionals will be emphasized to make them a key delivery system for both education and educational materials. Similar collaborations have been worked out with community organizations outside the health area such as youth, fraternal, and religious groups.

The formative research component is used to provide:

1. Baseline data on audience segments and profiles
2. Insights for program planning
3. Information about media components
4. Analysis of component performances

Both the formative and the quantitative (core questionnaire) research are conducted simultaneously but for essentially different purposes though inevitable overlap is anticipated. To overcome weaknesses of self-reports of behavior, other indirect data-gathering methods are being tried. For example, food store sales of selected items will be audited as a potential gauge of food behavioral changes.

In seeming response to the media planning deficiencies of the three-community study, media values will be monitored. Focus group interviews are used for message testing. In referring to the available "wealth of research into message variables," campaign officials caution that while "these should not be ignored by campaign planners, however, they should use this body of research as a source of ideas for message strategies and not as directly applicable to a particular situation."[8] The evaluation procedures take note of the stern warnings that Manoff International social marketers have been stressing for years: impact evaluation is not enough. It must be combined with evaluation of campaign components to pinpoint signs of weakness, strength, and even failure.

The Stanford projects are a particularly fascinating subject of study for those who have come to health promotion from the marketing side. They represent a notable affirmation by the academic community of social marketing principles.

The Contraceptive Social Marketing Project in Bangladesh

The contraceptive social marketing project (SMP) is a straightforward demonstration of what social marketing can accomplish with products of social importance but restricted previous acceptance. Bangladesh is a traditional Moslem society. Yet for almost a decade the social marketing of condoms, pills, and foaming tablets has been successfully conducted there. It has effectively doubled the free contraceptive distribution of the health system. Highly visible advertising has been employed on TV, radio, hoardings, in the press, at point of sale, and in other high-traffic locations. Some media were newly invented—rickshaw tailgate posters and sails on boats.

Formative research has illuminated all phases of the operation— package, price, name and message testing, media planning, trade distribution, and sales strategies. Despite the obvious delicacy involved, successful research has been conducted with consumers. It was not easy nor could it observe the usual research conventions. But ingenious adaptations made meaningful inquiries possible. This project proved that even under severely constraining social and cultural circumstances an appropriately designed social marketing enterprise is possible. True, ultimate objectives need to be balanced against present possibilities and realistic objectives and timetables set. But every unfolding phase creates an increasingly hospitable environment for expanding the possibilities of the next.

The Bangladesh SMP is managed by Population Services International (PSI) under USAID funding. The measure of its success may be gleaned from one significant statistic; in the 12 months from October 1982 to September 1983, SMP sold through commercial channels enough contraceptives to provide annual protection to some 985,000 couples.[9]

The SMP was inaugurated in 1973 but national commercial distribution of contraceptives did not get underway until 1975. The objective was to distribute nonclinical contraceptives through the wholesale and retail outlets supported by the traditional marketing mix of the commercial world—mass media consumer advertising and promotion, publicity, merchandising, trade promotion and discounts, consumer and market research, and sales audits. Condoms are marketed under the brand name Raja and, despite initial trade and consumer reticence, sales of Raja reached 9.7 million units by the end of 1976. By 1983 sales had increased to more than 82 million, a dramatic reflection of the public acceptance of an item that could only be whispered about even among men less than a decade earlier.

The advertising budget for Raja (and the other products) is now one of the biggest. Though the advertisements are still subject to rigid censorship restraints, they are today far more explicit than in 1976. So severely restricted were those that consumers could scarcely comprehend them in pretesting. Today, hardly a soul on the streets of Dhaka (almost certainly a male) can be found who does not know Raja or, in fact, the symbol, SMP. Messages about SMP brands redound from the radio, TV, the press, billboards, sound trucks, and even cascade from the skies in leaflets dropped from airplanes. But advertising can be wasted when distribution is incomplete, so SMP is constantly expanding the number of Raja's outlets. The sales force has been expanded, the number of area managers increased from four to eight in the special effort to broaden distribution to the more distant, less accessible rural areas.

A 1981 survey commissioned through a local agency showed that though Raja enjoyed broad consumer appeal, it had good penetration of lower socioeconomic groups. This confirmed the premise that subsidizing the right price point could create a market of population segments most in need.

Maya is the local brand name of the imported oral contraceptive repackaged in Bangladesh. Sales grew rapidly the first year, reached a plateau in 1977 to 1979 and then started to decline. A low-dose pill introduced under the Ovacon brand name in 1980 reversed the trend, which has since moved steadily upward. More than a new product was involved in the turnaround. A radically altered marketing strategy shifted sales emphasis from over the counter to the indigenous medical establishment of licensed doctors and rural medical practitioners—the doctor-sahibs of the countryside.

It had become apparent that a contraceptive designed for women could not easily overcome the hurdle of their isolation from the marketplace where all shopping is done by men. This made usage instruction even more complicated. In addition, rumors of side effects had aroused widespread fear of the pill provoked by sensationalized news reports. In fact, research suggested that apprehension about the safety of all devices may very well have been aroused entirely by concern over the pill.[10] These fears could not be competently dealt with at point of sale given the impersonal nature of over-the-counter transactions. Some form of face-to-face contact with an appropriate authority was clearly needed. Government family-planning workers were already distributing some half-million free cycles per month through home visits. The social marketing project needed another distribution system to augment this network.

The new-improved product, the low-dose Ovacon, promised greater user satisfaction and fewer complaints. Ironically, the network chosen for its distribution were the 150,000 rural medical practitioners who until then had been a major source of opposition to the pill, together with the much smaller corps of professionally qualified doctors. Their recruitment was carried out in two stages, first, by acknowledging their authority through the missionary task of presenting the full information needed to win their approval and second, to enlist them as suppliers of the pill on their customary paid professional basis. Retail distribution of Ovacon was withheld until acceptance was general among these practitioners in each area. A slow but steady increase in sales is evidence that the new strategy, in effect since 1980, is working.

Neo-Sampoon, a foaming tablet, has proved a less satisfactory product strategy. According to consumer reports, it is both less comfortable to use and less reliable in preventing conception. Sales of Neo-Sampoon have leveled to about 500,000 units monthly with no immediate prospect of an increase without major product improvement.

Overall results have been dramatic (Figure 10.3). By the end of 1983's third quarter, SMP had sold more than 290 million condoms, 7 million cycles of pills, and 25 million foaming tablets. Its share of nonclinical contraceptives had grown from 8 percent in 1975 and 1976 to over 50 percent in 1982 and 1983. According to other reports of the program 25 percent of current users of modern family planning methods are buying and using SMP products, and all the growth in modern contraceptive usage in the eight years since 1975 has come from consumer acceptance of SMP products.

Cost effectiveness is impressive. Of all the nonclinical family planning operations in Bangladesh, it is by far the most cost effective per couple/year of protection (CYP). SMP's CYP net operating cost of $1.67 (excludes cost of contraceptives) is far less than the comparable $3.00 to $18.00 range of other programs. Including cost of contraceptives, SMP's CYP cost is $6.37. Only the voluntary sterilization program is more cost effective and by a considerable margin. But this reflects the much lower cost of a single surgical procedure when amortized over the years of its effectiveness despite the initial higher expenditure. SMP's nonclinical devices need replacements after each use, entailing a much higher aggregate outlay. The comparison hardly suggests that one strategy should re-

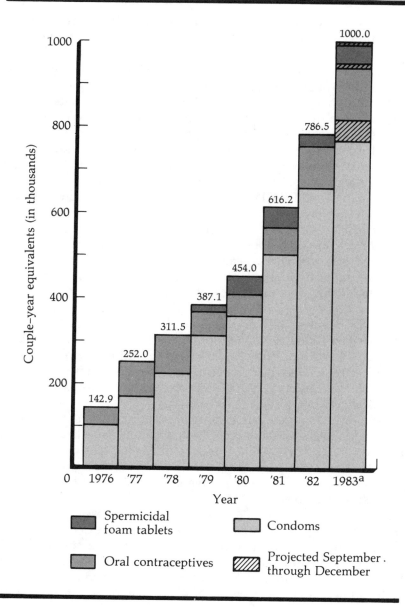

Figure 10.3.   PSI/SMP distribution, 1976 to 1983.

place the other for cost reasons. Both are obviously necessary to satisfy different population segments. Sterilization may be the least costly but for fertility-prevention purposes, it could be less effective in terms of the number of couples accepting.

SMP has two notable operational elements. One is its organization system and the other is the special social marketing motivational component introduced in 1982 under subcontract to Manoff International. SMP is organized on the commercial marketing model..Its project director is Anwar Ali, a Bangladeshi marketing professional from private industry who is also chief executive of operations. Under him are five senior managers for processing, warehousing and distribution, sales and marketing, and financial controls. The PSI resident adviser also acts as liaison with the government and USAID. The country is arranged in eight sales divisions, with each divisional sales force under an area sales manager. Of a total staff of 290, one-fourth is in direct sales. In the beginning, SMP could have contracted distribution with an existing commercial organization but the only arrangements available left uncertain the extent to which the sales force and distribution plans could be controlled. SMP is, in effect, a vertical marketing organization capable of handling other social products. It has already begun to distribute ORS packets.

USAID donates the contraceptives, which are repackaged and warehoused in Dhaka for transshipment to area depots or direct to 22 wholesalers. In all, more than 100,000 outlets of various size are served including 5,000 stockists who then job the merchandise to retail customers. Special medical missionary representatives direct sales to pharmacies and the medical network.

The motivational campaign was instigated in 1982 at the recommendation of Manoff International, SMP consultants, in anticipation that sales of contraceptives might be approaching the limits of existing demand. What was needed in addition to SMP's advertising was a market expansion advertising strategy to convert the considerable latent demand into purchase decisions.

The overall objectives of Manoff International's assignment was to develop a campaign that would persuade more people to practice family planning with modern contraceptives and deepen awareness of family planning with the rural populace. Some 40-odd research reports dealing with contraceptive attitudes or behavior were examined for clues to the need for additional research. From these, the Manoff International team was able to identify these critical concerns

1. *Religious Conservatism.* A prevailing interpretation that the Koran does not sanction the use of mechanical or chemical contraceptives has been accepted by most devout Muslims.

2. *Observance of* Purdah. Seclusion of women is highly prevalent and for the most part strictly observed, presenting a major obstacle to new concepts and ideas.

3. *Low Status of Women.* Women generally have little voice in important family decisions. Their attitudes tend to mirror those of their husbands.

4. *Sexual Taboos.* There is little open discussion of sexual matters among family members. Husbands commonly forbid contact between wives and family planning workers.

5. *Cultural Conservatism.* For most rural villagers, life-style, customs, habits, and mores have not significantly changed over many generations.

6. *Economic Distress.* The abject poverty in this agricultural society puts a premium on many sons.

7. *Child Mortality.* Infant and child mortality rates are high.

Serious shortcomings in the research raised doubts about the findings. For future research special safeguards were devised to ensure proper training and supervision of field staffs. New validation techniques were prepared. Members of the team undertook trips into the countryside for first-hand knowledge of rural conditions. Informal focus groups were held with village residents, shopkeepers, pharmacists, local government officials, and family planning workers.

Identifying *resistance points* was the primary objective of the formative research. The methodology was qualitative. Quantitative research of the knowledge/attitude/practice (KAP) type typically describes behavior; qualitative research seeks the reasons for behavior through loosely structured open-ended questions, in-depth probing of responses, indirect questioning, and the use of projective techniques. The delicate nature of the subject made reliance on individual in-depth interviews necessary when focus groups proved difficult to arrange.

Projective techniques are particularly useful to overcome reluctance to discuss personal experience of an intensely private matter. They can be used both within a focus-group environment and in individual interviews. In this case, they relied heavily on indirect questions about photos of individuals from different population strata (e.g., how would a friend react to this?). Respondents were asked to separate the photos two ways: people they felt would practice family planning and those they felt would not. They were asked to select the person most likely and the person least likely to practice family planning and to give reasons. Then, all the photos were shuffled together and each respondent asked to select the person (of the same sex) most desired as a friend. This technique offered easier access to respondents' true personal feelings by directing their attention from themselves to others. By matching the choices, researchers were able to assess positive or negative inclinations toward family planning and the reasons why.

Validation procedures included tape-recording all interviews, checking questionnaires against the tapes by a validation team of university students, and spot-checking field work by two observers. Tape-recording interviews ensured the quality of field work and minimized dishonesty. It also provided message designers with the words, phrases, and anecdotes used by real people. Tape transcribers were instructed to select verbatims that were unusual, interesting, colorful, or rich with imagery. Market Research Consultants of Bangladesh, Ltd. (MRCB) was selected from among three potential suppliers recommended by SMP, USAID, Unilever, Bangladesh Tobacco Co., and others.

The research team was trained in the four principal reasons for probing (getting specific, complete, clear answers that reflect the respondent's true feelings). They were also taught when and how to apply specific probes (i.e., Any other reason? In what way? What do you mean by that? Could you be more specific?) and techniques of establishing rapport with respondents. The field staff was college-trained and of middle-class background and had to be made sensitive to ways of bridging the cultural gap to rural respondents. They were given guidelines for dress, speech, behavior, and ways to put respondents at ease and to justify the use of tape recorders. Pilot interviews were conducted and coworkers critiqued the performances. Pretests of the question guides were conducted in urban and rural areas and interviewers debriefed afterward. Based on previous experience, interviews were conducted when men were unlikely to be home and women would welcome the opportunity to air their views.

The research identified these main *resistance points*

1. Birth control is contrary to Islamic law.
2. There is an absence of communication between husband and wife.
3. Fear of detrimental health effects from contraceptives including condoms and contraceptive foam. This exaggerated fear may be a function of illiteracy and reliance on word of mouth and irrational generalizations from the reports of occasional discomfort caused by pills. Some respondents believed they could lead to childlessness.
4. Ignorance about contraceptive options (despite a positive attitude toward limiting family size) because of lack of awareness of qualified information sources, lack of access to them, or reluctance to use them.

Determination of target audience strategy left no alternatives because

1. In the rural areas where 90 percent of the population lives, the family is male dominated.

2. *Purdah* is strictly observed. Virtually all purchases, including female undergarments and contraceptives, are made by men.
3. Radio is the only mass medium and is monopolized by the men. Women will listen when the men are out but with some apprehension.

Consequently, men were chosen as the primary target, and women secondarily, to convert their latent acceptance into a means of leverage less likely for the men to resist than if it came from other quarters. The sensitive religious issue remained unresolved. Plans to explore the implications of Islamic law with religious leaders were abandoned. Health fears were interpreted from the verbatims to be grounded in ignorance and were, therefore, deemed not rational. Consequently, the strategic conclusion was that rational, method-specific information in the messages was an irrelevant response. Emotional resistance points require emotional rebuttals.

What is to be done about misinformation concerning contraceptive safety and fear of detrimental health effects? Conventional wisdom is to avoid negatives for fear of reinforcing them. However, there are times when the pervasiveness of the issue requires a challenge to its validity, to confront the issue head-on, and to debunk it with a force equal to the one that implanted it. Intrusive creative messages plus saturation media exposure were called for.

The most delicate *resistance point* was a couple's reluctance to discuss family planning among themselves. Objectives could not be furthered without legitimizing such discussion between husband and wife. An acceptable dramatic demonstration of such an exchange—sensitively treated—became a mandatory element in the creative execution.

Each message had to promise tangible benefits, not offer vague or weak incentives like a happy family but the economic and maternal health benefits most frequently mentioned by male respondents. In addition, an immediate emotional benefit to men had to be proffered; an enhanced sense of pride as the head of the family was the singular male status value inferred from the research. Messages had to have an environment inviting to the target audience. This is message tonality—a dramatically compelling setting capable of provoking a visceral response—to be *intrusive*, capable of captivating audience attention and stimulating empathy with the message content.

The creative approach clearly needed to shake up smug, even arrogant, male self-confidence, confront the dramatic male prototype with doubts about his competence as a planner of his family, and force a reexamination of his attitudes on the subject. The task called for new images, new word combinations foreign even to the standard family planning lexicon.

The format? A minidrama in which the protagonist (always a male), accepted as a wise man, confesses to behavior as a fool. The reason? He had believed family planning devices to be unsafe. Why? Because he had been listening to ignorant tales told by ignorant people. By realizing his foolish error in time, he looks into family planning (the condom, the pill, and other safe methods), finds it safe, discusses it with his wife, and with her selects a method, his self-esteem as a wise man thankfully restored.

Certain key phrases were fixed features of every message:

- Do not listen to ignorant tales from ignorant people.
- I have not always been a wise man. Once I was a fool.
- Use condoms, pills, and other safe methods.
- Be a wise man—do the right thing.

The Bengali language is inordinately complex and operates on several different language levels: the language of the poet, playwright, and writer; the chaste Bengali used by the educated person as well as by Radio Bangladesh; and the vernacular of the average, uneducated, or illiterate Bangladeshi. Key words, like fool or wise man, became the subject of analysis to determine the Bengali words most closely approximating the desired meaning for the target audience. Message pretesting led to the inevitable revisions. The censorship process led to others. In the end the messages were produced both for radio (the primary medium) and for TV (the supporting medium for urban audiences).

As of this writing, all messages have been on the air for well over a year and are continuing. Evaluative tracking gives indication of positive behavioral impact and contraceptive sales are at new highs, but the full effect will not be decisively known until the impact evaluation is concluded some months after this writing.

The North Karelia Project

Much has been written and said about the difficulties of mounting effective antismoking campaigns and not enough about the potentialities. The cigarette companies are not among the doubters. When the U.S. Congress took up consideration of a ban on TV and radio cigarette advertising, the companies were among its most militant lobbyists. This was no beneficent gesture. The ban carried with it the likelihood under the Fairness Doctrine (guaranteeing both sides of an issue a fair airing) that anticigarette messages would also disappear from the air. The cigarette companies were willing to forego their privilege to forestall the opposition.

Antismoking campaigns can work, as some have demonstrated. Perhaps the most notable of these has been the North Karelia Project in Finland, which set out to employ TV for education on the risk factors identified with coronary heart disease (CHD). It chose smoking as the first to deal with because it was the most widely accepted.[11] Its innovative use of TV was to present on air over a five-week period seven sessions of a smoking cessation course with ten volunteer smokers. Each session lasted for 45 minutes, three of them the first week but only one a week thereafter. Content was derived from years of experience with smoking cessation therapy groups similar to such efforts in many countries. These have achieved cessation rates averaging 38 percent six months after course completion. This apparently provided the formative basis for the programs, making more formal formative research unnecessary. (The results achieved would seem to confirm the assumptions.) Could something like this be achieved in sessions transferred to TV? This was the question the project sought to answer with its first TV experiment in 1978.

Two experts were chosen to conduct the TV sessions with volunteers of mixed social origins, age, and sex. The two moderators followed the group therapy pattern of talk and discussion but interspersed these with comments directed to the TV audience as well. Members of the TV audience were urged to form tune-in groups and during each session to follow all instructions as though they were participants in the on-air session.

The project did not rely on TV alone. Publicity to attract as large a target audience as possible was launched in all media. Health services were indoctrinated in advance as were voluntary organizations working with health care and education programs. In North Karelia county, intensive field work was carried out. More than 200 volunteers undertook widespread missionary work with the public to form self-help groups timed to take advantage of the TV program for initiating smoking cessation. About 100 such groups were formed, though the effort was described as difficult to organize.

The program sessions, following the tried methods of smoking cessation, emphasized

1. The desire of most smokers to quit
2. The aim of the program to help them try
3. The practical skills in quitting that previous experience had proved effective
4. Real life situations
5. Encouragement for outspoken expression of personal problems
6. The short-term positive experiences of the group
7. Group pressure
8. Advice about social support systems

Conventional knowledge about the effects of smoking was played down and, in fact, deliberately avoided, when possible. When awareness of negative health consequences is already high, past experience had indicated little residual benefit is derived from harping on them further. The project was repeated a year later in spring 1979, with an additional session devoted to an update on the group from the 1978 program. Evaluation consisted of national surveys by mail of random samples of the adult population covering both the 1978 and 1979 programs. Sample size in each survey was approximately 6,000; the participation rate was 85 percent. Media audience evaluation showed that about 10 percent of the adult population followed the 1978 program but in North Karelia it was twice that amount. The 1979 repeat audiences were perceptibly higher on both counts.

Of the more than one million smokers in Finland, approximately 19 percent followed the program along with 15 percent of the nonsmokers. In real numbers, 14,000 quit and resumed and 8,000 quit permanently. In effect, the project whose centerpiece was a TV program broadcast only seven times in five weeks had helped almost 1 percent of Finland's smokers to kick the habit. The results of the 1979 repeat were even better. The number of quitters and those who had not relapsed several months (but less than a year) later was almost 13,000. Cost effectiveness was evaluated at less than $1 U.S. per successful cessation.

The question that is difficult to resolve is what would have happened had the program been of longer duration, of greater in-week frequency, repeated during the year, or continued regularly every year? There are other questions a social marketer is obliged to raise. Nevertheless, granting the project its normal degree of human imperfection, the results affirm the contribution that innovative social marketing can make even to the most difficult tasks of health education. The North Karelia Project is notable for its demonstration of the potentialities of the TV medium, in this case the live transfer to the TV screen of a real-life interpersonal group experience. This was no reach-and-frequency format employing short messages, no soap opera, no program designed expressly for TV but a moving-out from TV to embrace the country as a whole in an intimate group search for better health. Could this technique work for every problem? Probably not. But it worked for smoking cessation and probably can be made to work again and again—and better each time. The nature of the problem and the special group session therapy technique made the transfer to TV ideal. It was a creative judgment, an inspired linkage of two discrete elements—the smoking cessation group session on the one hand, the TV screen on the other. No amount of research intelligence can substitute for the ingenuity of the human mind and its capacity for invention. Social marketing disciplines cannot assure great leaps of discovery but they can help to produce the environment that enhances its possibility. This is creative social marketing.

The North Karelia Project has since repeated the program but broadened it to include weight loss and other dietary and life-style changes. The format remained essentially the same. Ten biweekly sessions over a longer, four-month period accommodated on-air monitoring of weight loss among group members and the TV audience. A workbook used by the TV group was made available to the TV audience through publication in cooperating national magazines. Reprints were widely distributed and, once again, volunteers in North Karelia mobilized tune-in groups.

Evaluation procedures were the same but a telephone survey was added to interview those whose mail responses identified them as weight-losers and/or smoking quitters. According to the results obtained, 40,000 Finns lost an average of roughly 4.5 kilos (9.9 lbs.) by the six-month follow-up; 5,000 more stopped smoking permanently; 3.4 percent of all the men and 5.2 percent of all the women in the country reduced fat and increased vegetable consumption; 2.8 percent of all the men and 5.2 percent of all the women reduced salt intake. Again, the results in North Karelia itself were 50 percent to as much as 100 percent better on all counts.[12]

Notes

1. Manoff International Inc., "Nutrition Communication and Behavior Change Component of the Indonesian Nutrition Development Program," Manoff International, New York.

2. Ho, T.J., "Economic Issues in Assessing Nutrition Projects: Costs, Affordability and Cost Effectiveness," staff technical report, International Bank for Reconstruction and Development (the World Bank), Washington, D.C., 1984.

3. Maccoby, N., Solomon, D., "Experiments in Risk Reduction Through Community Health Education," in *Health Education by Radio and TV* (ed. M. Meyer), K.G. Saur, Munich, 1981, pp. 140–166.

4. Ibid.

5. Farquhar, J.W., "Interdisciplinary Approaches to Heart Disease Prevention," American Association for the Advancement of Science Meetings, New York, 1975.

6. Maccoby, N., "Achieving Behavior Change via Mass Media and Interpersonal Communications," American Association for the Advancement of Science Meetings, New York, 1975.

7. Maccoby, N. et al., "Reducing the Risk of Cardiovascular Disease," *Journal of Community Health,* March 1977, pp. 100–114.

8. Maccoby and Solomon. Op. Cit.

9. Schellstede, W.P., Ciszewski, R.L., "Social Marketing of Contraceptives in Bangladesh," *Studies in Family Planning,* the Population Council, Vol. 15, No. 1, January/February 1984.

10. Manoff International Inc. and Market Research Consultants of Bangladesh Ltd., "Qualitative Research on the Concept of Family Planning," under subcontract to Population Services International, 1983.

11. Puska, P., "The North Karelia Project," WHO Regional Office for Europe, Copenhagen, 1981.

12. Puska, P., "Experiences with the Use of TV in National Health Promotion in Finland," in *Health Education by Radio and TV* (Ed. M. Meyer), K.G. Saur, Munich, 1981.

11

Cultural and Structural Impediments to Social Marketing

A minor German poet by the name of Heinz Jost once wrote: "Whenever I hear the word culture I reach for my gun." The quotation has since been erroneously attributed to Nazi Field Marshall Goering apparently because he liked it so much and used it so often. What both the poet and the field marshall had in mind, of course, was not culture but the arts of refinement—painting, music, *hoch literatur*—which comprise a crucial, but by no means the most important, expression of culture. The distinction is important to the social marketer.

Culture is the product of the human processing of environment. It combines useful adaptations to the demands of the environment with inventive formulas to modify the environment to human requirements. It is a constant process. The health of a society and its capacity for vigorous survival depend on appropriate cultural response and change.

In modern times, our enlarging authority over the physical, social, and economic environment accelerates the rate of change. The burden on culture is accordingly made heavier. Is the change in society's best interest? If so, what measures are needed to ensure an appropriate rate? If not, what restraints are necessary to forestall it?

The response of the social system unfolds through a procedure of cultural arbitration, which renders judgment for or against the change. This may come about through a governmental decision, an action of the private sector, or response to citizens' demands. Once rendered, it undergoes a process of cultural mediation. Legislators hold hearings to decide the manner of its implementation, the company sets the budget and timetable for its investment, or citizens' groups initiate lobbying efforts with government or the private sector. In the process, the rate of its adoption and the way it will be managed and monitored are decided.

251

In centrally planned socialist societies, this is a rigid procedure carried out with state mechanisms. In the nonsocialist world, the process is left to the workings of the free market system. The marketplace is the arbiter and mediator of new ideas, products, and practices.

In either case, culture and society are indistinguishable. Change in the one inevitably affects the other. The change is more desirable when it is internal, a venting by the society of its self-determined needs. When the change is external, there is risk of disturbing the arbitration and mediation processes with consequent social shock and damage.

Julius Nyerere of Tanzania, a strong and respected voice with African peoples, once said to me, "The choice is not between change or no change; the choice for Africa is between changing or being changed—changing our lives under our own direction or being changed by the impact of forces outside our control."

The quality of a culture can be measured by the appropriateness of its changes. The source of social decay is in the widening gap between culture and reality, the irrelevance of cultural response to social needs. The signs are easily detected: growing social dissonance, discontent, and upheaval.

Not long after World War II, Professor Lyman Bryson of Columbia University broached the subject to a student gathering. He placed a describing compass on a map of the world and anchored its needle on the island of Hong Kong. Extending its writing arm to a radius of 1,000 miles, he spun a circle. Within the circle, he said, lived more than half the population of the world and its average person dwelt in a shack with a thatched grass roof and no floor. Its sanitary facility was a pit at the edge of the clearing, the nearby stream, or some other haphazard arrangement for human waste disposal. Yet, Professor Bryson reminded us, the Voice of America was engaged in assuring the people of the circle that the United States would help guarantee free speech, a free press, and the right freely to assemble.

Professor Bryson's average person of what was later to be dubbed the Third World still lives in the same condition—the same housing, same no floor, same no sanitary facility, and, if anything, even worse water. The Voice of America is still heard but more prominent voices have joined the chorus: international aid organizations and, most resonant of all, the overwhelming decibels of multinational enterprise.

Since the health of a society can be measured by the appropriateness of its cultural response to change, there is a basis for distinguishing the good from the bad, the procultural from the anticultural. Who can question, for example, the contribution of medical science and aid agencies in helping to reduce death rates? Or the technological breakthroughs that now make possible notable advances in crop yields and food preservation, diversity, and distribution? But the question also prods us to examine the appropriateness of these achievements; have people been helped or hindered in their adaptation to the social, economic, and physical environments?

The dissonance of socially antagonistic practices cannot always be ameliorated by countervailing education interventions. Some problems defy educational solutions because they result from frictional behavior patterns of the system demanding structural changes. Social marketers have the obligation to recognize the difference so as not to engage in futile educational exercises and to support public policies needed for the desired change. When health and nutrition depend on factors other than individual will and enlightenment, health professionals and their social marketing allies become concerned.

The Public Health Paradox

The third era of public health (see Chapter 2) and the fourth since then have shifted the focus from social reform to behavior modification in the individual. According to Starr, "Narrowing the objectives of public health made it more politically acceptable . . . a movement away from the broad advocacy of social reform toward more narrow judgments that could be defended as the exercise of neutral authority."[1] The implications were even more profound. Emphasis on personal hygiene shifted the burden of disease prevention from the state to the individual despite ample evidence that argued for the priority of selected social reforms. As Starr reported, the new tubercular test revealed that tuberculosis was latent throughout the population though it struck down only a minority. The key protective factor was health capacity to resist disease. This argued for better nutrition, housing, sanitation, and working conditions at least as much as for education in personal hygiene and the universal medical examination. In fact, the latter was merely a disease detection device rather than a preventive measure.

But social reform is always a more costly strategy than education. The latter transfers the reform responsibility from the state's budget to that of the individual. This has had burdensome implications for public health in the Third World countries. Aid from developed nations, particularly the United States, comes packaged with their philosophies. In health this means medicine and Western medical practice, on the one hand; emphasis on personal education, on the other. These have produced their benefits—the eradication of smallpox, the cyclical successes against malaria, and growing awareness of positive health practices—but the effects have also been negative. Still, improvement of environmental conditions like water, sewerage, and sanitation systems are pressing health priorities that until recently were virtually ignored.

One Brazilian health authority characterized this situation as typical of the philosophy of developed countries. "You people," he said once to a Pan-American Health Organization (PAHO) representative in my presence, "are always recommending cultural solutions to our health problems because the economic solutions are just too costly."[2] He called it "the Economic Bias."

What makes the matter even more complicated is our growing awareness that the universe of environmental conditions and structural factors is constantly expanding. It now embraces not only the fixed physical environment—water, land use, air, and waste disposal—but also the unpredictable health implications of new inventions. A WHO Expert Committee called for reorientation of the health education approach from a singular focus on changing individual behavior to embrace consideration of the social context—"the political, economic and environmental factors that have a negative or neutralizing effect on health behavior."[3]

Stresses of the Marketing Culture

The climate is not hospitable to social marketing ventures, and social marketers who blind themselves to the enemy risk inevitable failure. The public health enemy is not only disease and malnutrition but social and economic constraints like antithetical marketing practices, faddist and unhealthful life-styles, poor water and sanitation facilities, lack of supportive public policies, divided opinion among health authorities, inappropriate food production priorities, and discoordination of health agencies' efforts. Social marketers must include in their planning the means to neutralize their enemies' impact. This will call for political strategies not directly related to the social marketing venture but pivotal, nevertheless, to its success.

Studies at Khartoum University, sponsored by Oxfam and the British Overseas Development Administration, indicated that kwashiorkor can be caused by aflatoxin, a fungus that damages the liver and blocks protein synthesis. It often forms on crops stored without protection from heat and humidity. The fungus could be prevented by proper storage—the kind used by well-established commercial food distributors—and by ensuring that cooking oil is processed only from oilseeds not contaminated with the fungus.[4]

In India, the major food problem is not food scarcity but distribution—a similar lack of warehousing, roads, transportation, and an organized marketplace. These necessary marketing methods are available in India but they are devoted to less essential foods unrelated to the needs of the typical Indian consumer. They serve the commercial marketer whose preferred target is the moneyed middle class. Marketing system energies are reserved for a small urban minority with profound negative effects for the rest.

Take the farmer I met one day on his way to work in the fields outside Amritsar in the Punjab. A traditional noonday repast of a Punjabi farmer is *chapati* (a flat wheat bread) and curd (yogurt). This man carried a small pot of tea, a package of commercial biscuits, and a radio. Economically, he was on the rise thanks to the Green Revolution but, nutritionally, he was heading for trouble. Tea and biscuits may be rationalized for the calorie-counting upper middle class in the city but not for a farmhand. The village is being sold new ideas from the city but these can be damaging to village life (as well as to disadvantaged urban people). *Advertising Age,* the prominent American journal of marketing, acknowledged that "even when marketers ventured into politically and economically less stable places . . . it was mainly to serve urban populations, leaving out people on the fringe."[5] For such countries, it is a case of getting what they don't need and needing what they can't get. For example, a Duke University sociologist in his book on drug marketing practices in the Third World referred to filiariasis, malaria, and dysentery as the three most prevalent diseases in India and then declared that "of the 15 leading pharmaceutical products in terms of sales in 1978 [in India] not one was used in the treatment of those diseases."[6]

A counterpart situation in Guayaquil, Ecuador, is that of a working-class woman who had given up breast-feeding in favor of store-bought dry milk, though she has neither the proper water to mix it with, the sterilized bottles to pour it into, the refrigeration to preserve it, or, in fact, the income to afford it. Like our Punjabi farmer, she was seeking to satisfy her rising expectations with something new and better. It is not surprising, therefore, that breast-feeding should be on the decline. In addition to the detrimental effect on the health of children, the implications for population growth may be serious. It has been estimated that "if rural women adopted the urban breast-feeding pattern, their total fertility would increase 0.5 births, from 4.9 to 5.4 births per month [or more than 10 percent], other factors remaining constant."[7]

In the United States, where breast-feeding has been reported rising after a long decline, "the return to . . . breast milk is not the trend among low-income women," according to a petition of Public Advocates.[8] This public interest law firm reports that less than 5 percent of the new mothers at the District of Columbia General Hospital were breast-feeding in 1981; only 1 percent among Mexican-Americans in Del Rio, Texas in 1980; and 3 to 12.8 percent among the ward service and clinics in New

York City. Only 18 percent of all clinic patients in Chinatown, San Francisco, planned to breast-feed; and of all WIC program (Women/Infants/Children) clients among the Navajo nation in Arizona, only 26 to 38 percent planned to breast-feed.[9]

Yet, Dr. Audrey Naylor, director of the Lactation Program at the University of California, San Diego, declared that 95 percent of mothers can produce sufficient milk for their infants—"Most nursing failures are the direct result of incorrect information . . . and of hospital procedures which interfere with normal physiology." Discharge packs of infant formula samples, she said, create "doubt at a time when confidence is most critical. Patients presume that something given by a health professional is to be used. The discharge pack promotes formula sales, not successful breast-feeding."[10]

Dr. Derrick B. Jelliffe was among the first to identify bottle feeding as a source of diarrheal infection. A former head of the Caribbean Food and Nutrition Institute, he labeled such infection a "commerciogenic disease," saying, "The pediatric nutritionist is left increasingly frustrated by the well-financed, steam roller, marketing techniques of the food industry to sell totally unaffordable and inappropriate infant foods in impoverished communities."[11] Ross Laboratories, a division of Abbott Laboratories, and Mead Johnson, a division of Bristol-Myers, reportedly donate nursery equipment, incubators, bottles, and nipples and give away free samples of formula to over 90 percent of U.S. hospitals. Ross has offered an architectural design service for hospitals that always provides for separate nurseries in the maternity section thereby discouraging rooming-in and making bottle feeding an almost certain routine.

The promotion of breast-feeding is a good example of a public health problem that on close examination proves to be complicated by structural factors beyond educational influence and that are, in fact, serious obstacles to it. There are at least four major structural constraints the social marketer would identify as strategic impediments to education:

1. Birthing practices in hospitals where newborns are separated from mothers in nurseries and artificial feeding is introduced
2. The unbridled promotion of breast-milk substitutes
3. No provision for maternity leaves for salaried mothers
4. Lack of nursing facilities in work establishments

These are obstacles to breast-feeding and no amount of education and promotion can totally overcome them.

Brazil's massive breast-feeding promotion in the early 1980s illustrated the difference strategic attacks on these structural constraints can make.[12] In eight of the nine maternity hospitals in Recife, rooming-in replaced the nursery. The results were

1. Whereas 76 percent of the mothers had been unable to breast-feed under the old system, virtually all mothers are now able to do so within the first 12 hours after birth.
2. Diarrheal infections that previously affected 10 to 15 percent of the infants have practically disappeared.
3. Child abandonment, a serious past problem, rarely occurs.
4. The use of breast-milk substitutes has fallen by 80 percent and is now reserved only for cases of respiratory disease in the mother, child abandonment, or lack of a milk bank.
5. Where four nurses were required to care for the 70 infants in the average nursery, only one is needed.

In addition, paid maternity leave for three months and crèches in every work establishment with more than 30 employees are mandatory by law. But legislation without enforcement is meaningless. So in the state of Santa Caterina where only 2 percent of affected firms were complying, enforcement steps by the state government raised compliance in one year to 85 percent, with 60 percent of the employed nursing mothers using the crèches. Curbing detrimental marketing practices by commercial milk companies has been undertaken by drafting an adaptation of the WHO/UNICEF Code.

At the Bronx Municipal Hospital Center in New York only 13 percent of new mothers ended up breast-feeding on discharge after 48 hours until these changes were made in maternity routines

1. Babies were put to the mother's breast at birth.
2. Babies were breast-fed on demand.
3. Babies were given no supplementary bottle feeding.
4. Formula gift packs were eliminated.

As a result, within six months the breast-feeding rate doubled even without rooming-in.[13] These are essential strategies of breast-feeding promotion and characterize the social marketing discipline of identifying and dealing with *resistance points* to health education, whether in the behavior of individuals or in social and economic systems.

In 1974 and 1975, a social marketing campaign in Nicaragua to educate mothers in the home preparation of an oral rehydration formula for treating diarrhea revealed the widespread use of *purgantes* (purgatives) for diarrhea, the result of overzealous promotion of milk of magnesia for stomach and bowel illness and cramps.[14] The irony, of course, is that there is nothing wrong with commercial or infant formula milks, tea, biscuits, or laxative drugs when used as directed for prescribed conditions. The problem is created by misdirected efforts that put them into the hands of the wrong consumers for the wrong reasons.

This is inevitable when large food companies are primarily marketing enterprises and their new products are conceived out of positioning and advertising copy appeals rather than significant consumer benefits; when emphasis is on lowered cost of goods to maximize profit and marketing margins with inevitable downward pressure on product quality. Such overzealous pursuit produces excesses antithetical to public health and welfare. When American models are exported they have an impact on the whole world. These become structural impediments to health education goals.

Proposed Guidelines for Consumer Protection promulgated by the U.N.'s Economic and Social Council provide for:

1. Food product standards, limits on additives and contaminants, and rules for marketing
2. Chemical product standards for pesticides, pharmaceuticals, and drugs as well as rules to prevent dumping of hazardous items
3. Consumer participation in developing such standards and rules
4. Consumer access to product information and consumer education materials and sources

Like the WHO/UNICEF Code for the Marketing of Breast-Milk Substitutes, these guidelines are intended to assist member states in drafting local laws and regulations.

In 1980, a primary objective of the Mexican government's Food System was to control the marketing of nonbasic and nontraditional products. Snack foods and alcoholic beverages were singled out for priority attention, although cigarettes and infant formulas were also included. In summer 1984, partial implementation of this initiative went into effect restricting certain aspects of liquor and cigarette advertising. Neither the advertising nor sale of these products was permitted at parks, stadiums, sport centers, theaters, and in the vicinity of schools. The standing prohibition on alcohol and cigarette advertising on TV is unchanged. No alcohol advertising is permissible before 10:00 P.M. nor can cigarettes be advertised after 9:30 P.M. All packages of these products now must carry a warning: "Excessive consumption of this product is dangerous to a person's health."[15]

The concern is by no means confined to Mexico. There is growing apprehension among the Eskimos in Frobisher Bay, the Northwest Territories, over excessive sugar consumption by a people who until recently had never used it in their diets. The local Ikalut candy store offers 243 different kinds of candy causing Marc Andre Levesque, the local dentist, to declare that Inuit children eat too many sweets "and as a result their teeth are rotting."[16]

In the United States, an 11-year study by the Food and Drug Administration determined that of 700 key ingredients of over-the-counter drug products only one-third were actually safe and effective.[17] Nor are all food ingredients safe or useful. Marian Burros, a food writer for the New York *Times,* wondered how "we ever got to the point where we thought it essential to color food in order to sell it" and answered, "to make artificial foods look real (Tang, Jell-O), and to make cheap substitutes look expensive (caramel coloring in bread to simulate whole grain flour, yellow dye in cakes to simulate eggs)."[18]

The results are far from frivolous. People have been led to believe that imitation ingredients and products are the nutritional equal of the real things. Tang advertises itself as containing more vitamin C than orange juice; yet, says one authoritative nutrition publication, "it contains little else besides sugar and Vitamin C" without the "significant amounts of potassium, folacin, thiamin and Vitamin A of orange juice."[19] It also admonishes manufacturers of nondairy creamers who "promote their products as a *replacement* for milk on cereal and fruit. Some parents give it *instead* of milk to their children—not realizing that it could have adverse health consequences. . . . Four children in Southern California developed kwashiorkor recently after their physician prescribed a non-dairy creamer to treat milk-protein sensitivity." Eli Lilly's false and misleading promotion of the now-banned arthritis drug, Oraflex was "a key element in many of the lawsuits filed against Lilly on behalf of people injured or killed" by the drug, wrote one observer of the marketing scene in *Advertising Age.*[20]

Food manufacturers have been responding to demand for health-related foods—calorie-reduced, sugar-free, salt-free, and those made of whole grains and rich in fiber. But in the enthusiasm for the new nutrition market, some have gone to extremes to exploit every slight nutrition claim in products of limited total nutritional value. A Campbell's Soup Company campaign to the effect that "Soup is Good Food" has been criticized by the Center for Science in the Public Interest as "false, deceptive and unsubstantiated. . . . On the contrary, the excessive sodium content . . . increases the risk of high blood pressure."[21]

Seven-Up, hardly a symbol of a nutritious libation, sought to polish its image among soft drinks by launching one advertising campaign attacking colas for their caffeine content, then followed with another attacking their artificial coloring and flavoring. This may be clever competitive marketing but hardly nutritionally enlightening to the consumer. Jello-O Brand Pudding Pops proved a successful new product from General Foods in 1982, leading President Philip L. Smith to forecast $100 million worth of business for that fiscal year from what he calls the "better-for-you-sweet-snack-business." The Beef Industry Council, seeking to stem the decline in red meat consumption, promoted the theme that "Beef Gives Strength" and trumpeted the nutrient richness of beef (protein, phosphorous, niacin, vitamin B-12, iron, riboflavin, zinc) to veil its high-fat, high-cholesterol disadvantage at a time when nutrition authorities urged a reduction in animal fat consumption.

In the Third World, marketing behavior dropped this finesse with the practice of "dumping hazardous consumer goods, dangerous technologies and toxic drugs . . . by some multinationals [that] discovered that faulty goods, banned in the North could be dumped in Third World countries."[22] In 1974, an antidiarrheal drug that produced blindness and paralysis in "several thousands in Japan" was being marketed "in Third World countries for spurious complaints, with higher recommended doses and incomplete warnings." Sweetened condensed milk banned for infant feeding in Britain since 1911, is still being sold for that purpose in many Third World countries despite a widespread ban, including a specific prohibition in the International Code for the Marketing of Breast-Milk Substitutes adopted at the 1981 World Health Assembly.

Attempts to control detrimental marketing practices meet with considerable pressures. Three major American pharmaceutical manufacturers summarily ended their operations in Greece in late 1983 when the government's National Drug Organization imposed pricing and other controls. The government described pharmaceuticals as a "social industry of public interest" and intended for its new agency to engage in the production of drugs and related items that private firms find uneconomical to make.[23]

Market Dominance of Mass Media

Even in the world of information, media messages from the United States dominate developing societies. When I was in Iran in 1972, the most popular TV program was "Peyton Place," then the number 1 TV show in the United States. That same year, more than 60 percent of all TV programming on the major station in Lima, Peru, consisted of reruns of old American programs with virtually no relevance for Peruvians, neither in story line, characters and their conduct, or in the issues they dramatized. The most popular program in Dhaka, Bangladesh, in 1982 was "Dallas," the hit show in the United States. The preponderance of such frivolous entertainment in the United States has long been deplored as a squandering of TV's more constructive potential. Even Japan, the most media-saturated nation in the world, has

> created what is probably the world's most diverse . . . television system shared between private owners and . . . the public Japan Broadcasting Corporation (NHK). Half the stations run by NHK are devoted . . . to educational and cultural fare. On the other hand, less than 30% of the time is given to entertainment. Even the privately-owned stations, . . . approximately 25% of all the TV outlets and are devoted mainly to enter-tainment, are required to devote at least 30% of their time to education and culture.[24]

The media messages coming the other way—TV coverage of Third World culture—present a distorted picture: "Television brings these people into our living rooms when they revolt, riot or starve, but rarely when they are just going about their daily lives, steadily trying to improve them. This may explain why Americans tend to perceive the Third World villagers as . . . inert—or as objects, statistics, things to be manipulated."[25]

TV advertising in Third World countries is a retread of commercials familiar to Americans dubbed-in with local languages. But, as Patwant Singh, an Indian publisher, said to me, "you can dub-in the local lan-guage, but you can't dub-out the cultural dissonance." Even in the United States, advertising messages are rarely harmonious with public health. One sports hero, Ryne Duren, "a country boy who could throw a baseball faster than anyone ever seen" and who had his career as a star pitcher with the New York Yankees destroyed by a bout with alcoholism said, "the problem is the image of the macho man who . . . could drink all night and play baseball the next afternoon. And the message kids get from beer advertising is 'The pros are drinking and playing. Why not you?'"[26]

The direct influence of commercial advertising by international mar-keters is multiplied many times by its indirect influence on the patterns of Third World businesses. The heaviest advertiser on the government-owned Karachi, Pakistan, TV station in 1975 was the cinema industry. Food and beverage advertising was prominent for tea, commercial milks for children, and biscuits. The second most important advertising cate-gory on radio was for soap and cosmetics.[27] This could be a description of radio and TV advertising on almost any day in the United States. Adver-tisements for health and nutrition, prepared by public interest groups, are aired at the discretion of networks or station operators. For the few ac-cepted, exposure is haphazard and at times when audiences are minimal. Media systems of the Third World are generally more accessible to the so-cial marketer but the pattern has been set for exploiting its potential as a source of revenue.

One view of the free enterprise system is of an anonymous dictatorship that, once set in motion, runs by its own immutable rule. It may have validity for achieving prosperity and enrichment at home but not necessarily for Pakistan, Brazil, Zambia, the Philippines, or Morocco. Yet the history of international business expansion is an account of its unvarying replication, country after country. Product names, packaging, and language may vary but these are mere surface transformations. The same enterprise is doing business at a different stand.

This raises a question for the social marketer—to what degree does this marketing behavior negate the aims of health and nutrition education? An old African proverb says: "Let a guest come so the host may benefit." The source of growing hostility toward foreign enterprises is that its benefits accumulate for a select few. Increasingly, business behavior at home and abroad is expected to evidence greater responsibility to social priorities.

The "Marketization" of Agriculture

In an East African country like Kenya, the competition between food- and cash-crop agriculture has an agonizing cultural impact. The men are lured by the prospect of cash income to seek employment on export crop farms. This leaves the women in charge of farming for food. But it is the huge export agricultural enterprises that benefit most from technological advances and from the help of the farm extension service. Meanwhile, food crop agriculture, left to the women, languishes under primitive methods and a shrinking share of arable acreage. The symbol of the woman farmer is the *jembe*—the Swahili word for hoe—because this ancient hand tool remains practically all she has to work with. One Kenyan woman puts it this way: "You see these women working hard in the fields. They suffer. Their husbands may be working in town, drinking beer, spending their wages, enjoying themselves."[28]

In Kenya, I learned that in 1983 57 percent of the time farm extension service agents spent was with 7 percent of the farms—the most modern, most productive, and most devoted to export crops. One official explained: "It is more interesting for the agents and more rewarding for their efforts. Besides, there are political pressures from the large landowners"—of whom the late Jomo Kenyatta was reputed to be the largest. The late Bruce MacKenzie, former secretary of Agriculture and a close friend and business associate of Kenyatta, boasted of his more than 100,000 hectares of land, a good part of which was devoted to cultivating carnations for the European market. This is not an unusual situation. In

Sarawak, Malaysia, "efforts to mobilize agricultural development have foundered on the existing power structure in the villages with the better-off farmers tending to monopolize outside aid."[29]

Quite apart from its inequitable distribution, much of agricultural technology exported to the Third World is inappropriate. One of Angola's leaders reports a "deal with the Bulgarians or the Russians to grow cotton and we bought their machines. But the machines turned out not to work here; they're not suitable for Angola. Again, I saw a giant machine for pineapple cultivation. It had never been used. You see that kind of thing everywhere. We need to do things our own way."[30] Obviously, cultural irrelevance is not a monopoly of Western democracies.

Flawed agricultural policies are also the bane of developed countries. Consider the range of American farm supports and the indirect cost they impose on American consumers: price support and reserve loans by the government that enable farmers to withhold their crops from the market during a period of price decline; subsidies in a depressed market; paid diversion of land—"idling the land"—from cultivation of overproduced crops; payment in kind with government surplus crops for idling land; milk price supports by USDA purchase of unsold milk, butter, cheese, and dried milk for use only in food aid programs in the United States and abroad. Legislation implemented in 1983 provided for the first payments for dairy farmers not to produce milk. In 1983 the total cost of these programs amounted to $21.8 billion, nearly twice that of the year before and more than four times the annual average for the 1970s, keeping consumer food prices inordinately high. Moreover, this policy of government support of high-fat dairy products contradicts efforts of nutrition education from the Department of Health and Human Services and the USDA, urging reduction in fat consumption. "Among the goofier new strategies decreed by a frustrated Congress," a November 18, 1983, New York *Times* editorial says, "is a Government ad campaign to push milk products on the nation—in direct opposition to other Government ad campaigns that warn of the hazards to health in consuming too much fat."

Subsidies to tobacco farmers conflict with warnings by the U.S. Surgeon General that "cigarette smoking is injurious to your health." Such contradictions led James Hightower, Texas commissioner of Agriculture, to declare at the 1983 National Food Policy Conference that "it is not a matter of evil individuals or evil companies, but a system that is out of whack."

Some segments of the business community are objective about it. An article in *Advertising Age* noted the "need for new 'partnering' to clean up the morass of counterproductive regulations, price supports, grading and marketing orders . . . grading of beef based on fat content, paying the dairy industry on the basis of butter fat . . . artificially limiting available market supplies to keep prices high."[31]

The new Nicaraguan Government appears to have made progress against this problem, having learned a lesson from the luckless experiences of the Castro revolution in Cuba. The state purchasing agency deals with the problem under a twofold policy—it competes with private food retailers by offering more to farmers and motivating them to greater production, and then subsidizes consumers with lower prices as an incentive for them to buy. This grow-it-and-eat-it policy enables the government to maintain a flexible support for selected crops and provides an opportunity to integrate agricultural production policy with nutrition objectives.[32]

The Green Revolution in Asia, born of the ingenious breed of new strains of rice and wheat, has been a mixed blessing. Dependent on heavy inputs of fertilizer, pesticides, and water, it automatically favored the wealthy landowner. Moreover, it meant abandoning the traditional diversified seed bank in favor of concentrating on a single strain. Both alien dependencies introduced a new fragility into their economies. When oil prices soared in 1974 and 1975, the cost of fertilizer and pesticides—petrochemical derivatives—soared with them. But the shift to single-seed-variety cultivation greatly reduced the flexibility of operation. Many small farmers ended up worse off than before. To prevent this kind of experience Karl Eicher called for "location-specific research by multi-disciplinary research teams." The failure to develop appropriate agricultural policies is a legacy, he believed, of "hundreds of foreign economic advisers who have imported inappropriate models and theories of development . . . a failure to provide a convincing understanding of the motivations of rural people."[33]

The Baited Trap of Technology

The importation of industrial technologies frequently fares no better. Ruth Vermeer, development officer of the International Organization of Consumer Unions (IOCU), advised judging consumer products not only for performance but also for their manufacturing method. "We feel Third World consumers should also ask themselves if the product they are buying is, from a broader and longer term perspective, an appropriate one," she said. She cited Raleigh bicycles whose manufacturing technology in Malaysia was found "not the most appropriate." The bicycle of a local manufacturer proved to be more labor-intensive but still met "the basic need of reliable transportation at a price acceptable to low income families."[34]

The issue of labor-intensive production methods is far more than a matter of local pride. In Third World countries, labor-saving technology from industrialized nations is an invitation to economic disaster. In the 1970s, though Brazil was the shining example of Third World development, the signs of economic dissonance were already evident. For example, on one visit in 1972, I was told the GNP had advanced more than 11 percent, a rate second only to Japan. But population had increased almost 2.5 percent while employment had grown only 1.5 percent. In effect, employment was growing at roughly half the rate of population despite an economic growth rate almost four times as high! Less than a decade later Brazil was to become a serious economic problem in South America, overburdened with a foreign debt it could neither repay nor service.

Lionel Brizola, governor of the State of Rio de Janeiro, blamed it on the foreign businesses. He argued that they shape the economy to their own interests:

> I'll give you an example. We have a great seacoast and river network, but the multinationals wanted us to create an automobile industry, so now our commerce has to move by truck over roads, which is much more expensive. . . . If Americans had the kind of capitalism we have here today, they'd send for Lafayette and have another revolution.[35]

"Economic and political progress may be possible," declared Tom Wicker in commenting on American aid programs for Central America, if "aid is administered in accord with Central American political and economic dynamics, and in cooperation rather than conflict with the region's existing institutions and systems—above all recognizing Central America's aspirations and goals."[36]

Even the aid given by outside nations to ameliorate the fallout of inadvisable development policies can exacerbate the problem. In the Philippines, I interviewed a woman who had been recruited into the family planning program. She had nursed all her previous children but bottle-fed the last because the birth control pills she had been given inhibited lactation. In the United States or the Soviet Union this might not be a serious, though undesirable, situation, but among the poor in countries like the Philippines, it produces malnutrition and death for infants.

Laying Waste the World

Industrialization and free enterprise evolved in response to need and with little regard for aftereffects. A free market depends on meeting pressing needs first, regardless of all other considerations, because they were the most profitable to satisfy. But only in recent years have we discovered the price we have had to pay for certain past practices that are now known to have devastating effects on our environment and public health. In 1980, a U.S. Environmental Protection Agency "report listing hundreds of industrial sites in 33 states where dioxin might be found received little or no attention until dioxin was discovered [in 1983] at one of the locations."[37] Dioxin is one of many industrial pollutants whose deleterious effect on health have received notice only in recent years. Asbestos is another. Though concern about this industrial product's link to cancer has been growing since the early 1970s, it was not until almost ten years later that protective measures were first instituted. In England, reaction was "deeply depressing that the best the Health and Safety Commission can do now is to produce its modest proposals for 1984."[38] Ironically, to escape even these modest proposals, some firms apparently considered transferring operations to—guess where? "The threat to export jobs—and deaths—to Third World countries with less stringent regulations should be jumped on hard," the Manchester *Guardian* editorialized.

It took the U.S. EPA ten years to do something about EDB (ethylene dibromide). It issued guidelines to states on safe levels for the deadly pesticide in bread, baked goods, and grains but the response of state authorities has been anything but uniform. Under EPA's new standards, Dr. Samuel Epstein of the University of Illinois Medical Center, gloomily estimated that we "could expect some 3,000 new cancer deaths a year."[39]

Acid rain was first identified in industrial England in the 1870s and has become a serious problem in the United States. The National Academy of Sciences and the White House Science Office urged that "immediate action was needed lest environmental damage reach 'the point of irreversibility.'"[40] But the threat is now perceived to extend directly to human survival. First believed to be the product of sulfur dioxides and nitrous oxides emitted from coal-burning plants, acid rain is now known also to include metals like aluminum, cadmium, copper, lead, and zinc—all varyingly toxic—the result of industrial emissions into the atmosphere. Though regulatory response in the United States has been slow in emerging, public awareness has mushroomed.

Though business has become sensitive to this new public consciousness in the United States, there is little evidence of it in the business and marketing strategies pursued in the Third World. This has provoked nationals of these lands to ask, Is this the right way to do business, to ignore the needs of the marketplace in favor of the needs of the marketer? Isn't it true you don't do it that way at home because the marketplace would reject you in favor of your competition? Because we are incapable of mounting competitive alternatives should this relieve you of your obligation to our needs and a timetable compatible with our development capacities?

"The time is long since past," a Tanzanian official said to me at dinner in Dar es Salaam, "when you can pursue a strategy designed to win short-term profits but to lose you the world."

Some environmental health dangers occur naturally but even in such cases, the hand of man occasionally magnifies the peril. What goes by the Hindi name of *kesari dal* in the Indian state of Madhya Pradesh is a toxic pulse (bean) identified as "the dietary cause for nervous irritation and loosened joints of the leg" causing lameness in thousands every year.[41] Because it grows easily, landowners find it an inexpensive way "to pay wages in kind to the landless workers especially in the rural interiors who remain virtually bonded in their service. . . . Or, they make quick and unconscionable profit by adulterating costlier pulses mostly exported to other states." Attempts to establish a safe level of consumption, reduce the toxic content, or breed out the toxins have proved unsuccessful so that "nothing less than an effective and total ban on its cultivation will do . . . [which] might also help to influence landlords to put their land to socially justifiable use."

The Politics of Malnutrition

When a Latin American director of agrarian reform arranged for a video recording of a training program, one of the subjects was oil palm cultivation and some of the farmers opposed this industrial crop in favor of expanding food production. He gave in but his superiors took a dim view of this "undermining of government policy." The director was transferred. His successor summarily terminated the video program and vigorously enforced oil palm production leaving the farmers with reduced rather than expanded capacity for food production.[42] Politics is not always so crass but crass or not, it is always operating and, as in this case, can have profound public health implications.

Malnutrition used to be considered:

1. The result of not enough food or of deficiencies in nutrients and/or
2. The result of poor utilization of available food. This limited view of the problem restricted it to agricultural experts on the one hand—to grow more and better foods—and nutritionists and nutrition educators on the other—to help people to eat better—and to food aid programs; we have learned that these are not the only adjustments necessary because malnutrition is also.
3. An income (poverty) problem
4. A problem of potable water
5. A land-tenure and land-use problem, involving policies affecting the balance between export and food crop production
6. A technology problem in the effort to improve food crop production

7. A distribution problem calling for roads and storage facilities
8. An economic problem of appropriate credit and fiscal policies for farmers
9. A problem of commercial manufacturing and marketing practices detrimental to proper diet and health
10. In general, a problem of structural impediments in the system

The poverty rate in the United States has for years been in stark contrast to our affluence. For the past 25 years it has ranged from 9.5 percent to a high of 15 percent in 1982 or about 34.4 million Americans, according to Rudolph G. Penner, director of the Congressional Budget Office. If these Americans lived in a land of their own it would be the world's twenty-second largest nation and among the poorest. Alice M. Rivlin, while director of the Congressional Budget Office before Penner, reported in 1983 that one-fourth of all children in the United States "lives in near-poverty"[43] while one-fifth lives below it.[44] The impact of poverty on public health has been widely reported around the world. WHO disclosed that in the late 1960s and 1970s the rate of mortality decline slowed in many less-developed countries with the slowing of economic growth.[45]

While the infant mortality rate (IMR) in the United States continues to decline, it is still far higher for blacks than for whites and the gap is widening. In 1982, white infant mortality was 9.9 per 1,000 births compared to 19.3 per 1,000, or 95 percent higher for blacks. This contrasts with 12 per 1,000 for whites and 22.3 per 1,000, or 86 percent higher for blacks in 1978. Dorothy Rice, former director of the government's National Center for Health Statistics and an adviser to the study, related it to the fact that "the U.S. is no longer making as much progress in reducing the incidence of low birth weight as it did" before 1978. Dr. Arthur Hoyte of Georgetown University said that "until five years ago the gap between white and black infant mortality had been closing. . . . That progress has stopped."[46] He suggested that if health departments recorded infant deaths by family income, it would show that the problem is not race but poverty. Carl Eicher, director of the African Rural Economy Program at Michigan State University with 20 years of African experience, could not agree more. "The hunger and malnutrition problem is caused by poverty," he said. "Even in areas where per capita food production is not declining, the poor do not have the income or the resources to cope with hunger and malnutrition."[47]

The head of the Public Health Association of New York City, Dr. Victor W. Sidel, summarized to a congressional subcommittee the results of a study among the poor that "lack of income, not nutrition misinformation, seems to be the major reason for poor diets."[48] Dr. Larry J. Brown of the Harvard School of Public Health declared that his research revealed that food stamp allotments last "only to the third week of each month."[49] Surveys conducted in England reported that men unemployed at the time of the 1971 census suffered higher mortality in the subsequent four years than those employed. Professor Harvey Brenner of Johns Hopkins University concluded that unemployment causes a rise in mortality. For every 1-percent increase in unemployment in England, he estimated there has been a 2-percent increase in mortality, representing approximately 17,000 deaths annually.[50]

Penner's suggestions for legislative actions necessary to ameliorate the punishments of poverty included a national minimum benefit level for Aid to Families with Dependent Children, expanded Medicaid eligibility to all poor families with children, and, despite charges of wastage, increase in the maximum food stamp benefits. The charge of food stamp wastage was disproved by data from the 1977 and 1978 Nationwide Food Consumption Survey of USDA. Households below the poverty level were found to have lower average home food costs per person with more nutrients per dollar than higher income households. Peterkin and Hama of USDA's Consumer Nutrition Division, and authors of the survey report, concluded that "food shopping expertise of households with low food costs, with low incomes, and receiving food stamps was as good or better than that of other households." Moreover, as Jean Mayer has pointed out, food stamps and other feeding programs constituted an indirect subsidy to farmers. Cuts in these not only are damaging to the health of poor people but also hurt America's farmers.

The same is true of international aid. The total from all industrialized democracies has dropped to 0.35 percent of GNP and lower in recent years. The recommendation of the Brandt commission was that aid should be at least 0.70 percent of GNP or double the current rate, which would represent only 25 days of the world's military spending. Aid from the United States has been declining. In 1965, it was 0.50 percent of GNP and in 1980 declined to 0.20 percent, a performance that, in the words of the late Barbara Ward, is "highly unlikely to put fresh heart into other poorer donors."[51] The Soviet Union's pitiful contribution to international food aid is 0.03 percent of GNP to countries other than Cuba.

There are other drawbacks. The programs are voluntary and 75 percent of their budgets are allocated to bilateral aid.[52] The premise behind bilateral aid is its use "as a weapon" to quote the Reagan administration's secretary of Agriculture, John Block.[53] Thus, U.S. bilateral aid does not favor countries that need it most—the low-income nations. They were receiving only 19 percent of it as of 1983 while "politically motivated" aid "has nearly doubled to 41% in the past ten years."[54] Yet other industrial countries like Japan, West Germany, and England go about their business without insistence that recipient countries pursue policies consistent with free enterprise philosophy.

The food deficit of developing countries continues to worsen. In 1960, it amounted to 20 million tons. By 1980, it grew to 80 million tons and is estimated to be 145 million tons by 1990.[55]

On the other hand, Frances Moore Lappé referred to food assistance as "aid-as-obstacle" when it competes with and discourages local farm production and spurs the trend to food imports even among countries capable of food self-sufficiency.[56] Ironically, the poverty that makes food aid necessary in the first place is also exacerbated by it. According to the USDA, food-importing countries increased grain imports from 1.2 million tons annually in 1960 to 1963 to 8 million in 1980 for a cost of $2.1 billion, a growth rate three times greater than the population. This shifts tastes from locally available grains like cassava, millet, corn, sorghum, and yams to imported wheat and rice, in their processed forms as well—bread, snacks, cakes, and ready-to-eat cereals. "Given the linkage of hunger and malnutrition to poverty, economists and food production specialists are coming to agree that food and poverty problems should be tackled together," Carl Eicher declared.[57]

The economic plight of Third World people is exacerbated by short-ages of natural resources on which they could historically depend. In 1980, almost three-fifths of the world's two billion rural people dependent on wood as their primary fuel did not have enough. If present trends continue, the FAO estimates that by the year 2000 the number will more than double.[58] Necessary measures include expansion of forestry planta-tions, reduction of waste in felling trees and in converting wood to char-coal, widespread planting of trees outside forest areas, and improving the design of traditional wood-burning arrangements in the home.

This litany underscores once again the futility of goal-setting without multisectorial collaboration or needed public policy initiatives. Certainly, planning for social marketing programs on behalf of health and nutrition education must weigh these constraints seriously. Will they ultimately represent insuperable obstacles and make the social marketing program a futile exercise? What is the point in initiating campaigns to promote breast-feeding in the face of the aggressive promotion of commercial milks for infant feeding whether in the United States, England, or in Chad, Botswana, or Chile, or when a birth control pill inhibits lactation? Why be satisfied merely to teach mothers to rehydrate their infants when the real solution to diarrhea is potable water and better sanitation—not education but economic improvement?

One health educator went so far as to suggest that health education's primary goal should be changing the social structure in order to achieve "a society in which each individual feels both the right and responsibility to be healthy."[59] The 1979 conference of International Union for Health Education (IUHE), in emphasizing that the goal of health education is to inform, influence, and assist individuals to assume greater responsibility for their health, also declared that "politicians and government departments must be a prime target audience for health educators" and that legislative changes must be seen not as an alternative but as a complement to other health education measures.[60]

Changing the Role of the Private Sector

The international controversy over infant formula and other breast-milk substitutes and the adoption in 1981 of the WHO/UNICEF code to control their marketing has underlined the new social responsibilities of industry. In the same year the government of Mexico's attempt to regulate food marketing practices was further evidence that Third World countries are taking the example of the consumer movements in the United States, England, and Sweden in designing their consumer protection laws and regulations; if such laws and regulations are proper for guiding marketing practices at home, why shouldn't they continue in force when the companies go abroad? Business faces the choice of being subject to regulations drafted with little sympathetic understanding of business problems or of making changes on their own in practices patently disharmonious with local needs. Both business and government ought to ask some new questions, including, How can food companies reexamine their products and marketing methods to contribute to local nutritional needs and do so profitably? What can governments learn from food businesses and their marketing methods as a social technology to achieve some of their food and nutrition goals?

The size and influence of the commercial food market system is increasing as rural cultures change to urban ways and as the mass media and mass markets penetrate remote rural areas. The commercial marketplace manages a growing share of the food supply and an even greater influence on food value systems. Supermarkets are common in upper- and middle-income neighborhoods; open-air markets are filled with processed and packaged foods and the output of radio and TV stations— even state-owned stations—is cluttered with commercials for processed foods. The comfortable stereotype of the commercially isolated peasant may soon be a myth; all families are being drawn into and influenced by the commercial food system. Industry and government can join in special food production activities to help combat specific nutritional deficiencies: iodine enrichment of salt to prevent goiter; vitamin and mineral enrichment of refined cereal products—a standard procedure in the United States for 40 years—to deal with local nutrient deficiencies, vitamin A enrichment of food to prevent blindness, and iron enrichment of foods or marketing of low-cost iron supplements.

The point is that there is no alternative to the special responsibility that marketers and governments must assume. Though governments have vital instruction to give to business on the conduct of its affairs, there is much they can learn from business. The government of Ecuador, with support from USAID, undertook a program of health and nutrition education in 1972 for the rural poor. Radio was the key medium and endemic goiter one of the priority health problems to be dealt with. The campaign was timed to coincide with the distribution of free sample packets of *sal yodada,* iodized salt—a time-honored marketing device—arranged for through ECUSAL, a Morton Salt Company affiliate.[61] After one year of broadcast, 40 percent of the mestizo and 20 percent of the indigenous households knew about *sal yodada* and could repeat all or part of the radio message. By the end of one year, nearly all the mestizo housewives interviewed could point to a bag of *sal yodada* in their homes and salt sales data confirmed the penetration. Among indigenous families, more firmly bound to the *sal engrano,* about 15 percent of the interviewed homes had the new salt at the end of one year, though none had used it before.[62]

Social marketing adapted to the conditions of the developing countries can have an impact on health behavior, farm practices, and child care, but only when social and economic circumstances are conducive. It is a self-imposed constraint for health authorities to accept the confines of existing rules and regulations as the limit of their sanction. Laws and regulations incompatible with public health need to be modified. "Rules," a sage once said, "are made to be broken."

Changing Agricultural Imperatives

Twenty years ago, governments, international organizations, foundations, and the private sector joined forces to found the International Rice Research Institute in the Philippines. Simultaneously, the famous Norman Borlaug wheat experiments were going on in Mexico. Both ventures produced revolutionary new seeds. But an intersectoral alliance could join resources to improve other crops even more certain to benefit the poor. A fraction of the resources spent on improvements in rice, wheat, and other cash crops might be spent on corn, cassava, legumes, potatoes, and quinoa, which are lower in cost and less likely to be diverted into the international market. India, for example, has in the 1980s become a net exporter of wheat. Yet millions of Indians still live in a deficit food condition. In Africa, "many colonial regimes focused their research and development programs on export crops and the needs of commercial farmers and managers of plantations."[63]

Alan Berg, senior nutrition adviser of the World Bank, estimated that a 10-percent increase in the supply of beef in Colombia

> would add three times as many calories to the daily diets of the already adequately nourished group as to the diets of the calorie-deficient group. In contrast, the benefits of a 10% increase in the production of cassava would be received entirely by the calorie-deficient group. In Indonesia . . . the lowest three income deciles obtain about 40% of their calories from cassava and corn. . . . The upper three get about only 14% of their calories from these foods."[64]

Also, he reported, the balance between protein and calories in the diet of the poor is surprisingly good if they get enough calories, which is why emphasis on calories is important.

Most small farmers and families are landless or near landless. Thus, programs designed to boost production of small farmers might benefit them and there is justification for doing so. A World Bank cross-sectional study of 41 developing countries showed that output per acre is higher with the smaller farmer.[65] In Mexico, the production of beans and corn—centuries-old staple foods—has been declining. Advances in the technology of production of these staple foods have not kept up with the methods of producing cash crops. Land devoted to their production has been turned over to truck gardens whose produce—lettuce, tomatoes, and cucumbers—is shipped to the United States.[66]

Advances in technology do not carry guarantees of advances in the human condition. Advances in the human condition come about primarily as a result of profound policy decisions for structural changes in social and economic systems as necessary. Yet there is a disinclination to accept the frictions and unpleasantness sometimes incurred by social change. But of all the inputs and interventions developing countries, in particular, must consider, the need for such social change may very well be the most important and the sympathy and support of the developed world may be the most vital aid it can provide.

Water, Water Everywhere But . . .

Among needed improvements in living conditions, none is more important than clean water and sanitation. More than 80 percent of infections in the Third World are spread by water and poor sanitation. For half the world's people, there exists no reasonable access to safe and adequate drinking water. Water-related diseases may claim as many as 10 to 25 million lives a year and cause untold illness. Urban slum families frequently give up 10 percent of their earnings to the water vendor.[67] UNICEF estimated that about 15 million children below the age of five die in the developing countries every year, some 6 million from infections caused by bad water. With access to safe drinking water and sanitation, the estimate is that infant mortality could be cut by as much as 50 percent worldwide.[68] According to the World Health Organization, approximately 80 percent of all sickness and disease can be attributed to inadequate water or sanitation and contributes to the death of up to 18 million people.[69] Babies are starved in the womb, the milk of mothers dries up, and child care suffers. In Upper Volta, 88 percent of those in rural areas have no clean water readily available.[70]

Water is the universal medium for disease organisms. The same streams that millions draw on for water are also the dumping ground for human waste. The cycle of infection and reinfection continues. The realization has grown that vertical health programs, like nutrition, family planning, water, and sanitation, cannot succeed because they impinge on each other. Even the conservative British publication, *The Economist,* in summarizing current scientific opinion said that "if these diseases were to be eradicated from a community, not only water supplies and sanitation will be needed but better housing, nutrition and education as well."[71] "My own personal attitude is that health for all will fall by the wayside," said WHO's Halfdan Mahler, "unless we succeed with nutrition and water and sanitation."[72] James P. Grant, executive director of UNICEF, in his 1983 report on the state of the world's children, gave an even sharper focus to primary health care by singling out its key interventions: growth monitoring, oral rehydration, and breast-feeding, and immunization, as well as family planning and food production (GOBI-FF).

WHO has lowered its expectation for "the Decade of Water" (1980 to 1990) now to provide clean water for 95 percent of the urban population and 85 percent of the rural (coupled with sanitation for 80 percent of the urban). The World Bank cost estimate is $30 billion annually but in the first year of the decade only $7 billion was expended on water and $3 billion on sanitation. There is little likelihood of meeting the goal. The problem is aggravated by lukewarm interest of governments. As of the end of 1983, only 26 countries had announced programs with another 39 having them under study.

Economic constraints obviously play a part. Governments must weigh the alternative demands for development funds, and this imposes agonizing decisions. Yet money shortages seem not to obstruct rising military expenditures. According to Ruth Leger Sivard in her *World Mili-*

tary and Social Expenditures (1983), military expenditures are US $660 billion or $1.26 million a minute.[73] The $30 billion a year required for "the Water Decade" is only 5 percent of this military outlay. In the past two decades (1963 to 1983), combined U.S.-U.S.S.R. military expenditures amounted to $3.1 trillion. Only 20 percent of this average annual expenditure would have been sufficient if not for a tap and a toilet for every home, at least reasonable access to them. The tragedy deepens when we discover that in a poor country like Pakistan where "public expenditure per capita on the military is $15 per annum . . . expenditure per capita on education is only $5 and on health care a bare $1. Infant mortality rate is . . . 126 per 1,000 and life expectancy only 51 years. The same is true of India, Bangladesh and a host of other Third World countries."[74]

There are other, sometimes sinister, forces at work. In Nicaragua in 1975 when I served as a USAID consultant to the Health Ministry nutrition education programs, I had the opportunity to discuss the water problem with President Anastasio Somoza. Nicaragua was a small country of 2,500,000 people, 80 percent of whom resided in rural areas. Engineering studies concluded that potable water could be provided for most of rural Nicaragua for a cost ranging from $6 to $20 million. A preliminary geological survey to confirm conditions would run to only $100,000 and appeared to be a worthwhile investment. Health authorities had identified diarrhea as the number-one concern.

The reaction was lackluster. After the meeting, my companion from the Health Ministry dashed any hope for the project. "It will never happen," he said with some vague explanations of "other priorities." But not until later did I discover the real reasons. Good water means lives saved and that means more schools, housing, food, and jobs. Bad water was one of this government's effective population control programs. This wretched cynicism recalled the words of Dr. Walter Santos in Brazil two or three years earlier that cultural solutions to health problems are often popular because economic solutions are just too costly. Though Somoza was overthrown in 1979, his philosophy survived elsewhere in misplaced priorities that give macroeconomic development goals precedence over basic human needs. A World Bank study ascribes the "deepening crisis" affecting the African Region to domestic policies set by the African nations themselves.[75] It suggests that the priorities accorded to steel mills, international airports, and industrialization should be reassigned to agriculture and food production.

Myths, Madness, Make-Believe, and Malarkey

For a number of misguided years environmentalists in the United States inadvertently supported the notion that the spoliation of our environment resulted from individual indifference and neglect. They implored us not to be litterbugs as though wanton discard of emptied food and beverage containers were the major cause of our ecological decline. A TV public service announcement showed a proud, stalwart American Indian chieftain sadly surveying the beer-can-littered terrain of his once glorious domain. As the camera panned moodily into a lingering tight shot of his noble profile, a tear drop formed in the corner of his eye and slowly threaded its way down the weathered creases of his cheek. Who can recall a message of such emotional impact—or any message, in fact—imploring community action about the truly major causes of pollution—the industrial poisoning of water resources, the fouling of the atmosphere, the threats to food supplies from the profligate use of pesticides and processing chemicals?

Environmental degradation, as the scientists say, is not monogenic in origin. It has many causes and, surely, careless handling of the leftover debris of human consumption is one. But what conclusions may we draw from an educational effort that focuses on surface littering in the face of the profound internal dislocations of our ecological systems from the litter of unwise agricultural and industrial processes?

Myths, madness, make-believe, and malarkey are familiar attributes of America's public life. President Reagan makes no bones about fitness. He pursues it and is more than willing to share the secrets of his special regimen, including his diet. He advised the American people in *Parade* magazine, December 4, 1983,

> Here the key is moderation [and] I do watch what I eat. For example, at breakfast I pass up the pancakes and sausage in favor of cereal and fruit, skim milk and decaffeinated coffee. For lunch I have soup and a salad. But when I do have the big lunch (a Mexican plate—tacos, enchiladas, beans, rice), I cut down in the evening. Our evening meals usually consist of fish, chicken or meat with fresh vegetables and a salad of some kind.

He gave up salt while governor of California when a doctor asked if he wanted to live 15 years longer. "In less than a week I cured myself of the salt habit."

This is better advice than the American people get from his secretary of Agriculture. John Block doesn't believe it's the government's responsibility to advise the American people on what to eat. However he may choose to eat on his own, he has all but publicly disowned the Dietary Guidelines though the president seems sensibly disposed to them. Block, a hog farmer, is in favor of having his agency promote, rather than discourage, meat and dairy products high in animal fat.

We are a genial people with a tradition of amused tolerance for the antics of our knaves. Come election time, we throw the rascals out, promptly replace them with new ones, and when the fun is over, go back about our business. But in recent years, our ire has been aroused by an awareness that this jejune political behavior is not so funny. We are suffering a deepening malaise from neglect of our national purpose and one of its symptoms is stress in the state of public health. We are recovering the realization that the game of politics is serious business. It's not so much who wins that counts but what they do with the victory once they leave the field. We have allowed our winners to get off with a feeble account of themselves.

We are an immoderate people, given to improbable dreams and impossible extremes. No aspect of our national life more clearly manifests this than the muddled state of our public affairs. As we have seen, there is a warp of madness in the woof of our agricultural policies that reward farmers not to farm and makes their customers pay for it. Our industrial policies, originally intended to enrich our environment, have ended up despoiling it. Marketing practices emphasize food as a vehicle of business profit rather than human nourishment, and drugs as items of consumption rather than treatment.

In the past, advertising of ethical (prescription) drugs was confined to professional medical journals and has totaled $2 billion annually. But manufacturers have always dreamed of a chance to advertise directly to the consumer. In justification they present findings from their consumer research that consumers want to know more about these products. Though there is considerable reason to doubt that proprietary advertising is the best way to accomplish consumer education, the Food and Drug Administration, which regulates the industry, in 1983 permitted the Cable Health Network to accept ethical drug advertising. Boots Pharmaceuticals Inc. seized that as a precedent for regular TV advertising. Subsequently, according to Tony Malara, CBS TV president, the network was approached by "a number of drug companies with storyboards . . . and a desire to go on the air." William Grigg of the FDA indicated that FDA will probably go along but under guidelines promulgated from its research. Professional and consumer groups, he said, fear "that such commercials would end up promotional rather than informational."[76] It hardly seems likely that the companies would be eager to expend millions of dollars for any other purpose.

We are mythists, leaving to moral suasion (in which we have a waning faith) the job of contending with antisocial behaviors that only firm administration of law can curb. It is make-believe to delegate the awful problems of cigarette smoking and excessive alcohol consumption to health educators when the evidence is clear that education is not enough. And it is mythic of health educators to believe it. In some states, sanity has prevailed in the form of tough drunk-driver and uniform drinking age laws. New York City has pioneered the legal requirement that liquor stores must exhibit posters warning that alcohol can cause birth defects.

WHO, after studying the alcohol problem for 15 years (1960 to 1975) in Canada, Finland, Ireland, the Netherlands, Poland, Switzerland, and the United States, recommended in its 1983 bulletin on the subject that governments restrict the availability of alcohol and resist it as a source of tax revenues. However, it found that instead of dealing with these roots of the problems, governments have increased their involvement in alcohol production and promotion and have chosen to expand treatment facilities for alcoholics.

Myth, madness, and malarkey are intertwined in the cigarette problem. The best that the federal government has done thus far is the law requiring a warning on cigarette packages and in advertising. Tobacco subsidies flow to farmers despite the surgeon general's determination "that cigarette smoking is a danger to your health." The myth is exposed in the glare of these realities: lung cancer has surpassed breast cancer as the major cause of cancer death among women; cigarette advertising now exceeds $1 billion annually; annual tobacco subsidies amount to nearly $15 million; smoking-related illness costs $38 billion in health care, lost wages, and decreased productivity; 53 million Americans still smoke and 340,000 of them die annually from smoking-related disease.[77] Yet, the Reynolds Tobacco Company ran an advertising campaign compounded of unprecedented make-believe and malarkey (and chutzpah!) asking for public understanding of the rights of smokers. But the campaign was really an effort of the cigarette industry to preserve its misbegotten consumer constituency from the social pressures that threatened to deplete its ranks. Its self-righteous criticism of the methodologies and conclusions of studies linking smoking and ill health cast the industry in the unlikely role of defending the holy faith of scientific inquiry. More malarkey.

Combating smoking only with education is aiming a garden hose at a forest fire, and aroused Americans are seeking recourse in the law. Not all legal measures have the desired effect. Congress doubled the cigarette tax in 1982 and though the number of cigarettes sold decreased for the first time in five years, more Americans were smoking than the year before. Taxing as a disincentive, as with alcohol, often has the contrary effect. "Nearly one-third of the almost $23 billion Americans spent on 624 billion cigarettes," reported Newsweek, (more than 2,000 cigarettes per capita/per annum or more than seven-a-day for every man, woman, and child in the United States), "poured into the tax coffers of federal, state and local governments—making most of them less than eager to restrict consumption."[78] But other kinds of measures are evolving: restricted smoking areas, fines as high as $500 a day for violations, and outright bans in certain public places as with the Minnesota Clean Indoor Air Act. Social pressures against smokers will probably prove more important than the prohibition and the threat of penalties. Smokers are the new pariahs. Eventually, they will have to choose between kicking the habit or being kicked for it. Status and self-image are likely to prevail. This is a useful insight for health educators and social marketers.

The established health care systems cannot always be depended on for support of the right strategies. In fact, they are sometimes the source of the problem. The publicity on the dioxin hazard in the United States prompted an American Medical Association resolution condemning the media for conducting "a witch hunt" leading to "unjustified public fright" and "hysteria."[79] But what is the social marketer to do when, on the other hand, prominent environmental scientists insist that there is cause for concern? Samuel S. Epstein, an authority on hazardous waste and cancer at the medical center of the University of Illinois, called the AMA's resolution "a travesty" because there is "more than enough evidence to warrant extreme concern."[80] Federal officials at the Centers for Disease Control and also at the Environmental Protection Agency agreed while acknowledging the difficulties in determining what is "appropriate caution and what's excessive alarm."[81] Paul Wiesner, assistant director for medical affairs and environmental health at the centers, declared that "most of what I've seen . . . in the media has been a fairly reasonable statement of caution."[82]

High-cholesterol, high-fat dietary intake poses a similar conundrum. The medical and scientific communities are not of one mind as to what advice to give the American people. Should they be advised to reduce fat intake because of accumulating indications of its relationship to cancer and cerebrovascular morbidity? Some authorities like E.H. Ahrens of Rockefeller University said "no," the evidence is not conclusive.[83] Others, including the American Cancer Society and the American Heart Association, disagreed. More than a conflict over the facts, this is a clash of philosophies as to what ought to be done.

The social marketer's imperatives are markedly different from those of the scientist. For the former, prudence is the guiding principle; for the latter, exactitude. While admitting that dioxin constitutes a hazard or that high-animal-fat consumption may be perilous to health, the scientist's responsibility is to certitude and probabilities of effect. The social marketer and the health educator cannot wait until the absolute evidence is in. They are concerned with present possibilities. Until such time (years, perhaps, never) prudence suggests that warning signs go up to the public. This counsels caution, not alarm, based on full disclosure of the facts as best we know them. Those whose vested interests are radically affected are bound to view such notice with alarm and their hysteria can easily be misrepresented as unjustified public fright.

Notes

1. Starr, P., *The Social Transformation of American Medicine,* Harper & Row, New York, 1982.

2. A remark made by Dr. Walter Santos on May 19, 1972, then minister of health in the State of Sao Paulo, now president Sociedade Brasileira de Nutricao, Rio de Janeiro.

3. "Two Major Events," in *Education for Health,* the WHO newsletter, WHO, Geneva, Switzerland, inaugural issue, 1984.

4. Sakr, A., "Kwashiorkor's Fungus Link," *South,* November 1983.

5. Nunzio, J., "Third World Healthcare: Uncultivated Market?" *Advertising Age,* September 26, 1983, p. M-29.

6. Gereffi, G., *The Pharmaceutical Industry and Dependency in the Third World,* Princeton University Press, 1983.

7. Monteith, R.S., Anderson, J.E., Mascarine, F., Morris, L., "Contraceptive Use and Fertility in the Republic of Panama," *Studies in Family Planning* 12:10, 1981.

8. Hauck, A.S., "A Danger to Infant Health . . . at Home," *Food Monitor,* March–April 1983, p. 21.

9. Ibid.

10. From testimony before committee hearings of the Washington, D.C. Council, April–May 1983.

11. Jelliffe, D.B., Jelliffe, E.F.P., "The Urban Avalanche," *Journal of the American Dietetic Association,* August 1970, p. 116.

12. Manoff, R.K., "The Brazilian National Breast-Feeding Program," Manoff International Inc., New York, 1982.

13. Hauck, A., op. cit., p. 24.

14. Manoff, R.K., Cooke, T.M., Romweber, S.T., "Radio Nutrition Education—Using The Advertising Technique to Reach Rural Families: Philippines and Nicaragua," final report, December 1977. Manoff International Inc. was engaged as technical consultants to this project, which was supported by the Office of Nutrition, Technical Assistance Bureau, Agency for International Development, Washington, D.C.

15. "New Mexican Law Restricts Liquor and Cigarette Ads," *Advertising Age,* April 9, 1984.

16. Kaufman, M.T., "Eskimos Try to Take Essence of Past into Future," the New York *Times,* August 8, 1983, p. 2.

17. "Study Finds a Third of Drug Ingredients Effective," the New York *Times,* (UPI), October 9, 1983, p. 26.

18. Burros, M., "De Gustibus," the New York *Times,* October 22, 1983, p. 48.

19. "Nutritional Aspects of Fabricated Foods," *Nutrition and the M.D.,* 9/7, July 1983.

20. Wolfe, S.M., "Commentary Corner," *Advertising Age,* September 26, 1983, p. M-12.

21. *Nutrition Week,* Community Nutrition Institute, Washington, D.C., December 8, 1983.

22. Islam, S., "Red Alert on Corporate Crime," *South,* October 1983, p. 50.

23. Howe, M., "Drug Makers Balk at Rules in Greece," the New York *Times,* February 6, 1984, p. D6.

24. Christopher, R.C., "Japan's Media-Mad Society," *Asia,* July-August, 1983, Vol. 6/2, p. 8.

25. Critchfield, R., "Science and the Villager: The Last Sleeper Wakes," *Foreign Affairs,* Fall 1982, Vol. 61, No. 1, p. 18.

26. "Duren's New Pitch: Look Out for Booze," *Newsweek,* June 20, 1983, p. 13.

27. Manoff International Inc., "Mass Media and Nutrition Education: Report of the Assessment Visit to Pakistan," for USAID, Manoff International Inc., New York, March 5, 1975.

28. Critchfield, R., op. cit., p. 21.

29. Rowley, J., "Self-Help in Sarawak," *People,* Vol. 10/3, 1983, p. 16.

30. The New York *Times,* February 8, 1981.

31. "Grocery Marketing: Tough Questions Line Every Aisle," *Advertising Age,* March 15, 1982.

32. Steele, J., "The Grassroots Democracy that Sets Nicaragua Apart," the Manchester *Guardian Weekly,* September 4, 1983, p. 8.

33. Eicher, C.K., "Facing up to Africa's Food Crisis," *Foreign Affairs,* Fall 1982, Vol. 61, No. 1, p. 163.

34. Quoted by Isham, S. "Red Alert on Corporate Crime," *South,* October 1983, London, p. 51.

35. Hoge, W., "Brazil's New Governors Find the Cupboard Bare," the New York *Times,* July 7, 1983, p. A2.

36. Wicker, T., "U.S. Aid Must Be Relevant," *International Herald Tribune,* January 10, 1984, op-ed page.

37. "1980 Dioxin List Drew Little Action," the New York *Times,* (AP), June 27, 1983, p. A13.

38. "A Late and Lame Response," the Manchester *Guardian Weekly,* editorial, September 4, 1983.

39. Boffey, P.M. "The Debate over Dioxin," The New York *Times,* June 25, 1983, p. 1.

40. Clendinen, D., "Concern on Acid Rain Extending to Public Health," the New York *Times,* June 29, 1983, p. 6.

41. Wagh, J., "Lathyrism: What Is That?" *Future,* 1983, First Quarter, p. 4.

42. Fraser, C., "Adapting Communication Technology for Rural Development," *Ceres,* No. 95, September–October 1983, p. 23.

43. "Sharp Rise is Seen in Poor Children," United Press International, April 28, 1983.

44. *Nutrition Week,* Community Nutrition Institute, Vol. 13, No. 31, August 14, 1983.

45. "Mortality and Death," *People,* Vol. 10, No. 3, IPPF London.

46. Cohn, V., "U.S. Racial Gap in Infant Mortality Grows," *International Herald Tribune,* January 7–8, 1984.

47. Eicher, C.K., op. cit.

48. Pear, R., "Three Doctors Tell House Panel of New Medical Data on Hunger," the New York *Times,* October 21, 1983.

49. Ibid.

50. Miles, I., "Joblessness and Health," *New Scientist,* London, May 12, 1983.

51. Ward, B., "Another Chance for the North?" *Foreign Affairs,* Winter 1980.

52. ul Haq, Mahbub, "Negotiating the Future," *Foreign Affairs,* Winter 1980.

53. "The Good Samaritan Was Not Using Food as a Weapon," as quoted by Lane Vanderslice, the New York *Times,* January 14, 1981, op-ed page.

54. Maynes, C.W., "We'll Sink with Them," the Manchester *Guardian Weekly,* October 2, 1983, p. 17.

55. ul Haq, Mahbub, op. cit.

56. Lappé, F.M., Collins, J., Kinley, D. "Aid as Obstacle," Institute for Food and Development Policy, San Francisco, 1980.

57. Eicher, C.K., op. cit.

58. "Fuelwood Supplies in the Developing Countries," *FAO Forestry Paper,* No. 42, Rome, Italy.

59. Kaprio, L., "Health for All by the Year 2000: The Role of Health Education," *International Journal of Health Education,* 22/3, pp. 136–37.

60. "Theme 1: Public Policy," The Conference Reports, *International Journal of Health Education,* 22/3, pp. 170–73.

61. Manoff International Inc., "Mass Media and Nutrition Education," Ecuador, USAID, 1975.

62. Ibid.

63. Eicher, C.K., op. cit., p. 157.

64. Berg, A., "A Strategy to Reduce Malnutrition," *Finance and Development,* World Bank, March 1980.

65. Ibid.

66. Riding, A., "Food is Challenge for Mexican Regime," the New York *Times,* January 9, 1979.

67. "Decade Dossier," *UNDP,* United Nations, New York.

68. Ibid.

69. Ibid.

70. Ibid.

71. "Cleaning Up Third World Diseases," Science and Technology Brief, *The Economist,* September 10, 1983.

72. Mahler, H. "Rescue Mission for Tomorrow's Health," *People,* Vol. 6, No. 2, 1979.

73. Gauhar, A., "Bang Goes US $600 Billion," *South,* December 1983, p. 9.

74. Ibid.

75. Weinraub, B., "World Bank Says Africa is Creating a Crisis," the New York *Times,* September 18, 1983, p. 6.

76. Dougherty, P.H., "Ethical Drugs and Television," in advertising, the New York *Times,* February 13, 1984, p. D10.

77. Sewell, E.M. president, American Lung Association, New York City, in a letter to the New York *Times,* January 26, 1984.

78. "Showdown on Smoking," *Newsweek,* June 6, 1983, p. 60.

79. Reinhold, R. "A.M.A.'s Dioxin Stand," the New York *Times,* July 4, 1983.

80. Boffey, P.M., "The Debate Over Dioxin," the New York *Times,* June 25, 1983, p. 1.

81. Ibid.

82. Ibid.

83. Ahrens, E.H., "Dietary Fats and Coronary Heart Disease: Unfinished Business," *The Lancet,* 22/29, December 1979, pp. 1345–1348.

Index

About the Author

Richard K. Manoff is president of Manoff International Inc., the pioneering social marketing firm responsible for several of the important projects reported in this book. In 1956 he founded Richard K. Manoff Inc., which became one of the leading marketing and advertising agencies in the United States, representing outstanding firms like Kraft Inc., Welch Foods, Castle & Cooke, National Car Rental System, American Cyanamid, and Cargill.

He first became involved in public health and nutrition activities when he served on the U.S. delegation to FAO in 1965. Following a USAID mission on nutrition education to India in 1967, he formed Manoff International to handle continuing assignments in Ecuador, the Philippines, Nicaragua, and other nations of the Third World. He has also been involved in similar activities in the United States for the Office of Economic Opportunity and on behalf of the first national family planning campaign in the United States. Manoff International's services have been employed by USAID, the World Bank, the U.N., and the Ford Foundation, among others.

Mr. Manoff himself has served as special adviser to the heads of both WHO and UNICEF expressly for the development of the International Code for the Marketing of Breast-Milk Substitutes, which was adopted by the World Health Assembly in 1981.

Mr. Manoff has served as an adjunct professor in the Department of Health Sciences of Sargent College of Allied Health Professions of Boston University and as Adjunct Lecturer in Public Health at Physicians and Surgeons School of Medicine, Columbia University, New York. He has published widely in the area of nutrition education, family planning, and public health with particular emphasis on communications strategies and the application of marketing techniques for their implementation.